Praise for Alister McGrath

'McGrath's style is scholarly yet accessible and engaging, and he presents a convincing case for replacing the old "narrative of conflict"... Anyone with an interest in the science-religion debate, whatever their level of expertise, will welcome this balanced and thoughtful contribution.'

Adrian Read, *Independent*

'*Enriching our Vision of Reality* is elegant, erudite and animated by a constant enthusiasm for its subject. There is everything here – science, theology, philosophy, biography, even some poetry – all enlisted to help us to see the world as it is, both more clearly and with greater delight.'

Revd Andrew Davison, Starbridge Lecturer in Theology and Natural Sciences, University of Cambridge

'McGrath is a clear-eyed, learned companion... illuminating.'

Philip Womack, *Telegraph*

'Many of us thought we knew most of what there was to know about C. S. Lewis. Alister McGrath's new biography makes use of archives and other material that clarify, deepen and further explain the many sides of one of Christianity's most remarkable apologists... penetrating and illuminating.'

N. T. Wright

'Alister McGrath's new biography of C. S. Lewis is excellent. It's filled with information based on extensive scholarship but is nonetheless extremely readable. It not only devotes great attention to the formation and character of Lewis the man, it offers incisive and balanced analyses of all his main literary works.'

Timothy Keller

Why We Believe

Finding Meaning in Uncertain Times

Alister McGrath

ONEWORLD

A Oneworld Book
First published by Oneworld Publications Ltd in 2025

Copyright © Alister McGrath 2025

ISBN 978-0-86154-921-4
eISBN 978-0-86154-923-8

Typeset by Geethik Technologies
Printed and bound in Great Britain by Clays Ltd, Elcograf S.p.A.

Oneworld Publications Ltd
10 Bloomsbury Street
London WC1B 3SR
England

Contents

Introduction

Why believe? Surely this idea is a relic from the past, a hangover from a superstitious age that is totally out of place in today's rational and science-led culture? The dominant social rhetoric of our age now dismisses any form of belief as lying somewhere on a dark spectrum between weird and toxic. While the Age of Belief may linger on in primitive societies, it has been discredited and displaced in the West by the Age of Reason. We don't need to go beyond the realm of reason and science and, if we do, we end up in the Badlands of superstition and irrationality. Belief is *weird*, a symptom of mental deficiency, an inadequate education, or a fundamental incapacity to reason properly.

Perhaps more worryingly, belief is *toxic*. If you believe something that is unevidenced, you will end up believing *anything* that is unevidenced, falling victim to a kind of 'blind faith' which is socially and politically dangerous. Maybe it is faintly amusing that some less evolved human beings believe in a sky fairy. But what if this delusion leads them to fly airplanes into buildings? Surely something needs to be done to eliminate such backward and destructive ways of thinking? Richard Dawkins expressed the deep cultural anxieties of many about belief and faith which crystallised around the turn of the millennium: 'I think a case can be made that faith is one of the world's great evils, comparable to the smallpox virus but harder to eradicate.'

Inevitably, the tone of the discussion of belief shifted as a result of the terrorist attacks of 11 September 2001. Many political commentators saw this as the outcome of American foreign policy and military interventionism in the Middle East, which generated a demand for retribution in this region. One analysis suggests that western sanctions against Iraq in the period between the two Gulf Wars caused more deaths than 'all so-called weapons of mass destruction throughout history.'[1]

Christopher Hitchens, Richard Dawkins and Sam Harris, however, reframed this event as a demonstration of the dangers of *religion*. Religion was denounced as the 'opium of the people', impairing proper mental functioning and thus inducing extremism and violence. They say that nothing can stop an idea whose time has come; for many, these were the prophets of a new worldview that had been waiting for its moment in the sun.

New Atheism encouraged a discriminatory rhetoric which turned a longstanding academic discussion on the reasonableness of religious belief into a political lightning rod in which conventions of thoughtful debate and personal civility were set to one side. Bumper slogans appeared, unconstrained by any consideration of truth or morality. 'I think, therefore I am an atheist.' Or, 'God doesn't kill People. People who believe in God kill People.' The target of these denunciations was no longer simply religious *ideas*, but religious *people*. These, it was argued, are deluded and dangerous and therefore should be socially marginalised, excluded from positions of influence. Perhaps it was inevitable that religion, as the writer Marilynne

Robinson observed, has 'dropped out of the cultural conversation'. It seems that religion has been shamed into the margins of our culture, embarrassed out of the public square.

Not everyone greeted this development with equanimity. Greg Epstein, humanist chaplain to Harvard University, was one of many who protested against shaming people for their faith.

> While atheism is the lack of belief in any god, anti-theism means actively seeking out the worst aspects of faith in God and portraying them as representative of all religion. Anti-theism seeks to shame and embarrass people away from religion, browbeating them about the stupidity of belief in a bellicose god.[2]

There now seems to have been a shift in the cultural mood, however, partly in reaction against this unnecessary dehumanisation of religious believers. The feminist atheist blogger Ashley Miller distanced herself from her more dismissive colleagues who suggested that 'people who are religious aren't worthwhile and are certainly too stupid to be respected'. Atheism had become, in her view, *tribal*.[3] 'We dehumanize people who disagree with us instead of arguing about ideas.' Looking back on the meteoric rise of the New Atheism, the New Zealand blogger and cultural critic Giovanni Tiso wondered how 'such a transparently flawed intellectual project' managed to hold sway 'for so long among so many?'[4] For a while, this view seemed to represent the future, only to end up relegated to the long list of discarded pseudo-certainties that didn't make the final cut. It is an idea whose time is gone.

Yet perhaps a deeper, if less obvious, shift was taking place at the intellectual level – the growing realisation within reflective atheist circles that the great eighteenth-century Age of Reason must now be seen to have failed in its quest to provide meaningful universal truths.

There was also some discomfort arising from how the rhetoric of ideas was being policed and manipulated before our very eyes and with no higher standard of proof. While many remain sceptical of Nietzsche's view that there are 'no facts but only interpretations', there is a suspicion that many of the alleged 'certainties' of our age are simply influential opinions which have become benchmarks of cultural acceptability today, but may well be abandoned in the future.

In her scathing assessment of the credulity of western culture in the closing years of the twentieth century, the novelist Doris Lessing denounced the 'great over-simplifiers' who imprison us in facile and shallow accounts of the world, ridiculing those who suggest things might be more complicated (and interesting) than they believe. For Lessing, recent developments within western culture represent a series of 'boilings up of emotion, of wild partisan passion', that everyone knows will one day be seen as 'ridiculous and even shameful' – but which nobody seemed able or willing to challenge at the time.[5]

This book argues for a recalibration of the notion of 'belief', and a more nuanced understanding of the positive role this plays in the lives of individuals and communities. I shall explore why certain unevidenced beliefs are much more acceptable than others. As might be expected, this is not a simple question; facing up to its complexity, however, helps us better understand what it means to be human, and the challenges we face inhabiting a world of uncertainties.

⁎⁎

I grew up in Northern Ireland during the 1960s and experienced at first hand a culture characterised by ingrained political, religious and social divisions. My first love was the natural sciences, evoked by a profound respect for the world around me, a longing to understand both how it functioned and what it meant. Perhaps because I was intolerant of uncertainty, I believed that the natural sciences might provide me with indubitable answers to life's big questions. I went on to study chemistry at Oxford University, specialising in quantum theory, and followed this with a doctorate in the biological sciences.

Yet the natural sciences served another purpose for me as a teenager. To study science was like stepping into another world, governed by rules of evidence and the courteous disagreement that is essential to scientific progress. Here, political and religious tensions could be put to one side; what mattered was the quality of your proofs, furnished by experimentation. A classic example of this eirenic role of the natural sciences can be seen in the role of natural scientists in building bridges across political and religious divisions, which helped heal the cultural wounds caused by England's Civil War.[6]

I was an atheist back in the late 1960s, with a strong interest in Marxism. Although I took the stubborn austerity of my teenage atheism to be a reliable indicator of its truth, I began to have anxieties about the stridency with which I now began to assert my views. The force of my conviction of the non-existence of God seemed to me to bear an inverse relation to the evidence available. I began to have private doubts, not simply about my atheism, but about *any* beliefs, in that these seemed to lack rigorous intellectual justification. So, for a time I condemned myself to some form of agnosticism, conceding that nothing could be known.

While reading Bertrand Russell's *History of Western Philosophy* at eighteen, I came across this remarkable statement that seemed to hint at a more gracious way of making sense of our world: 'To teach how to live without certainty, and yet without being paralysed by hesitation, is perhaps the chief thing that philosophy, in our age, can still do for those who study it.'[7] Russell helped me realise that it might be possible to hold beliefs without being able to prove them, opening the way for me to create a grander view of life than was possible by relying only on the sciences.

At Oxford, I came to appreciate the intellectual merits of Christianity and have since spent my career reflecting on its core themes, and particularly how science and faith can be brought into a meaningful conversation. Having grown up in the politically and religiously polarised context of Northern Ireland, I came to doubt those with strident views, believing it was possible to have civilised conversations despite divergent beliefs. I forced myself to talk to people with whom I disagreed across disciplinary, religious and ideological frontiers. The aim wasn't to achieve consensus, but to understand the issues more fully.

A key question for me was how it was possible to maintain my own beliefs with integrity, when I could not prove them. Russell's comments led me on a journey of discovery, in which

I began to appreciate how it was possible to live meaningfully in a world of uncertainties. This is precisely what I hope to explore in this book.

Somewhere along the way 'belief' became synonymous with '*religious* belief', thus unleashing a predictable torrent of anti-religious invective directed against 'belief' in general, rather than being attentive to the multiple specific forms that belief takes, and its important and legitimate place within humanity's attempts to make sense of our world. Belief, as I shall argue in this work, is *ordinary*, a routine aspect of the business of living and reflecting.

Ambivalence towards religious institutions or 'organised religion' has led many people in recent decades to identify as 'spiritual but not religious' or as 'religious Nones'. In both cases, these groups tend to avoid labelling themselves as 'religious' or affiliating with religious organisations such as churches. However, scepticism about religion need not lead to the rejection of the category of 'belief'. Many of the twenty-two per cent of Americans who identify as 'spiritual but not religious' turn out to have sophisticated personal belief systems. For example, eighty-eight per cent of this group believe that there is something spiritual beyond the natural world and fifty-five per cent believe that deceased individuals can provide assistance, protection or guidance to the living. The issue is not belief itself, but rather the type of beliefs considered acceptable.[8]

As Professor of Science and Religion at Oxford University, I have had time to reflect on the scientific study of beliefs, which calls into question the cultural oversimplifications of recent polemics. One of the most fruitful outcomes of recent scientific research in the field of belief is the clear indication that 'belief' is a generic category, which includes religious and secular forms. To draw on biological taxonomy, belief is the *genus*, and religious belief one of its many *species*. From an empirical point of view, the evidence suggests that it is the act of believing – rather than the substance of what is believed – that is of critical value for human existence. Despite their obvious differences, religious and secular beliefs both play similar psychological roles, and often lead to the same benefits – such as giving structure to life, providing reassurance, reducing anxiety and facilitating social integration.[9] This suggests that 'any belief system that provides explanations of the world will afford comfort and assurance'.

This book explores the nature of belief and maps out some approaches which I think might be helpful – not necessarily as firm conclusions, but certainly as lines of thought that have the potential to be illuminating. It explores the phenomenon of belief as integral to living. Although I shall explore some religious themes, this book is not a defence of the generic notion of 'religion' or of any specific religion, or even of my own beliefs. It is a reflection on what is perhaps the greatest paradox that we face as human beings: that we only seem to be able to prove shallow truths, but not the great truths of meaning, goodness and significance that lie at the heart of our existence which give order and meaning to our lives. Accepting the ambiguities of existence and respecting their complexity may not solve all our problems, but it might at least help us avoid slick and superficial answers to life's deepest questions, and cope with the plurality of beliefs and values. Our world is strange and hard to make sense of. This does not mean we shouldn't try to find meaning in our brief time here.

Chapter 1

Believing: A Mental Experiment

To believe is to be human; it undergirds our ability to imagine, experiment, relate to others and the world. From an evolutionary perspective, our capacity for belief is rooted in our histories as primates.[1] Although we tend to think of it as unique to human beings, it can be argued to emerge from certain primate traits, such as an ability to experience beauty and awe.[2] This spiritual sense is part of our configuration.[3]

For most people, 'belief' provides 'a framework for explaining the way things are (or should be), and is capable of influencing our behaviour, feelings, attitudes and decisions'.[4] Beliefs can lead to graciousness, inclusiveness, hospitality and love. Yet beliefs are dangerous, we are told. They inevitably lead to discrimination, tribalism and hatred. They certainly can. Yet it is not the *category* of 'belief' that is a problem; it is the *specific beliefs* which shape your way of living, whether for good or bad.

In any case, are we sure that we *know* what is 'good' and what is 'bad'? Surely this involves a value judgement – a belief which lies beyond proof? What I think is 'bad' might be seen as 'good' by someone else. Food etiquette rules illustrate this point neatly. In China, it is polite to leave some food on your plate (in that this implies your host is generous); in Japan, this is seen as rude (in that it violates *mottainai*, the principle of respecting resources and not wasting them).

The great eighteenth-century Age of Reason proposed a universal rational framework through which humanity could objectively resolve moral, political and intellectual questions, to learn to live in peace and harmony. The frontispiece to Christian Wolff's 1720 manifesto *Rational Thoughts on God, the World, the Human Soul and All Things in General* depicted a smiling sun illuminating a landscape, dispelling clouds of superstition. The Enlightenment immodestly proposed that, thanks to its unprecedented deployment of human reason, intellectuals in western Europe could see the universe objectively, as it truly is, for the first time in human history.

Yet what these Enlightenment intellectuals failed to recognise was that their idea of a 'universal rationality' was not universal at all, but a distillation of their own European, largely Christian, notions of morality. The evidence of such was already present in the 'voyager' literature of the seventeenth and early eighteenth centuries. British travellers and explorers reported on cultures whose notions of morality and rationality diverged significantly from those of England.[5] The empirical evidence pointed to a multiplicity of understandings of what it meant to be 'rational'. Yet English Enlightenment writers tended to dismiss such alternative ways of reasoning as 'primitive' or 'savage', instead of questioning their own assumptions about a universal human rationality.

The Enlightenment thus failed to set out a criterion that stands *above* human practice, by which rival visions of rationality could be judged. If reason is the supreme judge of beliefs, how can it adjudicate authoritatively and unaided between competing views of what it means to be 'rational'? As Hilary Putnam observed, the Enlightenment relied on an unattainable 'God's eye view' of reality. In his landmark study *Whose Justice? Which Rationality?* the philosopher Alasdair MacIntyre concluded that the 'legacy of the Enlightenment has been the provision of an ideal of rational justification which it has proved impossible to attain'.[6]

MacIntyre argues that prominent rationalist writers – such as David Hume, Denis Diderot and Immanuel Kant – were unable to establish a firm rational foundation for their views on morality that would enable them to demonstrate the correctness of their own perspectives. For MacIntyre, philosophy rests upon commitments whose truth cannot be demonstrated and hence must be defended, based on assumptions that carry weight for some, but not for all.[7] In the end, we are left wondering whether Nietzsche might be right in suggesting pragmatically that morality is simply the views of those in power, a herd instinct rather than a coherent rational position. 'If there is nothing to morality but expressions of will, my morality can only be what my will creates.'

Since there was an unacknowledged diversity of views within the Enlightenment concerning what was 'rational', there was no means by which these disagreements might be resolved, or how a universal rational morality might be developed. This clearly raises a problem for any suggestion that the term 'Reason' denotes a single universal set of norms, independent of history or culture. The dark side of the European Age of Reason was that it believed that it was in possession of precisely such a master set of cosmic rational norms, which it proceeded to impose on 'primitive' societies (such as India) in what are now recognised to be acts of intellectual colonialism (but were seen as 'civilising' projects at the time). It was an ethnocentric delusion, privileging some distinctively western beliefs as if they were universal human truths. Anyway, why should human reasoning lead to universally accepted beliefs about everything? After all, everyone has the same taste receptors, but we don't all like the same foods.

In the end, the Wars of Religion of the seventeenth century were replaced by the Wars of Ideology of the twentieth, in which religion played a much smaller role. Religion can certainly be violent, but there is no evidence that it is uniquely and particularly so, as recent history makes clear. The First World War, perhaps the most destructive conflict to date in human history, was driven by multiple ideologies, none of them religious. The intrinsic human capacity for violence, which plays a critical role in Thomas H. Huxley's discussion of human evolution, found new ways of expressing itself in secular ideologies such as Stalinism.

Christopher Hitchens, who believed that religion possesses a necessary and characteristic propensity for violence, argued that this evidential awkwardness shows that Stalinism was really a religious movement.[8] Ba'athism – an absolutist Arab nationalist ideology – posed similar problems for Hitchens, who solved them by redefining this secular ideology as a 'religion', which seems a little pat to me. The Cambodian genocide of 1975 to 1979, in which up to a quarter of the country's population was liquidated, was also clearly primarily motivated by a political ideology.

So, what about science? Can it offer us universal and objective accounts of morality, or settle debates about cultural and social norms? The influential philosopher of science Karl Popper introduced the term 'ultimate questions' to refer to the great 'riddles of existence'[9], for example, 'what is the point of life?' or, 'what is the good life, and how do I lead it?' Popper declared that these questions lay beyond the scope of the natural sciences; if they could be answered, it could not be based on logic or science. Ultimate questions simply don't find scientific answers. In the end, such ultimate questions (and their answers) lie beyond logical or scientific demonstration, eventually resting on our beliefs about the nature of life.

Albert Einstein took a similar view, insisting that scientists ought to be moral people, while pointing out that their science couldn't determine moral values. These had to come from somewhere else. For perfectly understandable reasons, science rules out consideration of 'value' and 'purpose' from the outset of its enquiry. Science might help us illustrate or apply moral values; it couldn't establish them in the first place. Human beings, Einstein declared, need more than what a 'purely rational conception of our existence' can offer.[10]

Sam Harris disagreed. In his *Moral Landscape*, he argues that science can and should determine human values, thus enabling humanity to dispense with mere moral beliefs. He argued that the scientific notion of human wellbeing can easily be mapped on to traditional ideas of morality, both displacing these and offering rational certainties in their place. Suffering is morally bad and flourishing is morally good; morality is thus about abating suffering and enhancing flourishing. Yet to his critics, it seemed as if Harris had simply smuggled in moral values originating from somewhere else and pasted them on to his own preconceived ideas about human wellbeing. More seriously, there seems to be a category error here: 'moral behaviour' and 'subjective wellbeing' are planets that orbit different intellectual suns. As Harris himself concedes, it is perfectly reasonable to suggest that 'rapists, liars and thieves' might 'experience the same depth of happiness as the saints', breaking any obvious or plausible link between the notions of 'being good' and 'being happy'.[11]

A more consistent approach was developed by the philosopher Alex Rosenberg. In his *Atheist's Guide to Reality: Enjoying Life without Illusions,* he sets out the view that that science is 'our exclusive guide to reality',[12] offering us reliable certainties about our world and ourselves. In response to the question 'What is the difference between right and wrong, good and bad?' Rosenberg declares that 'there is no moral difference between them'. This alarming response needs unpacking. Rosenberg is advocating that the natural sciences are an 'exclusive guide to reality' – which precludes any moral values, in that these are not scientific notions. Science offers a descriptive account of how things function; it does not offer prescriptive declarations about what ought to be done. We need more than science to inform our ethics.

Happily, science can answer most of our questions about the natural world, even if it can't give us definitive answers to moral or existential questions. Science can certainly offer explanations for why we consider morality to be so important.[13] For example, it could be argued that our evolutionary history predisposes us towards pro-social behaviour, in that this enhances our prospects for survival. But why should science be expected to teach us *moral* values? Or answer existentially important questions such as 'How should I act?' or 'How should I live?' It's science, after all, not philosophy. Science has its own distinct toolkit, which enables it to answer its own spectrum of questions with unique authority and reliability. That's one of the reasons why I love and respect science so much. But it doesn't mean that science can answer all our questions, or that those that lie beyond its reach can be dismissed as pseudo-questions.

Here's the point: we feel that we *need* to answer moral questions – to be able to declare that certain acts are good and others bad; to name what we consider to be destructive to human wellbeing or the environment, and invest these judgements with deeper significance than a personal indication of distaste. Something deep within us whispers that these questions are important and need to be respected and answered. While modern psychological research does not (and *cannot*) tell us what it means to be 'good' or what we ought to believe about purpose or meaning in life, it makes it clear that these beliefs matter to people, and that they are integral to their wellbeing.

And what about philosophy? Does it allow us to reach secure and certain conclusions, or should we think of it as offering us a critical tool for evaluating and calibrating our beliefs? Most philosophers are somewhat pessimistic about the 'persistent and intractable disagreement' within their discipline, often reflecting the difficulty in finding undeniable premises for philosophical arguments.[14] The diversity and disagreement within the field is such that 'most philosophical views are minority opinions,' and there is typically 'nothing approaching a consensus on the correct alternative'.[15]

Yet these concerns do not detract from the role that moral philosophy plays in forcing us to think critically about our beliefs about right and wrong. It confronts the metaphysical and epistemological presuppositions and commitments of moral thought questions, such as 'Is morality more a matter of taste than truth?' or 'Are there moral facts?' It helps us engage grand theories about the origins of morality – such as Thrasymachus' view, reported by Plato, that morality was invented simply to keep elites in power.

It also helps us reflect on questions about the nature of morality itself. In asserting a particular 'moral truth' was A. J. Ayer right in suggesting that I am doing no more than expressing my own individual feelings and attitudes? Or should I concur with Iris Murdoch and Philippa Foot in asserting that there are standards independent of my attitudes and feelings, by which I may judge whether a certain course of action is 'good'?

Moral viewpoints lie beyond proof and verification. They may be well-founded beliefs, developed in a full knowledge of the criticisms and objections that could be raised against them – but they are still *beliefs*, part of the necessary fabric of motivated and informed judgements that underlie much of human culture.

Philosophy, in my view, remains a useful tool in developing and critiquing our beliefs. But can we *dispense* with beliefs – whether philosophical or otherwise? It is a tempting possibility, perhaps opening the way to metaphysical and moral certainties that eliminate the uncertainties of human judgements and reasoning. Or is belief something that is forced upon us by the limits of our nature and the complexity of our world? Perhaps the best way to explore this question is through a thought experiment.

The Experiment: Inhabiting a Realm of Certainties

Albert Einstein, probably the most celebrated scientist of the twentieth century, used mental experiments to help him to explore some major scientific issues. In an autobiographical reflection written shortly before his death in March 1955, Einstein recalled an experiment of this kind that had intrigued him while he was a high school student in the Swiss city of Aarau. What would it be like to move so quickly that it was possible to catch up with a beam of light? As Einstein played around with this imaginative scenario, he realised that surfing a beam of light seemed to raise difficulties with prevailing understandings of the nature of light, laying the ground for his own pioneering contributions which transformed physics in the early twentieth century.

My own thought experiment has three parts. First, I would like you to imagine a world in which we only accept truths that can be proved – what ancient Greek philosophers termed *epistēmē* (knowledge) rather than *doxa* (opinion) – and work out what this world would look like. Second, we will reflect on what convictions would *not* be allowed into this world. And finally, I will invite you to step into this world of certainties and ask whether you think it is fit for meaningful human existence. Can we *flourish* in this environment? Is it existentially habitable?

Let's begin this experiment. Imagine a paradise of certainties, a realm populated only with ideas that can be proved to be true, and are thus devoid of intellectual risk or damaging controversies. What convictions would be allowed into this imagined world of secure convictions? Here are four statements that I think rightly belong there:

1. $2 + 2 = 4$.
2. The whole is greater than the part.
3. The atomic mass of chlorine is 35.453.
4. The British monarch Queen Victoria died on 22 January 1901.

These four examples are taken from the worlds of mathematics, logic, science and history; more could easily be added.

I would consider these four statements to be *facts* – that is to say, statements that can be shown to be true by publicly acceptable norms and are not dependent on my own prejudices or biases. I can see no good reason to doubt any of them. I'm sure that my readers can easily add more truths of this kind, thus expanding the very basic contents of this world into a kaleidoscope of certainties.

But here's the point we have to face up to: *So what?* What difference do they make to anyone? Something can be *true* without being relevant; that is, something can be right, without having any traction on our hopes and fears, our attempts to live our moral lives in a strange and dangerous world, or to flourish amid adversity and uncertainty. These are *shallow* truths, easily proved yet nevertheless disconnected from the ultimate questions of life. Would it make any difference to the serious business of working out how to live authentically in this strange and confusing world if Queen Victoria died on 22 *February* 1901?

Factuality, it seems, is not in itself a guarantor of existential traction. Some facts, however, seem to occupy an intermediary zone. These take the form of observations that hint at a deeper order or interconnectedness in the world, possibly pointing beyond themselves to significant truths awaiting our discovery. Why is the sky dark at night? Why do the fundamental constants of our universe seem fine-tuned for life? These are like clues calling out for interpretation. Their importance lies not simply in their observational actuality, but their theoretical potentiality. When rightly understood, these facts might turn out to be gateways to a richer understanding of ourselves and our world. Yet they might equally turn out to be dead ends.

Let's move on to the next stage of my mental experiment. We've already explored what might be *included* in this imagined world. But what convictions would be *excluded* from this world of certainties because they are beliefs? Because they cannot be proved to be true? In my view, a list of such excluded beliefs would (unfortunately) include the following:

1. All people are created equal.
2. It is wrong to torture people.

First, we must exclude the statement that 'all people are created equal'. This is clearly a belief, not a fact, perhaps reflecting a profound human desire that it should be true when accidents of birth clearly continue to shape our social status and prospects. It is for many a deeply attractive belief, calling into question social constructions of value, significance and intrinsic merit. For Christians, for example, the belief that all are created equal is a social leveller, demanding that we look beyond how society values individuals and discern something deeper, more significant beneath the surface. Yet the statement that 'all people are created equal' is ultimately a *belief*, not something that can be publicly demonstrated to be true.

The American philosopher and statesman Benjamin Franklin would disagree with my judgement. He confidently declared that this was a 'self-evident' truth – most famously, in his landmark statement in the American Declaration of Independence. But why is this view 'self-evident'? After all, Thomas Jefferson's original version of this statement, which was modified by Franklin, spoke more cautiously of holding certain truths to be 'sacred and undeniable'.

A 'self-evident' truth is basically an intuition, in which someone just 'sees' or 'senses' that something is right, without relying on evidence or argument.[16] Yet these 'intuitions' are self-evident only *within* certain cultural contexts and *because of* those cultural contexts. Franklin's assertion that this belief is a 'self-evident' truth is little more than an intellectual ploy, designed to fend off criticism or critical evaluation of this decidedly under-evidenced assertion, no matter how culturally desirable or politically convenient it might be. It is a defiant assertion, not an evidenced conclusion, a decision to present a belief in such forceful terms that it will be treated as if it were a fact.

Why have I excluded the conviction that 'it is wrong to torture people'? Surely any right-minded and liberal person would affirm this without reservation? I happen to believe this is true, but that's not my point. This ethical conviction has the status of a moral *judgement*, a *belief* rather than a statement of fact. It is contestable in theory and is contested in practice. For example, Sam Harris argues that 'some propositions are so dangerous that it may even be ethical to kill people for believing them'.[17] Killing such people, he tells us, could be regarded as an act of self-defence. As part of his overall argument, Harris offers a defence of torture, based on his assessment of the relative de-merits of collateral damage on the one hand, and torture on the other.[18] Now many people (and I certainly include myself here) will disagree with Harris and the arguments that he sets out in support of his view.[19] Yet while I think he is wrong – in fact, I believe passionately that he is wrong – I cannot *prove* this.

Now, some might suggest that my belief that torture is wrong is a *blind* faith, as I cannot prove it to be true. If this were the case, we would have to write off humanity's richest and most noble statements about the meaning of life, the nature of good and how to live meaningfully. Yet this disparaging category of 'blind faith' is simply a rhetorical device, increasingly used to limit human thought to the rationally demonstrable by rid-iculing those who realise we need to go beyond what reason can prove in the quest for human flourishing. It needlessly and irresponsibly limits the human quest for truth, beauty and goodness to a highly desiccated and impoverished set of rational certainties.

My view that torture is wrong may be held by many well-regarded people, whose social influence places them in Aristotle's category of the 'wise' – a group of people whose beliefs were considered exemplary and hence culturally deter-minative. Yet Aristotle invented this category primarily to lend social approbation and moral force to what he knew could not be proved to be true. The assertion that it is wrong to torture people is an opinion, a *belief* and not a fact. No matter how many intellectual luminaries pile in to support it, it remains a belief – even if it might be a particularly influential or wide-spread belief, or one that is enforced by social controllers. Sadly, it has to be excluded from our imagined world of certainties.

At this point, it becomes clear that this realm of certainties that we have been exploring in our thought experiment might be rather small and emaciated, populated with pedestrian simplicities. A world that is free of beliefs excludes an alarming number of views about the nature of the good life and, crucially, respect for our fellow human beings. It's like a tone-deaf person writing a treatise on the significance of music for humanity that limits itself to the physics of musical instruments. Human beings deserve better than this.

What is 'The Purpose of Philosophy' (to borrow the title of Isaiah Berlin's celebrated essay)? Berlin argued that human convictions can be placed in three kinds of 'baskets': those that can be established by empirical observation; those that can be established by logical deduction; and a third basket 'in which all those questions live which cannot easily be fitted into the other two'.[20]

The third basket hence contains the moral, political, social and religious values and ideas that have shaped human culture and given human existence direction and purpose. Berlin writes:

> There is a plurality of ideals, as there is a plurality of cultures and of temperaments. I am not a relativist; I do not say 'I like my coffee with milk and you like it without; I am in favour of kindness and you prefer concentration camps' – each of us with his own values, which cannot be overcome or integrated. This I believe to be false. But I do believe that there is a plurality of values which men can and do seek, and that these values differ.[21]

One of the reasons why Berlin was so respected as an intellectual historian and philosopher was his willingness to acknowledge ambiguity and uncertainty – notice his use of the term 'believe' in the last few lines of this statement, where lesser philosophers or ideological activists might present these views as truths – something we *know*. The intelligent application of reason leads people to a plurality of defensible – yet *unprovable* – ideals or moral values, not to a single universal concept of 'the good'.

Berlin rejected the monist view that 'all genuine questions must have one true answer and one only, all the rest being necessarily errors'. This, he believed, simply gave a spurious intellectual legitimacy to some form of totalitarianism: 'To force people into the neat uniforms demanded by dogmatically believed-in schemes is almost always the road to inhumanity.'[22] Berlin's criticisms offer a powerful criticism of blind faith or obedience demanded by institutions, ideologies and charismatic individuals – including some that are clearly religious, but claim not to be.

We have a further question to explore in conducting our mental experiment, which is perhaps the most important: are human beings capable of meaningful existence within this imagined world of certainties? Suppose we limit ourselves to such certainties: can they provide a basis for a good life?

Shallow Certainties Don't Allow Humans to Flourish

Many philosophers argue that the best way of assessing beliefs is to consider their rationality. Do they make sense? Are there good reasons for thinking they are right, or at least defensible? This is entirely reasonable. But as I suggested earlier in this

chapter, being *right* does not necessarily mean being *relevant*.
Let me return to one of the certainties of our imagined world,
noted earlier: 'The whole is greater than the part.' I can be
absolutely sure of this truth. This is something that is *right*
and therefore can be *relied upon*. There can be a universal
consensus about this unassailable truth, where mere beliefs
might lead to social division and tension, or the incitement
of hatred.

Yet truth cannot be directly correlated with relevance. I
must confess I struggle to see how this truth might give me a
reason to get up in the morning, or yearn to make the world
a better place. It is rationally incontestable yet existentially ir-
relevant. As Wittgenstein noted, you can be certain about it,
but it seems rather pointless. 'Nothing would follow from it,
and nothing could be explained by it. It would not tie in with
anything in my life.'[23]

With this point in mind, I want to suggest that we reclaim
an older concern – namely, considering the *existential vitality* of a way of thinking, asking how a belief or worldview
enables human flourishing and fosters wellbeing. Is this way
of thinking *liveable*? Does this worldview create a satisfying
'way of life'? Does it account for our deepest longings and
desires, and help us achieve joy and peace? Does it help us
to find meaning in life? Or happiness? Or does it repress and
limit us, trapping us within a constrained and impoverished
account of human existence? In our own time, many people
choose to abandon their commitments to worldviews, whether religious or secular, because they find them oppressive in
their outcomes, rather than deficient in their intellectual
foundations.[24]

For instance, when many sought to challenge the moral philosopher Peter Singer's argument that it is permissible to euthanise severely disabled infants, they honed in on its consequences: the murder of disabled people. Singer's conceptualisation of the value of a human life – founded upon rationality and autonomy – went largely unquestioned, as did his figuring of severely disabled people as a moral category apart from 'normal human beings'. Disability advocates, however, protested his lectures – arguing that disabled people, like all people, are capable of being loved and finding meaning in life. Our revulsion at particular outcomes, in other words, can't be separated from what we think human life is about. And for most of us, intuitively, it doesn't come down to reason alone.

There is now a substantial body of scientific studies that has established links between finding 'meaning in life' in lessening anxiety and enhancing wellbeing. Individuals need to feel that their lives and their existence are of importance and value (a condition now known as 'existential mattering').[25] We do not know *why* this is so; the evidence simply indicates that it *is* so – and is thus important to us. As the writer Jeanette Winterson observes, human beings are clearly meant to do more than just *survive*; they need to *flourish*.

> A meaningless life for a human being has none of the dignity of animal unselfconsciousness; we cannot simply eat, sleep, hunt and reproduce – we are meaning-seeking creatures. The Western world has done away with religion but not with religious impulses; we seem to need some higher purpose, some point to our lives – money and leisure, social progress, are just not enough.[26]

Winterson is surely right here. The cultural anthropologist Clifford Geertz earlier suggested that human beings are 'symbolizing, conceptualizing, meaning-seeking animals', who are driven to 'make sense out of experience, and give it some form and order'.[27] Humanity 'cannot live in a world it is unable to understand.' Nobody is sure why human beings find the concept of 'meaning' to be so significant; what we do know is that humans flourish when they have it and wither when they don't.

As mentioned, I discovered Marxism in the late 1960s. It was exhilarating, offering me precisely what Winterson identified as central human needs – 'some higher purpose, some point to our lives'. So let me tell you a little more about my own teenage longings for certainty, how I once believed these were met in Marxism and what I learned from my encounter with this worldview.

Reflections of a Lapsed Marxist

I was a nerdy scientist during my teenage years, studying at the Methodist College Belfast, one of Northern Ireland's largest schools. I loved the natural sciences for two reasons: first, they allowed me to engage with the beauty and mystery of nature in an intellectually rigorous way and, second, because they seemed to offer me evidence-based certainties about life. My growing fascination with chemistry helped me grasp how a good scientific theory could organise and explain what otherwise was a jumble of observations. Dmitri Mendeleev's brilliant analytical tool of the Periodic Table of the Elements (1869) organised chemical elements in a way that both accounted for their distinct properties, while suggesting (correctly) that there were gaps in the scheme that would be filled with as yet undiscovered elements.

It seemed to me that, just as Mendeleev had found a way of bringing theoretical order to the otherwise puzzling habits of chemical elements, Marx had developed a way of thinking that brought order and meaning to the historical process, enabling not merely its comprehension but its acceleration through informed human intervention towards its inevitable goal. Marx's theory was my first experience of a big picture approach to reality and I found it deeply satisfying, even inspiring.

Marxism seemed able to make sense of the social world but, more importantly, it created space for *me*. It was not like a scientific theory, which offered a detached and spectatorial account of how the world functioned; it was a participatory account of things. Marxism invited me both to appreciate its rendering of reality and to locate myself within that account and live accordingly. It was not simply a set of beliefs to be affirmed but a promise of participation in a new kind of existence. On this reading of things, I was part of something bigger. My life had a meaning.

Empirical studies of meaning see this as 'the extent to which one's life is experienced as making sense, as being directed and motivated by valued goals, and as mattering in the world.'[28] Marxism offered me all of these. As far as I was concerned, without such an informing and interpretative framework, it was impossible to discern or construct meaning in life.

Marx also played an important role in solidifying my increasingly trenchant teenage atheism. I had embraced atheism partly because of books I had read suggesting that religion was the enemy of science. Yet as I look back on that fascinating but long-vanished world of the late 1960s, I can see that Marxism allowed me to reinterpret what was probably little more than a cultural distaste for the kind of religion I encountered in Belfast as an intellectual and moral crusade against an alien and oppressive 'other'. I could reimagine myself as a noble hero in a culture war, part of a brave intellectual elite advancing human dignity by eliminating enemies of freedom. It made me feel good about myself, for a while.

I subsequently read Karl Popper's *Poverty of Historicism*. Popper, like me, had been drawn to Marxism as a teenager on account of its apparent explanatory power. And gradually I found myself unable to overlook his exposure of Marxism's evidential deficits (it consisted mainly of unfalsifiable claims) and its alarming capacity to incite violence and intolerance. But I had learned something important – the imaginative and intellectual appeal of a big picture account of reality. If I were ever to embrace another worldview, I told myself, it would have to be one that developed a framework of meaning that would allow me to be an active participant rather than a passive observer.

Let's return to our imagined world, populated only with convictions that can be proved to be true. Could we live meaningfully in this environment from which beliefs about existential meaning and moral values have been excluded? The psychologist William James didn't think so. In a lecture entitled 'Is Life Worth Living?' given at Harvard University in 1895,[29] he gave his audience this piece of advice: 'Believe that life *is* worth living and your belief will help create the fact.' Yet James was clear that 'scientific proof' of this conviction was simply not possible. Life is only worth living if there exists 'an unseen order of some kind in which the riddles of the natural order may be found explained'[30] – and this is a *belief* which cannot be confirmed scientifically, even though James considered it reasonable and defensible.

James's point is that it is not enough to believe that a big picture of reality, or an unseen order of some kind, simply *exists* – you have to step into this, becoming part of it, and allowing it to shape and inform your life and thought. We both *discern* and *create* meaning, recognizing it as an external reality that needs to be internally appropriated and assimilated. We don't observe it with a cool indifference from outside, but step inside this world of meaning and *experience* it. As many ancient Greek thinkers recognised, we are not simply passive observers of some grand theory of the world; we are called to become active participants within this theoretical framework, and thus create meaning in our lives through enacting this theory.

I will come back to theories of meaning and their importance, as there is much more that needs to be explored. But let's reflect on where our mental experiment has taken us in thinking about the place of belief in life, and setting up the agenda for the rest of the book.

The Gradgrind Paradox: Why Facts Aren't Enough

What does a world without belief look and feel like? For some, this world might be a rationalist paradise, in which we have left behind the debilitating notions of belief and faith, suitable only for the feebleminded who are unable to grasp the certainties of pure reason and the natural sciences. For others, however, this world of factual certainties is a limiting domain. It constitutes a segment of the spectrum of human knowledge, rather than defining this in its totality. Human beings yearn to go beyond the factual, opening up new worlds of meaning and values. As I see it, this move from observed facts to beliefs about life is both natural and necessary if human beings are to transition from mere physical survival to mental, social and relational flourishing – which is what our evolutionary history, both biological and cultural, suggests has happened.

What exactly is 'flourishing'? Although some treat this as equivalent to finding happiness or experiencing wellbeing, it is a much richer concept, which has come to play a major role in the Positive Psychology movement.[31] It is often described using the PERMA model which describes human flourishing in terms of positive emotions, engagement, relationships, meaning and achievement. Flourishing is about people growing as human beings through both good times and life struggles. This rests on seeing ourselves and reality in certain ways that go beyond observable facts.

One of Charles Dickens' more memorable literary creations is Mr Gradgrind, a schoolteacher whose educational philosophy is as simple as it is misguided: 'What I want is Facts. Teach these boys and girls nothing but Facts. Facts alone are wanted in life.'[32] For Gradgrind, facts alone give rise to intellectual certainty. Yet Gradgrind's philosophy simply leads to an overload of information and an absence of wisdom. Gradgrind's vision of a rational paradise is a joyless world of factual fetishes and cold actualities which bypass the human imagination and emotions.

Dickens adroitly brings out the utter lifelessness of this purely informational world through the lens of Gradgrind's daughter, Louisa. She is portrayed as having a 'starved imagination', being inclined through her father's influence to view everything from the standpoint of 'reason and calculation'.[33]

Sadly – but perhaps inevitably – having been indoctrinated into her father's creed, Louisa finds herself trapped in a loveless world, unable to find happiness and security. She needs something deeper to bring stability and joy to her life.

That's the paradox which stands at the heart of this book. Facts are epistemically safe and reliable, yet frustratingly inadequate for engaging the serious issues of life. In going beyond them, we embark on a journey that is both risky and exciting, and to be fair, this is a journey of discovery which can indeed go wrong. It involves making choices and judgements that do not necessarily go *against* reason, but often go *beyond* reason. And sometimes we make bad choices, ending up trapping ourselves within intellectual prisons of our own making. But it doesn't have to be like this.

What we cannot do, however, is pretend that we exist in a purely factual, belief-free world. Christopher Hitchens clearly believed he occupied such a world, allowing him to deliver privileged thunderbolts of rationalist wisdom from on high to lesser mortals, whose failure to grasp the core ideas of the Enlightenment locked them into a superstitious darkness: 'Our belief is not a belief.'[34] Hitchens' *professed* world is a world of certainties, from which beliefs are excluded. Yet Hitchens' *actual* world is clearly a world of *belief*, in that his arguments and assertions are based on a network of unacknowledged and unevidenced moral values (such as 'religion is evil') which he is unable to demonstrate – and hence tends to assert verbally rather than defend evidentially. To be human is to *believe* – that is, to refuse to be confined to a limited and limiting world of facts, and instead search for a larger vision of the world enfolding the good, the true and the beautiful.

You might have noticed that I have not even touched on religion, other than indicating my ephemeral teenage distaste for this cultural phenomenon. My reason for postponing discussion of religion is that I want to show that belief is a normal, integral aspect of human existence in general, rather than being something weird, abnormal or limited to religious people. Humans are creatures who *believe* – and by believing, find they can make more sense of their world and themselves. From a psychological perspective, beliefs are a fundamental aspect of human cognition that fulfil important individual and social functions – not least in providing meaning, comfort and communality. We will come to religious belief in a later chapter, but first, we need to explore the importance of finding a 'big picture' in life.

Chapter 2

Seeking a 'Big Picture'

Human beings need Big Pictures of reality to anchor their lives, allowing them to live meaningfully in a complex society. Worldviews, implicit or explicit, serve as anchor points for our understanding of what is good and meaningful in times of crisis, providing stability as the cultural landscape undergoes significant shifts. The problem, however, is that we often find ourselves trapped in webs of beliefs that are ultimately oppressive and inadequate, making it difficult to break free from their toxic thrall.

The novelist and poet Hermann Hesse (1877–1962) had an 'uncanny ability to give expression to the emotional and intellectual problems of his time', offering penetrating reflections on the cultural disturbances of his age.[1] In 1926, Hesse published an article in *UHU* magazine, a modernist journal established in 1924, aimed at an urban bourgeois liberal readership in Weimar Germany.[2] Weimar Germany was an intellectual and creative hothouse, the home of Dada, Bauhaus, New Objectivity, and new institutes for sexuality. But frequent economic shocks, millions of war wounded and escalating political violence left Germans anxious, unable to anchor themselves in the present. Hesse set out to explain why so

many Germans yearned for a coherent worldview and why it
was so difficult to find one.[3]

Traditional answers to this craving for a secure basis for human
existence were being cast aside, discredited by the devastation of
the war. But the latest intellectual fashions were simply a synthesis of the values *au courant* at that moment, lacking in depth,
substance and stability, all things that emerge from having been
subjected to critical evaluation over an extended period.

Hesse also argued that the trend of privileging novelty has
resulted in a precipitate dismissal of the wisdom of the past
and the unquestioning adoption of new and untested ideologies in a 'frenzied search for new interpretations of human
life'. It's an important point. The Irish writer and philosopher
John Moriarty later offered an insightful critique of such a
dangerous preoccupation with the transient truths of the present moment. The wise person, he suggests, is not someone
who walks ahead of humanity, but *behind* it, 'picking up the
wonderful things it leaves behind it in its flight into a future'
that might well prove to be yet another costly failure.[4]

It is not difficult to work out which ideologies Hesse had in
mind. Marxism and Nazism were in open competition for the
spiritual and intellectual soul of Germany at that time, a struggle that grew increasingly bitter and culminated in the Nazi
seizure of power in 1933. Germany had undergone a transformation. An untested new ideology was in the ascendancy.
UHU did not survive this development and published its last
issue in September 1934.

Human beings, according to Hesse, experience a 'primal
need to know that there is meaning to their lives' that is 'as old
and as important as the need for food, love and shelter.' Many

commentators have failed to grasp the importance of this yearning for meaning and significance. George Orwell, for example, complained that 'all "progressive" thought has assumed tacitly that human beings desire nothing beyond ease, security and avoidance of pain.'[5] The rise of Nazism in Germany, he remarked, showed the falsity of this view. People seemed to want a deeper vision of life that speaks of meaning, significance and purpose, that might require sacrifice on their part, rather than merely meeting their physical needs.

Hesse's reflections frame the core themes of this chapter – the human longing for a secure and stable big picture, capable of creating and sustaining the good life; and the precariousness of the quest for such a worldview, which can easily go badly wrong. Some might be tempted to suggest that the risks involved are so great that the best strategy is to avoid any such commitment. Yet other options are available. The writer E. M. Forster, best known for *A Room with a View* (1908), was also alarmed by the rise of ideologies such as Nazism during the 1930s. What could be done to challenge them? His response was this: 'There are so many militant creeds that, in self-defence, one has to formulate a creed of one's own.'[6]

Forster's argument is that the best way of dealing with a bad creed is not to have *no* creed, but to develop a *better* creed – in Forster's case, 'belief in good taste, and belief in the human race.' Our search for truth may begin by identifying what is *wrong* – but that does not in itself help us determine what is *right*. We all believe something and need to be clear on what this is, why we believe it is right, and the difference that it makes to the quality and character of our lives. Believing nothing is not a serious option.

Meaning and Big Pictures

Psychologists have highlighted the importance of human intellectual and emotional wellbeing. We seem to cope better with our complex and messy world if we feel that we can create a sense of order.[7] It's as if we have some inbuilt desire to find a big picture which helps us feel that we are part of something greater than ourselves, enabling us to position ourselves within this larger map of reality and live accordingly.[8] As the American philosopher Michael Sandel points out, while 'we may resist such ultimate questions as the meaning of justice and the nature of the good life, what we cannot escape is that we live some answer to these questions – we live some *theory* – all the time.'[9] This theory may be implicitly assumed rather than explicitly articulated – but it is *there*, informing and determining our attitudes and outlook.

Human beings have an extraordinary instinct and ability to join up the dots, to weave threads together to construct a pattern, going beyond what can be seen to what we believe lies behind it. This process can – and often does – go wrong: we connect the dots improperly, or fail to realise how much our reasoning is subservient to our desires. We want to trust our closest friends and so deny their failures that others see all too clearly. We want humanity to be good and so blind ourselves to its many defects and wilfully ignore our darker side. We find ourselves drawn to the 'necessary illusions' and 'emotionally potent oversimplifications' that Noam Chomsky believed were constructed by governmental agencies to control public opinion.[10] We too easily allow ourselves to be cushioned against harsh truths by constructing worldviews that protect us from thoughts that we might find unbearable – such as the pointlessness of life, or the utter indifference of the cosmos to our presence. Yet the process of making connections is essential to the construction of beliefs, even if it can misfire.

The French mathematician and philosopher of science Henri Poincaré helps us grasp this distinction: 'Science is made with facts, like a house is made with stones, but an accumulation of facts is no more a science than a pile of stones is a house.'[11] Each stone is significant; yet we need to be able to see the grander structure of which it is part if we are to appreciate the wholeness of our world, without losing sight of its many individual aspects.

Yet even here, there are uncertainties about the significance of this process. In the natural sciences, the debate between 'instrumentalism' and 'realism' continues. Is this 'conceptual framework' simply a construction of the human mind, which is read into or superimposed upon the real world? Or do we discern something that is there in the world? Have we invented something, or discovered it?

Perhaps more worryingly, we often assume we must find a single master picture or narrative which makes all others redundant, exposing them as inadequate or even fraudulent. Yet while some worldviews demand exclusive control over our readings and interpretations of life, most are permissive, illuminating or interpreting aspects of life, and allowing supplementation from other perspectives. One of the reasons why I moved away from Marxism as a teenager was my sense that it imprisoned me within a controlling narrative and left me unwilling to acknowledge insights from other ways of thinking.

The evidence clearly indicates that human beings are deeply pragmatic, working and living with a variety of big pictures, seeing them as helpful informing guides to some aspects of their lives (but not to others). The sociologist Christian Smith has noted how modern Americans draw selectively on about a dozen competing metanarratives – such as a Progressive Socialism narrative, a Scientific Enlightenment narrative, and a Christian narrative – to make sense of their world.[12] As Smith points out, these narratives are quite different, have different concerns and lie beyond empirical verification. Given that a person may have a diversity of 'social identities', these different narratives or frameworks can seem contradictory, thus creating tension and uncertainty within the individual.[13]

Sean McCloud, an American academic who specialises in the mass media representations of religion, similarly notes that 'Americans live by picking, mixing and combining a variety of religious and cultural idioms (within a sphere of materials constrained by their social locations) to find what works for them in everyday life.'[14] This is not, however, a new or specifically American phenomenon. In late classical antiquity, Roman imperial culture showed a remarkable ability to accommodate multiple narratives and cultural perspectives, despite the intellectual tensions that this often created.[15] The solution to this problem is not to integrate these narratives, but rather to respect their specific domains of application and validity. If our experience of life is disordered, perhaps we have to expect the same from our attempts to represent it.

This ability to switch interpretative frames when moving from one area of social interaction to another (for example, from a laboratory to a synagogue to a local political committee) has its parallel in multicultural contexts, in which individuals feel that

they 'belong' to *multiple* communities, each with its own identity and norms. Cross-cultural studies, however, have tended to
focus on groups of individuals drawn from different contexts
and failed to take account of single individuals who have internalised more than one culture.[16] Studies of the dynamics of
'multiple cultures in the same mind' suggests that people use a
mechanism of 'frame switching', in which such an individual
shifts between interpretive frames rooted in different cultures in
response to cues originating within their social environment.

The empirical study of how human beings construct their
systems of meaning suggests that we have a remarkable capacity to hold together multiple narratives or pictures, even
when these might seem to be disconnected, if not mutually
exclusive. Individuals often develop accounts of life that are
more complex, fragmentary and situational than the terms 'religion' or 'worldview' might suggest.[17] This does not mean that
these personal (and idiosyncratic) constructions are perceived
as incoherent; in fact, individuals often find them remarkably
helpful in making sense of life and coping with its challenges.

While some limit themselves to a single coherent master
narrative, most people seem prepared to apply a range of
narratives or frames selectively to different aspects of life,
without a full resolution of their tensions and divergences,
perhaps reflecting a realisation that no single big picture or
grand story can address every aspect of the complexities of
modern human existence. That's why some Christians are
capitalists, some socialists and others politically disengaged.
Worldviews are often selectively appropriated, with certain
themes foregrounded and others marginalised. Individuals
tend to construct their own personalised versions of Big

Pictures, adapting them to their circumstances and correlating them in different manners.

Yet Big Pictures lead to different outcomes. Some provide an *explanation* and others an *interpretation* of our world. To explore this important distinction, so easily overlooked, we will reflect on scientific and philosophical Big Pictures and the significantly different outcomes that these generate. We begin by thinking about the natural sciences.

Explaining Our World: A Scientific Big Picture

A scientific theory offers a way of imagining or beholding the world, which enables its fundamental ordering and coherence to be discerned. Without this theoretical lens, this order cannot be discerned. Earlier, I mentioned Dmitri Mendeleev's 'Periodic Table of the Elements,' developed in 1869. The novelist C. P. Snow gives a fictionalised account of how using this table as an interpretative lens enabled him to see past the apparent chaos of a seemingly disconnected accumulation of chemical observations and discern the fundamental principles that lay behind them.

> I saw a medley of haphazard facts fall into line and order. All the jumbles and recipes and hotchpotch of the inorganic chemistry of my boyhood seemed to fit into the scheme before my eyes – as though one were standing beside a jungle and it suddenly transformed itself into a Dutch garden.[18]

One of the greatest achievements of science is the 'mathematisation' of nature – the representation of its relationships and structures using mathematical equations. One of the best examples of this mathematical mastering of nature is Isaac Newton's theory of universal gravitation. This was widely seen as an intellectual wonder of the early modern age, a stunning demonstration of the power of human reason to make the mysteries of the universe rationally transparent and intelligible. On being asked how he came up with the notion of gravity, Newton told his friends that the idea came to him in the summer of 1666 when an outbreak of the plague at Cambridge University forced him to hastily leave his rooms at Trinity College and retreat to the safety of his mother's house in rural Lincolnshire.

The story of what followed is well known, even if it likely involves a significant degree of poetic licence. While sitting in his mother's garden, Newton tells us, he observed an apple fall from a tree – and thereby made a connection with the way in which planets orbited the sun. If there was some fundamental force of attraction between physical bodies – which we now know as 'gravity' – this would explain the orbits of planets round the sun, the moon around the earth and the falling of apples to the ground.[19]

Some fifty years earlier, Johannes Kepler had shown that – for reasons he did not understand – the square of the orbital period of any planet was proportional to the cube of the semi-major axis of its orbit. Kepler had found this out by trial and error, superimposing all kinds of mathematical constructions on detailed observational data of the movement of the planet Mars provided by Tycho Brahe. Eventually, Kepler found a mathematical formula that seemed to work. Newton was able to show that the principles of universal gravitation and inertia explained Kepler's pragmatically reliable yet theoretically puzzling rules of planetary motion. Newton was able to set out a comprehensive Big Picture of how our universe functions which enfolded and explained these seemingly disconnected observations.

Yet understanding how our universe *works* does not necessarily tell us what it *means*. Scientific explanations are not interpretations of the world, which aim to discern its value or meaning; they are attempts to work out how it functions. Despite its great explanatory successes, scientific analysis does not lead to existentially or intellectually compelling *interpretations* of our universe or human existence. For Ludwig Wittgenstein, 'the meaning of the world must lie beyond it'.[20]

This interpretative pluralism helps us understand the grand diversity of metaphysical and religious beliefs evident within the scientific community. Consider, for example, three theoretical physicists, each with a shared commitment to scientific *explanation* yet holding divergent accounts of what a scientific *interpretation* of the universe might look like. For the atheist Steven Weinberg, human beings seem pointless, devoid of meaning and significance in a universe that is indifferent to our presence.[21] The more we know about the universe, the more pointless it seems. Sean Carroll develops a 'poetic naturalism' which respects the immense grandeur of the universe, while pointing to the emergence of humanity as bringing 'meaning and mattering into the world'.[22] John Polkinghorne, however, sees the 'rational transparency and beauty of the universe' as pointing to God as its ultimate ground.[23]

While Weinberg, Carroll and Polkinghorne adopt comparable scientific explanations of the universe, they offer quite distinct *interpretations* of our universe, which science can neither confirm nor deny. Though all three thinkers are distinguished scientists, their interpretations of what the universe means lie beyond the horizon of the scientific method. All three can argue that their worldview is *consistent* with what is observed. (A more sceptical neutral observer might suggest that all three are thus equally absurd, in that none is *demanded* by the evidence.) This suggests we need to look further at this idea of 'interpreting' the universe.

Interpreting Our World: A Philosophical Big Picture

Susan Wolf notes that we feel a need to get involved in something 'larger than oneself' to secure meaningfulness. While affirming the philosophical importance of these yearnings to live meaningfully and purposefully, Wolf concedes that academic philosophers now seem to have lost interest in the question of finding meaning in life.[24] Yet this philosophical disengagement with meaning is a recent development. As Pierre Hadot has pointed out, classical philosophy – both Greek and Roman – was intensely concerned about questions of meaning and value.

In making this point, Hadot draws a distinction between *philosophy* itself and *philosophical discourse*. Philosophy sets out a vision of reality; philosophical discourse articulates this in words. Perhaps we need to rediscover this vision of philosophy as enabling practical wisdom, and draw a distinction between empowering and informing vision on the one hand, and its formal expression in human words on the other. Hadot argues that we need to retrieve the classical vision of philosophy as a discipline of human flourishing, which emphasises the capacity of its beliefs to inform and sustain a meaningful and fulfilling 'way of life'.[25]

For example, Hadot notes that the Stoic philosopher Marcus Aurelius was 'trying to do what, in the last analysis, we are all trying to do: to live in complete consciousness and lucidity, to give to each of our instants its full intensity, and to give meaning to our entire life.'[26] This account helps us to understand why early Christianity was widely regarded, by both its practitioners and its critics, as a 'philosophy', as this term was understood in late classical antiquity.[27] While philosophy can be *enacted*, philosophical *discourse* often becomes trapped within arcane technocratic echo chambers, which may be cognitively interesting, yet are generally existentially barren. But it doesn't need to be like this. Søren Kierkegaard held that truth was not primarily something objective that we apprehend, but something that apprehends us, and so changes us inwardly.

Currently, as Wolf rightly notes, religion is one of the most important sources of meaning and value in our culture.[28] We will reflect further on the nature of religion and religious belief in the next chapter, but now it is enough to note that many consider one of the distinct characteristics of religion to be its integration of theory and practice. The philosopher Keith Yandell brings this point out clearly: a religion, he suggests, is a 'conceptual system' that provides an interpretation of the world and our place within it, leading to an account of 'how life should be lived given that interpretation', which is expressed or enacted in 'a set of rituals, institutions and practices.'[29]

It is, of course, obvious that such systems of meaning are found beyond the traditional category of 'religion' – for example, in Marxism or Darwinism. This partly reflects the problematic category of 'religion', which is a false universal, something that is regularly presented as a 'natural kind' when it is really a social construction. Yet my point here is that while this propensity is *characteristic* of religion, it is not *limited* to religion. As Mary Midgley pointed out, this helps us understand why Marxism and Darwinism – the 'two great secular faiths of our day' – display 'religious-looking features'.[30]

The point we have been considering in this section is that 'framing beliefs' are of critical importance to a meaningful human inhabitation of this world, yet cannot be proved to be true. This does not mean that they are arbitrary, delusional, or deliberately constructed falsehoods. Belief is an entirely reasonable option as we try to interpret the messy and mysterious world into which we are thrown, which fails to disclose its significance – or ours – in an unambiguous way.

In his late poem *The Ancient Sage* (1885), Alfred Lord Tennyson reflected extensively on his own struggles with faith and doubt, and the predicament of being immersed in a world of uncertainty in which many things were *important* but nothing was *clear*. 'It is hard,' he once declared, 'to believe in God; but it is harder not to believe.'[31] Yet Tennyson was at least clear about one matter: if a belief was important, if it genuinely mattered, then it could not be proved:

> For nothing worthy proving can be proven,
>   Nor yet disproven.[32]

Some will argue that, since the essence of human identity is our freedom to make choices, we are free to create such beliefs as we please in the absence of compelling, or even suggestive, evidence. Jean-Paul Sartre asserted that our beliefs, commitments and purposes are simply principles that we ourselves determine. We are what we choose to be. Richard Rorty similarly insisted that 'there is nothing deep down inside us except what we have put there ourselves.'[33]

Others, however, are disturbed by the absence of any transcendent grounding for our beliefs which might challenge what are often self-serving ideologies, privileging the views of certain individuals or social groups. Surely our beliefs need to be grounded in and accountable to something greater? The idea of 'natural law' is important here. It suggests that our beliefs, commitments and purposes are to be judged against a transcendent norm, which lies beyond human manipulation and control. Morality and meaning rest on some transcendent ground that is not our creation, but which we progressively discern and gradually enact.

The difficulties of these debates lead some to suggest that we ought to disengage from trying to interpret the world, in that questions of meaning and value lie beyond rational or scientific verification. Yet as Albert Camus pointed out, that amounts to a denial of an essential feature of the human condition – an inbuilt longing to seek meaning. Camus' Sisyphus had to live in the 'absurd' situation of having to believe in a world that is silent when questioned, declining to tell us what it means. There is an existential tension between our desire for meaning and the inherent meaninglessness of our existence, leading Sisyphus to push this boulder up a hill time and time again, determined to find the meaning that had eluded him up to this point.

We can, Camus suggests, only eliminate our distinctively human urge to find meaning through suppressing our exploration of the world on the one hand, or by ending our lives on the other. We have to work with human nature as we find it, rather than eliminate its distinctively human elements – such as the capacity and inclination to believe, often (though not invariably) expressed in religious faith. As Philip Pullman points out, 'the religious impulse is part of what we are and it always has been'.[34]

Human beings thus seem to be 'metaphysical animals', to borrow a phrase from the Cambridge philosopher Donald MacKinnon.[35] We are hardwired to supplement our biological instinct for survival with an existential instinct to find and enact meaning and value. Some seek to suppress this instinct, fearing its consequences; others dismiss it as a hangover from our evolutionary past which deludes us into believing in some greater account of reality that transcends mere functionality. Yet, clearly, meaning and values matter to human beings. We need beliefs to help us to navigate the complexities and cope with the ambiguities of life.

Weaving Beliefs Together:
Towards a Big Picture of Reality

Countless philosophical, spiritual and religious writers have commended an integrative account of human wisdom, bringing together the multiple dispersed elements of knowledge to yield a greater whole. The German philosopher Ernst Cassirer spoke of our ability to acquire 'a new dimension of reality', reflecting humanity's apparently unique capacity to construct 'symbolic systems' which extend our vision of the social world, and make its inhabitation meaningful. This means going beyond a mere accumulation of facts and observations, and finding a way of integrating them to see the 'big picture' that lies behind them. So how can we do this? How can we, for example, achieve a workable synthesis of ethics and physics?

In 1905, Albert Einstein published a seminal paper concerning the interchangeability of mass and energy, memorably expressed in the famous scientific equation, $E = mc^2$. Forty years later, this scientific principle was put to destructive use in the two atom bombs that devastated the Japanese cities of Hiroshima and Nagasaki. Although Einstein played no role in this technological development, he was alarmed at the way in which science was being used to develop new and more deadly weapons of mass destruction, such as napalm (developed in the Harvard laboratories of Professor Louis Fieser in 1942) or nuclear weapons.

Yet for Einstein, science by itself could not provide scientists with a viable moral framework: 'science can only ascertain what *is*, not what *should be*, and outside of its domain value judgements of all kinds remain necessary.'[36] David Hume, one of Einstein's two favourite philosophers (the other being Baruch Spinoza), had exposed the intellectual problems of moving from an account of the way things *are* and the way things *should be*, and Einstein could see no way round this disjunction of fact and value. In their quest to be moral, scientists would have to draw on ethical values that originated from beyond their own specialist field of studies.

Mary Midgley, perhaps the most significant public philosopher to deal with this question, highlighted the need to use all our 'philosophical tools to bring these distinct kinds of thought together.'[37] For Midgley, it was clear that 'all explanation, and particularly the explanation of human action, quite properly uses many non-competing but convergent methods.'[38] Difference in method does not entail incompatibility.

Neither does difference in *outcome*, in that each could be seen as a particular *perspective* on a complex reality – such as the nature of universe or the meaning of human existence – which resists reduction to simplistic categories or single levels of explanation. We have to try and use our tools of knowing as best we can to align our 'knowledge' with something that we encounter but cannot control, and that demands progressing beyond monochrome surface readings of reality.

Yet some insist that such a multidisciplinary approach is unnecessary and improper, in that the natural sciences can answer every significant question with a unique rational and cultural authority. This position is often known as 'scientism', which can be described as 'a totalizing attitude that regards science as the ultimate standard and arbiter of all interesting questions.'[39] I used to think this myself, so I can easily understand its appeal to anyone longing for certainty.

For the philosopher of science Alex Rosenberg, science offers 'irrefutably correct answers' (hence eliminating any need for belief or any anxiety about uncertainty) to 'persistent questions' such as 'What is the nature of reality?' (his answer: what physics says it is), or 'What is the purpose of the universe?' (his answer: there is none). Rosenberg graciously concedes that 'knowing the truth makes it hard not to sound patronizing of the benighted souls still under religion's spell.' But if you have discovered what you believe to be 'irrefutably correct answers',

I suppose it's irritating when others suggest you may have got things wrong.

In the light of his unassailable certainties about life, Rosenberg declares that it is pointless to try and find 'a good reason to go on living, because there isn't any.' Happily, Rosenberg has a therapeutic solution for those who might be troubled by the absence of morality or meaning from their worlds: if this 'makes it impossible to get out of bed in the morning,' you should try Prozac (other neuro-pharmacological fixes are, of course, available).

Rosenberg presents himself as a lofty, rational observer of other people's madness. Yet I am unpersuaded by his line of argument. Let me invite you to join me in a mental experiment that might be helpful in exploring this question. During the COVID lockdown of 2020–21, I regularly used a thermometer to determine my temperature. A raised temperature would not necessarily mean that I had COVID, but it was certainly an indication that I needed to check things out. Suppose I were to argue like this. My thermometer proved to be a reliable tool for checking my temperature. Since it worked so well in that role, why not use it for everything? Like working out what is right or wrong? Or whether I have free will? Or determining the meaning of life?

Now this will strike most of my readers as a ridiculous argument. I suspect (and hope) many will respond to my suggestion like this: a thermometer has been designed to check temperatures! It doesn't do anything else! It's not meant to be used for ethical or existential issues! But that's my point. Intellectual disciplines devise their own research methods to engage specific aspects of reality. A research method that works for one domain will be useless or misleading if used in another. Rosenberg is simply universalising a tool that was designed with other specific (and limited) purposes in mind.

Mary Midgley makes this point in a highly critical assessment of those who, like Rosenberg, demand that every intellectual domain should be subordinated to the methods of physicists. 'No one pattern of thought – not even in physics – is so "fundamental" that all others will eventually be reduced to it. Instead, for most important questions in human life, a number of different conceptual tool-boxes always have to be used together.'[40]

But I have a second problem with Rosenberg's approach, which he himself recognises: his argument for the exclusive authority of science is viciously circular, presupposing (indeed, relying upon) its conclusions. Imagine someone who makes the following assertion: 'science is the only reliable arbitrator of reliable knowledge, offering "irrefutably correct answers" to any meaningful questions.' Here's my point: if science is the *only* secure foundation and reliable arbitrator of human knowledge, it necessarily follows that we must use science to reliably evaluate *every* belief or proposal – including the belief that 'science is the only reliable arbitrator of reliable knowledge'. What experiment might show that science is the sole source of reliable knowledge? How could Rosenberg's claim be validated from outside a scientific perspective? Rosenberg's whole process of validation is ultimately self-referential and self-validating, allowing us to affirm the *internal consistency* but not the *truth* of this belief – and it *is* a belief, in that it cannot be proved to be true.

Furthermore, how can we *know* that there is no more to reality than the laws of nature that science discovers? Declaring that science is the 'ultimate standard and arbiter of all inter-esting questions' is making a second-order *philosophical* claim about science, which cannot be verified empirically. As the philosopher Edward Feser points out, Rosenberg is trapped in a circular argument. To break out of this circle, he suggests, 'requires "getting outside" science altogether' and verifying from an 'extra-scientific vantage point' that science alone offers a reliable picture of reality. Yet making this entirely reasonable intellectual move simply pulls the rug out from Rosenberg's argument. 'The very existence of that extra-scientific vantage point would falsify the claim that science *alone* gives us a ra-tional means of investigating objective reality.'[41]

Over the years, I have come to the view that there is a spectrum of human knowledge, which rests on the applica-tion of a range of different 'conceptual tool-boxes' (Midgley), each developed and adapted with specific research questions in mind. Some examples may help illustrate the rich diversity of questions that people consider significant, and which they hope may be answered.

What is the universe expanding into?

Why can't I be the good person that I know I ought to be?

How can I help deal with the world's environmental crisis? These are all real questions; yet they cannot be answered by a single disciplinary approach. For example, the expansion of the universe can be explained and justified through contem-porary cosmology; yet the real issue lying behind this question requires a different toolbox, in that it concerns the *psychological* question of how human beings can visualise four-dimensional space-time, when they have been habituated into three-dimensional modes of thinking.

Like the biologist Steven Rose, I consider that we live in a world that is an 'ontological unity',[42] while recognising that we must adopt 'an epistemological pluralism' if we are to investigate it responsibly and coherently. We use different research methods for each of its many aspects. The resulting forms of knowledge will have different characteristics and epistemic values – some capable of being proved (logic and mathematics), some well-evidenced yet open to revision over time through evidential accumulation and theoretical development (the natural sciences), and others taking the form of beliefs that may be trusted yet cannot be proved (ethics, politics and religion).

Knowledge of the world thus takes different forms; each of these has a different evidence base and form of reasoning, and consequently permits a different degree of epistemic confidence. But I can't force every aspect of human knowledge into the same epistemic container. I can't insist that ethics should be subject to the same methods and norms as physics. Nevertheless, it is reasonable to explore how these different forms of knowledge might be woven together, or at least be held together alongside each other.

The human quest for wisdom involves an interdisciplinary correlation of these insights. Yet the mood of our 'debauched culture invites us to simplify reality, to despise wisdom' (Susan Sontag).[43] Achieving wisdom, for Sontag, demands a full and attentive engagement with the *complexity* of reality. But how can this be done in practice, when in theory it seems to be impossible, given the issues that we have just noted?[44] In what follows, we will consider how the British public philosopher Mary Midgley approaches this important question.

Mary Midgley and the Correlation
of Human Knowledge

The realisation that our world is too vast and complex to be fully grasped by any single individual can be traced back to Plato. No single method of investigation can provide us with a comprehensive understanding of our world. Mary Midgley was a champion of an intellectually respectful engagement with our universe, arguing that it requires the use of many approaches and perspectives to do justice to its many aspects, and avoid a distorting reductionism. She insisted that the quality of our thinking ought to be as deep and complex as the world itself, demanding an expansion of our intellectual vision to enfold our complex world, rather than reducing it to the intellectually manageable.

Midgley suggests that it is helpful to compare the world to a 'huge aquarium', with multiple viewing windows to allow us not simply to consider its many aspects, but to realise that these are elements of a greater interconnected whole. 'We cannot see it as a whole from above, so we peer in at it through a number of small windows. ... We can eventually make quite a lot of sense of this habitat if we patiently put together the data from different angles. But if we insist that our own window is the only one worth looking through, we shall not get very far.'[45] Our world demands using a wide range of windows and viewpoints if we are to fully capture its depth and complexity.

Midgley's anti-reductionist strategy of 'multiple maps' allows us to capture, represent and, ultimately, safeguard the complexity of our world. We need a collection of maps, each incomplete, to view alongside each other.[46] These maps complement, rather than contradict; they each offer distinct accounts of the same territory, providing their own specific information and insights. A political map of Europe is not the same as a physical map of Europe; neither makes the other redundant. The first discloses the political boundaries of its regions, where one nation-state ends and other begins – matters that would be appreciated by refugees seeking safety. The second discloses the location of rivers, mountains and lakes – matters that would be appreciated by tourists and nature lovers. Both serve their own distinct purpose, disclosing only certain aspects of the landscape of reality which can be more fully grasped and comprehended by superimposing these individual maps. Yet when taken together, these maps unfold an extended vision of our world and human existence, allowing us to locate ourselves within its existential landscape.

Much the same point was made by Iris Murdoch, noted for her emphasis on the 'calming' and 'whole-making' effect of beliefs,[47] which help us to see the world as coherent and capable of sustaining meaningful human existence. Like Midgley, Murdoch recognised the importance of finding a unifying picture which coordinates the metaphysical (what reality *is*) with the existential (what reality *means*). Where Alex Rosenberg believes that the universe is meaningless, recommending judicious use of antidepressants such as Prozac to cope with this unsettling insight, Midgley and Murdoch argue that we can achieve mental stability by discerning the richer vision of the universe that results from interdisciplinary reflection and allows us insights into how we can live more authentically in this complex world.

Moving On

In this chapter, we have explored the idea of a 'big picture', a way of understanding this world and our place within it that is attentive to its particularities, while still attuned to the grander vision of reality that lies behind or beyond them. It creates specifically an imaginative space within which beliefs can be interconnected and enriched, enabling not simply an *explanation* of how our world works, but an *interpretation* of that world that enables its meaningful habitation.

For Wittgenstein, authentic meaning and happiness arise when we think and live in accordance with something deeper and greater than ourselves – something to which we are accountable for our beliefs. 'In order to live happily I must be in agreement with the world.'[48] Similar views can be instanced from Chinese or Japanese philosophies of life and spiritual traditions. Confucianism, for example, stresses the importance of enacting a way of life that is in harmony with the way of the world.[49]

To believe is not to be religious (though that is certainly one possible outcome); it is rather to have discerned 'an unseen order of some kind' or grasped an intuited scheme of things, that enables us to understand our world and live a meaningful life. The case for faith or belief in sustaining meaningful human existence does not need to be made on religious grounds, nor is religion the sole example – or even the *best* example – of a way of thinking that requires faith. Yet since many consider that religion is the most obvious instance of something that is characterised by beliefs, we will explore the question of specifically *religious* belief in the next chapter, before moving on to consider how we might assess the reliability of our beliefs.

Chapter 3

The Case of Religious Belief

It is fatally easy to believe that something that has been *named* is something that is *understood*. Everyone thinks they know what 'religion' is. Perhaps this is why it remains such a viable category in public discourse and everyday life. But cultural familiarity is not the same as intellectual stability. We are all familiar with the term 'love', but people profess and embody this notion in vastly different ways from one culture to another, across age groups and even within the same home.

What is Religion?

Religion, we are often told, is a universal human phenomenon. This may be true, but the popular *conceptualisation* of 'religion' is decidedly western, shaped by the social and intellectual history of modern western Europe and North America. Allegedly 'global' definitions of religion are generally based on the views of present-day WEIRD (western, educated, industrialised, rich and democratic) populations, overlooking the views of as much as eighty-eight per cent of humanity today, and reflecting a disturbing disregard for how the concept was understood in the past.

So, what do we study when we study religion? After all, a psychologist of religion or a sociologist of religion needs to know what they are meant to be investigating. Yet to speak of 'religion' is to enter a definitional cloud of unknowing, a miasma of personal opinions, cultural prejudices and questionable inherited intellectual habits which shroud the landscape like a dense fog. For example, while Judaism can be described as a 'religion', and Jews understood as adherents of this religion, there is growing scholarly evidence that Jews are better understood as a 'people group' with ancestral practices and beliefs that have become normative over time.[1]

Take Ancient Rome. The Latin word *religio* did not originally refer to a set of beliefs, but rather to a social and cultural obligation to perform certain actions, such as worshipping the gods in certain ways, or perform certain cultural obligations which were deemed 'venerable' or 'appropriate', yet which many westerners today would not regard as 'religious' in any sense. *Religio* in its classic Roman form focused on practices, rather than beliefs.

The problem here is 'essentialisation' – the belief that 'religion' is a real thing which has certain fixed features that allow generalisations, both subtle and crass, to be made across the religious world. Happily, a good knowledge of history and the scientific study of religion can help correct this influential misjudgement. Religion is not a 'natural kind' – a grouping or categorisation that reflects the structure of the natural world, rather than the interests and actions of human beings.[2] The modern western category of 'religion' is clearly inadequate.

In an influential study of how we should define religion and distinguish it from its alternatives, the social psychologist Jonathan Jong argues that the empirical evidence suggests there are good reasons for 'abandoning the deep-seated and intuitive assumption that religion is a natural kind, a category with an identifiable essence.'[3] 'Religion' is not a 'thing' that can be observed and precisely defined. Where many people hold that individual specific religions (such as Christianity, Buddhism and Hinduism) are examples of this 'thing', 'religion' as a *category* must be seen as fluid and historically contingent. For this reason, the anthropologist Talal Asad argues that 'there cannot be a universal definition of religion, not only because its constituent elements and relationships are historically specific, but because that definition is itself the historical product of discursive processes.'[4]

Asad's point about the social location of definitions of religion is reinforced by the magisterial historical analysis of the notions of 'religion' and 'science' developed by the Australian intellectual historian Peter Harrison, who points out that modern western discussions of the notions of 'religion' and 'the religions' represent an objectification or reification of what was once understood as an interior disposition.[5] To adopt an 'essentialist' understanding of religion is to assume that it is defined by some intrinsic qualities. Yet, as Jong points out, those qualities can also be found beyond the accepted understanding of 'religion'.

The term 'religion' was originally framed in terms of the possession or enactment of certain interior qualities, such as piety or devotion; yet the rationalising tendencies of the early modern period led to it being seen as referring to adherence to bodies of doctrine or knowledge. This helps us understand one core feature of the New Atheism – its 'Americanized understanding of religion as an iteration of knowledge'.[6] Richard Dawkins and Daniel Dennett offer a highly cognitive view of religion,

defining it virtually exclusively in terms of 'belief in God'. Yet
a more reliable description of religion would acknowledge its
multiple aspects, which include knowledge, beliefs, experience,
ritual practices and patterns of social affiliation and personal
identity.[7]

While philosophers in the past may have thought of faith in
terms of propositional belief, such as 'I believe that there is a
God', in recent years there has been a significant shift towards
thinking of faith in terms of allegiance, trust or hope[8] – notions
that are more easily aligned with Christian notions of faith as a
trusting relationship with affective and cognitive dimensions.
New Atheism, however, has gone in a different direction. It has
degraded and rationalised 'faith', treating it as a set of beliefs,
as if it is simply a form of data.

Perhaps the inevitable outcome of this process of rationalisation is Yuval Noah Harari's vision of the religion of the
future, already emerging within Silicon Valley – a 'Data
Religion' whose algorithms will decide how we will be governed.[9] Religion, once seen as a form of humility in which
we live our lives and align ourselves with something that
is greater than ourselves, has been redefined by modernist
thinkers simply in terms of a quest for a controlling set of
beliefs.

Some have argued that we need a new definition of religion
to find our way out of this mess. I'm sceptical about this. Too
many recent attempts to redefine religion are constructed in
the pursuit of unacknowledged agendas and vested interests.
My solution is inadequate (but less so than its alternatives) – to
recognise that what we have come to mean by 'religion' is more
complex than any single definition can encapsulate.

I recall a meeting in London that I attended, discussing the future of religious communities in a changing culture. One speaker argued for the public repudiation of all forms of religion, based on the behaviour of the Taliban in Afghanistan. Jews and Hindus present in the audience vigorously objected to the vilification of their religious traditions based on the speaker's views about a *different* religious group. 'You're religious,' the speaker responded to these objections. 'You're all the same.' We see here both a somewhat uncritical formulation of the Enlightenment's belief that individual religions are representative of a universal concept of 'religion', along with the negative reaction that such crude stereotyping rightly provokes.

How did this influential misrepresentation achieve such cultural dominance? Why do so many still buy into this outdated idea that religion is a 'thing'?

How 'Religion' became a False Universal

It is well known that the concept of 'religion' varies from one historical and cultural context to another. Some historical examples highlight the problems in assuming that the term 'religion' is an unproblematically valid universal category. Pre-Columbian Mesoamerican inscriptions do not contain any words that can plausibly be translated as 'religion'.[10] Yet following the Spanish colonisation of this region, the Spanish term *religión* seems to have been used by early modern ethnographers working in seventeenth-century Mesoamerica as a self-evidently appropriate term to refer to a variety of indigenous cultural practices, which were then assimilated into this western cultural phenomenon. A European template was thus imposed on indigenous Mesoamerican ways of thinking.[11]

A century later, Britain established a commercial base in India, which eventually led to the colonisation of the region. Once more, western observers, noting certain Indian cultural beliefs and practices that did not easily fit into existing categories (such as 'philosophy'), designated these as forms of 'religion', and created the English term 'Hinduism' to enfold the variegated phenomena they witnessed in the Indian religious landscape.[12]

Many have argued that the very idea of Hinduism was a construct of the colonial enterprise, 'fabricated in the service of foreign interests, whether by European Orientalists or the British colonial regime.'[13] Others have argued that colonialism gave a new significance to indigenous Indian religions as a means of preserving Indian cultural identity during the colonial period, thus encouraging the idea that Hinduism was a multi-dimensional unitary faith. To this day, Hindu scholars regularly (and rightly) complain that a group of Asian cultural beliefs and practices are still being assimilated to European categories.

The same pattern can be seen in the western construction of 'Confucianism' as a religion, when it is better seen as a *philosophy of life* than as a *religion*.[14] Yet again, an indigenous cultural movement was forced into the preconceived ethnocentric framework of a colonial power, which misrepresents its historical particularities (above all, its own understanding and experience of the nature and social function of 'religion') as normative and universal. The universal concept of 'religion' is ultimately an outdated remnant of a colonial past, and needs to be recalibrated and rehabilitated, if not set aside as unhelpful and unreliable.

Defining Religion: The Problem of Platonism

It is often assumed that the recognition of a supernatural realm or transcendent dimension to life (such as belief in God) is a distinct characteristic of religion, and that the term 'religious' can be applied to anyone holding such a view. In conversation with Gary Wolf (the journalist who introduced the phrase 'New Atheism' in 2006), Richard Dawkins identified the key issue with religious believers as 'supernaturalism' – belief in something that lies beyond the empirical world.

Yet Dawkins' use of the word 'supernatural' is puzzling. People have believed in gods since the dawn of time, and developed a vocabulary adapted to this belief. Yet the Latin term *supernaturalis* only came into use in the thirteenth century to designate a 'mental geography' in which events or entities could be assigned to two possible domains – the 'natural' and 'supernatural'.[15]

Yet this belief is held, whether it is implicitly assumed or explicitly articulated, in the writings of many scientists and mathematicians who are struck by the remarkable ability of mathematics to represent the contours of reality.[16] In his important work *Our Mathematical Universe*, the physicist Max Tegmark sets out his 'mathematical universe hypothesis': our universe is not simply described or represented by mathematics; it *is* mathematics.[17] To many, especially those who believe that human beings construct our realities, it seems deeply counterintuitive to suggest that coherent mathematical structures exist *beyond the human mind*. Some rationalists have even used the argument that this seems *religious*, presumably assuming such an association might discredit the notion (it hasn't).

The mathematician and theoretical physicist Roger Penrose, who won the 2020 Nobel Prize in Physics, does not self-define as 'religious'; he nevertheless affirms the existence of a transcendent realm on the basis of his interpretation of the role of mathematics in the successes of the natural sciences.[18] Penrose argues that we need to expand our concept of 'real existence', refusing to limit this to physical objects by including mathematical structures which seem to exist before they are discovered.[19] While Penrose is open to these mysteries being explained (in ways that we presently do not know), his view that there exists a 'real' mathematical world that we discover rather than invent is a helpful reminder that such beliefs about a transcendent world exist beyond the world of 'religion', and that there are non-religious considerations that underlie their acceptance.

The same basic idea lies behind Plato's celebrated 'theory of forms', which emerged during the classical period of Greek philosophy. (Penrose's position is sometimes described as 'Mathematical Platonism.') Yet although Plato proposed a world that lies beyond that of everyday experience, this was not seen as 'religious' in the terms of the classical age. The gradual transformation of classical Greek religion from reflective social practice into a form of belief system dates from a later stage of classical antiquity.[20] Plato's approach was seen as *philosophical* at that time, offering a reliable way of seeing reality (which Plato expresses using the Greek term *theōria*) which leads into an appropriate way of living.[21]

It is difficult to see how Penrose's 'Platonic world' can be assigned to any category other than something that lies beyond nature, particularly given the distinction he draws between this 'Platonic' world and the 'mental world' of reflective human beings. Dawkins, as we saw earlier, identified supernaturalism as a core concern in his controversy with religious people. So, are Platonists *religious?* Forms of mathematical Platonism – such as that of Penrose – certainly have their critics, particularly social constructivists, but there is no doubting either the quality of the reasoning that leads them to their conclusions, or the intellectual resilience of this position. Yet I have not met a mathematical Platonist who equates their belief in a Platonic world with being 'religious'. There are no grounds for considering this to be a religious position, other than the lingering presence of discredited notions of 'religion' within less informed sections of western culture. Mathematical Platonism is a philosophical doctrine about a real world that is held to exist beyond the human mind.

There are, however, some who have found their way from a transcendent world of Platonic ideals to a specifically religious belief. The American philosopher Paul Elmer More, for example, was initially fascinated by the ideal world of beautiful Platonic forms, the silent and impersonal world of the purely ideal.[22] However, More began to experience a sense of unutterable bleakness and loneliness in this still and faceless realm. 'To be satisfied I must see face to face.'[23] More's yearning to find a personal reality was finally met through the Christian doctrine of the incarnation, which allowed the 'face of God' to be seen.

More's comments chime in with Salman Rushdie's declaration that it is difficult to describe or define human beings 'in terms that exclude their spiritual needs'.[24] More's personal narrative also helps us see how individuals are often drawn to religious faith for quite different reasons, reflecting the diversity of human needs and aspirations. While some flatten the spiritual needs of humanity, the evidence suggests a more complex set of factors that have the potential to draw individuals to faith. More's desire to see 'face to face' in a world of abstractions may not be representative; it is, however, illustrative of the many factors that incline people to explore religious faith.

Religious Belief: A Preliminary Exploration

Our familiarity with the word 'religion' has created a false sense of security in its capacity and legitimacy to represent the many complex human attempts to make sense of our world. The term cannot bear the weight that has been placed upon it in contemporary discussions about the place of religion in our world, and we have yet to find a way of dealing with this problem.

Suggesting that there is no defensible intellectual category of religion does not in any way disparage or devalue individual religions – whether we use that specific term or not – such as Christianity, Judaism, Islam, Buddhism or Hinduism. If anything, it allows us to focus on them as individual movements with their own distinct identities and histories, instead of feeling we have to force them into the predetermined (and problematic) category of 'religion', with the inevitable simplifications, associations, accommodations and distortions that this process of forced assimilation entails. Instead of offering anodyne and contrived generalities about religion, we can focus on appreciating and understanding specific faith systems, and on their own terms.

This consideration is central to the approach to religion that I shall adopt in this book. I will not offer potentially misleading religious generalisations, but will primarily reflect on Christianity, which I know and understand well. This focus on the world's largest religion as a worked example enables me to deal with most of the issues and concerns relating to religious belief by using the faith I have embraced, which is likely to be familiar, at least to some extent, to many of my readers.

This worked example allows me to look at many of the issues and concerns about religious faith in general, and I invite those who are members of other faith communities, or have knowledge of these, to supplement my own reflections with theirs. Let me make it clear that I have no institutional authority or representative status in this matter. I am simply an informed and reflective Christian who is well placed to explore the question of belief, and hopes to help others do the same. With this point in mind, we turn to consider the question of what it means when I say 'I believe …' from a religious perspective. And how might this differ from the use of this phrase in an everyday context?

One of the more frustrating aspects of discussing issues of belief, whether in friendly and productive discussions with academic colleagues or in sometimes fraught public debates with atheists, is that fundamental words like 'faith' or 'God' are conceptualised in completely different ways by both parties. I used to inhabit an atheist mindset and know its contours, its appeal. But I often wonder whether some of my atheist colleagues comprehend religious belief's purpose, often presenting their misapprehensions as if they are self-evidently true, lying beyond question or challenge. (I am sure the same problem emerges with atheism, which is much more diverse than many beyond this community realise.)

The philosopher Thomas Nagel once asked: what is it like to be a bat?[25] The point he was making remains important. If you *aren't* a bat, you can't tell what it's like to *be* a bat, as this demands a comprehension of the bat's first-person subjective experience. We may understand something about bats (such as the way they locate objects through echolocation), but that is an external third-person perspective, which doesn't clarify anything about what it *feels like* to be a bat. Thomas Metzinger made a similar point, emphasising the divergence of two completely different ways of thinking or experiencing: an 'inner' account (a 'first-person perspective') and an 'outside' account (a 'third-person perspective').[26]

I often feel that some atheist critiques of religion are based on uninterrogated external assumptions about what religion must *be* and how religion must *feel*, lacking any sense of intellectual curiosity or cultural empathy that might motivate them to understand what religious people think and mean by words such as 'faith' or 'belief'. Terry Eagleton is one of many cultural critics to make this point: 'imagine someone holding forth on biology whose only knowledge of the subject is the *Book of British Birds*, and you have a rough idea of what it feels like to read Richard Dawkins on theology.'[27] Philip Pullman is much more alert to the complexities of faith than Dawkins, highlighting the importance of a 'sense that there is a power bigger than us' which is 'deserving of attention and respect', while at the same time rightly expressing concerns about the entanglements of organised religion with money and political influence.[28]

This tendency to misunderstand or misread religious terms may help us understand why atheist critics of religious faith often focus on purely propositional understandings of belief, or interpret God in terms of imagined teapots orbiting distant planets, or 'sky fairies' that do not match up with either the self-understanding or experience of religious believers. As has often been pointed out, 'what the atheist rejects is seldom what the theologian or believer professes.'[29] The outcome is inevitable: the dialogue partners misunderstand each other, shooting past each other rather than engaging in a meaningful conversation.

Thinking of religious beliefs in terms of 'cosmic teapots' suggests that they are essentially a form of 'knowledge through description', along the same lines as scientific statements, making no personal claims on the person who holds these views. This view of religion as a misguided and outdated form of science, set out originally in James Frazer's *Golden Bough* (1890), misses the point completely.[30]

As Wittgenstein reminds us, we need to listen to how people use key words, and appreciate that they may understand them in ways that differ from our own intuitive sense of what they *ought* to mean. In discussing beliefs in public debate, I often find that my opponents present a mangled and muddled account of Christianity, sometimes derived from a somewhat uncritical reading of oracular atheistic writers (Christopher Hitchens seems to be a favourite) – not, I think, because they deliberately misrepresent it for polemical reasons, but because they don't quite grasp what it is all about in the first place, or assume that it is so obviously deficient that no further investigation is needed.

Most religions don't have any form of creeds – formal statements of the main points of faith. Judaism, from which Christianity emerged during the first century, has a simple affirmation of faith in God known as the 'Shema' – but not a detailed list of specific beliefs.[31] The main forms of Roman and Greek religion at this time do not appear to have felt the need for formal declarations of faith. Yet while Christianity is not typical in its use of public statements of faith, all religious traditions (and, of course, their secular counterparts) rest on certain beliefs, whether these are publicly affirmed or personally appropriated.

The so-called Apostles' Creed is thought to have emerged gradually within early Christian communities, particularly in Rome, apparently in response to the need for brief personal articulations of faith on the part of people who presented themselves for baptism. The Creeds set out the Christian vision of reality in dull, terse statements, each of which encapsulates an aspect of this greater vision that cannot be *proved* to be true, but which was *found* to be true and *made* to be meaningful by a community of people, who have passed down in the Creeds their collective witness to what they discovered.

Back in the 1980s, the Canadian philosopher Charles Taylor introduced his idea of 'articulation'. Every attempt to live a good life or develop a viable moral system depends on a set of background assumptions which need to be identified and put into words. 'Articulation' is about the 'bringing to light of that which is unspoken but presupposed'.[32] Taylor's point is that we need to put into words the grander vision of reality which shapes the way we think and live, despite the obvious inability of words to do justice or fully express this vision. A similar point is made by William James, who argued that religious doctrines are subsidiary to the way that religious people *experienced* the universe and *felt* about their place within it.[33]

The way we imagine the world – whether socially, morally, politically or religiously – needs to be expressed; yet paradoxically that very act of expression both diminishes and restricts that vision, precisely because it is a rich imaginative reality that cannot be reduced to words. These statements – such as 'I believe in God' – are too easily misunderstood as purely (and uninterestingly) *propositional*, when they are really descriptions of something that is to be encountered and explored, a map of a new territory to be inhabited, both intellectually and socially.

For Christians, faith is thus not a half-hearted hope that there might be a God, but a luminous vision of a God who brings meaning, coherence and joy. It is about 'getting' what things are all about in an epiphanic moment of seeing a oneness at the heart of things, allowing us to put everything together. Faith is about existential commitment. This is what I believe to be right and trustworthy. This is how I see the world.

The New Testament presents Christianity primarily as a trustworthy way of thinking and living; the Creeds subsequently expressed this more formally, focusing on the content of belief, rather than how it is to be lived out, and the difference that this makes. The Creeds are thus not so much a demand to believe as a *description* of what other Christians have found, an *affirmation* of its capacity to satisfy and sustain, and an *invitation* to explore, discover and inhabit this new world. To believe in God is to place trust in God and take up the responsibilities and expectations that come with this relationship.

Thinking of Creeds in this way allows us to see them as expressing frameworks of exploration and discovery. There is a constant and creative interplay between faith understood as a response to a vision of God on the one hand, and as a formally stated belief about God on the other. Rather than presenting us with a set of verbal formulae as 'givens', the Creeds point to a rich landscape that we can explore, identifying its landmarks that deserve our attention. They are like guidebooks, telling us what to look out for – and thus countering our natural tendency to limit ourselves to the familiar by pointing out what we have yet to discover.

While it is important to have verbal articulations of faith, these can too easily be misunderstood as defining the essence of faith when they are signposts to its core vision, which cannot be adequately expressed in words. For William James, religion is about 'felt knowledge' – an experience that isn't a thought, but feels as if it is.

If the Christian faith can be compared to a landscape, then its best guides are those who live there, having internalised its contours and incorporated them into their lives. There is a necessary and proper synergy between the statements of the Creeds and the personal experiences of Christians. The Creeds map the landscape of faith; yet individual Christian believers are best placed to explain and unpack its features, and the difference that this makes to their lives. The primary witnesses to the vitality of faith are ordinary Christians, who can connect the landmarks of faith with their personal journeys of discovery and living out their faith, and explain how these credal statements affect the way they live not merely how they think.

Let me gather together these reflections, and show how they help us give a Christian answer to the question, 'What does it mean to believe in God?' Is it like believing in an extra moon orbiting the planet Uranus – a factual statement about something just being there? No. For Christians, faith is trusting that there is a viable 'big picture' of life, leading into a decision to step inside this worldview, and live it out. The

Latin word *credo* (I believe) has the root meaning 'to trust or confide in something or someone'. While we now tend to think of belief in terms of a hesitant theoretical judgement, the creeds see it as a confident personal commitment. I cannot prove that this is true, but I know there is something here that I cannot let go of without losing my identity, significance and meaning.

Historically, early Christianity did not see itself as a 'religion' (as many now use that word) based on a set of beliefs to which we must assent, but as a way of imagining and living which we can trust, and are invited to enter. Perhaps for this reason, the early Christians were initially known as both 'believers' and 'followers of the way' – people who thought and acted in a new way.[34]

What is the difference between a 'religious' belief and an 'ordinary' belief? To begin with, there is an obvious similarity: like ordinary beliefs, religious beliefs lie beyond proof. Yet they are not individual disconnected affirmations; they are elements of a greater scheme of things which we are invited to trust, and make the basis of our way of thinking and living. Earlier, I mentioned the philosopher of religion Keith Yandell's definition of a religion, which captures this point without falling into the error of assuming that belief in God is integral to the identity of religion. His 'neutral definition' of religion needs to be quoted more fully.

> A religion is a conceptual system that provides an interpretation of the world and the place of human beings in it, bases an account of how life should be lived given that interpretation, and expresses this interpretation and lifestyle in a set of rituals, institutions and practices.[35]

Yandell chose this definition with some care, aiming to avoid bias in terms of its outcomes. Where the New Atheism defined religion in terms that were designed to facilitate its ridicule and destructive criticism, Yandell does not presuppose anything about the truth or falsity of religion, nor fall into the error of assuming that a religion necessarily involves belief in a god or gods. His concern is to place religion upon a conceptual map, and try to clarify at least some aspects of its distinct identity and functions.

One aspect of Yandell's analysis is particularly significant: his clear recognition that a religious 'conceptual system' leads to the creation of moral values and the emergence of a manner of living which is not based on some allegedly universal human rationality, but is an appropriate expression or enactment of the internal logic of this religion. We now know enough about the emergence of human rationalities to reject the notion that there is some universal normative pattern of reasoning, outside the specialist realms of logic and mathematics; cultural rationalities emerge historically, and are shaped by their social contexts.

Some believe that you can judge religions objectively – as, for example, in the Enlightenment's appeal to a universal human rationality, which transcends the limitations of any religious worldview. Yet there is no such neutral standard or standpoint, and we must always judge religions in light of some ultimate truth-commitment that lies beyond external proof. Judging a religion often seems to involve assessing one belief on the basis of another belief. Wittgenstein rightly points out that rationality has a history, and that it takes different forms in different social locations: 'What men consider reasonable or unreasonable alters. At certain periods, men find reasonable what at other periods they found unreasonable. And vice-versa.'[36]

Although Yandell does not engage Pierre Hadot's call for the revitalisation of philosophy as a set of practices arising from theoretical discourse, his approach suggests significant points of connection with the theme of 'finding spiritual nourishment'.[37] Yandell rightly sees that conceptual systems create and inform ways of life – one of the most characteristic aspects of major religions. This insight is affirmed by recent psychological studies of the distinctive role of religion in human life. In general terms, religion engages three deep human needs that seem to be essential for our flourishing.

> Religion is unique in that it can inform all three components of existential meaning for individuals and cultures: religion provides a coherent, encompassing narrative that has great explanatory power; it outlines specific values and goals that are to be pursued; and it conveys a sense of transcendence that goes beyond the mundane and the ephemeral.[38]

Religious Belief: Grasping a Vision, Not Just Accepting Ideas

Yandell's definition of religion as a 'conceptual system' suggests that it is something that is apprehended primarily (if not solely) through rational reflection. For many, this aspect of faith is of decisive importance. G. K. Chesterton, for example, returned to Christianity primarily on account of its capacity to make sense of the world. Yet there is ample evidence that many are primarily drawn to religious belief or commitment for imaginative, emotional, aesthetical or existential reasons – and subsequently discover, appreciate and internalise its rational virtues.

In an important reflection on the nature of belief in God, John Cottingham argued that the core divergence between atheism and theism does not lie primarily in matters of theoretical belief or philosophical argument, but rather in their differing affective responses to reality, and in the adoption of certain models for living.[39] An atheist and a theist live in the same physical world – a 'world of pain and loss, of vulnerability and danger, and, even in the case where the individual comes through unscathed, of eventual inevitable physical and mental deterioration and, finally, death.'[40] Yet they each *see*, *understand* and *experience* this world in very different ways, as a result of the different perceptual frameworks they use to interpret it.[41] Although this statement needs to be treated with caution, we could say that these two observers live in *different* worlds, in that each has a quite distinct vision of the world and their place within it. And this affects how we *feel* about ourselves and the world.

It makes no difference to me how many moons the planet Saturn has, or whether the scientific consensus about the age of the universe is 13.8 billion years or 13.797 billion years. These don't affect me. I don't connect with them. From a religious perspective, God is not an item of information but the basis of a meaningful life, evoking worship and adoration rather than an indifferent mental assent. Faith is affective, not simply cognitive, offering *transformation* and not merely *information*.

Religion in general has the capacity to create a new and intensified engagement with the natural world and the fundamental questions of existence. My Oxford colleague Mark Wynn has explored the ways in which religious ideas or frameworks can help stimulate and shape our sensory experience.

Wynn channels the Harvard psychologist William James, who noted that an individual's perception and experience of the world often shifted radically as a result of their religious conversion: 'It was like entering another world, a new state of existence. Natural objects were glorified, my spiritual vision was so clarified that I saw beauty in every material object in the universe, the woods were vocal with heavenly music.'[42]

This emphasis on a new way of seeing things, or a new quality of apprehending the world, needs further exploration. David Cooper suggests that a religious teacher or tradition offers not so much a set of ideas to be accepted but a 'vision' that is to be apprehended and inhabited – a way of beholding our world which, once it has been 'properly absorbed', leads to a new *attitude* towards the world.[43] While Cooper explores this question from a Daoist perspective, the same point is made repeatedly from other religious standpoints.

One of the most important recent discussions of this point is found in Charles Taylor's notion of the 'social imaginary', which shifts attention from abstract theories and ideas about reality to the way in which we imagine our world, and locate ourselves within it. The way we imagine the world is prior to what we believe about it, which is 'not expressed in theoretical terms, but is carried in images, stories, and legends',[44] more easily and naturally expressed using the language of 'seeing' than 'thinking'.

The Oxford philosopher of religion Austin Farrer saw this point as central to understanding why C. S. Lewis's way of commending Christianity was so effective, particularly in comparison with more abstract rational defences of faith. Lewis, he suggested, was not setting out an evidential case for

Christianity, appealing to the human reason. He was rather depicting and projecting its vision of reality, that it might capture the imaginations of his audience. Lewis allows us to 'think we are listening to an argument', when we are actually 'presented with a vision, and it is the vision that carries conviction.'[45]

For Farrer, this vision is encountered and experienced as real, significant and imaginatively desirable – and so people are drawn into it, absorbing rather than merely accepting its core themes, and finding that these inform and motivate their existence. We do not simply *observe* this vision as spectators; we find that we are caught up in it, and *participate* in its account of reality.

From a religious perspective, this leads to actions that express and enact this core vision of reality – in the case of Christianity, to prayer, adoration and worship, which are seen as authentic and natural ways of celebrating and expressing this 'religious imaginary'. This once more highlights the need for outsiders to empathetically 'step inside' religion, and try to grasp how it changes the way people see and experience the world, and offers a framework for living. We will have more to say about this later, as we turn to engage the role of belief in exploring the great human questions of finding meaning, value, significance in life, and developing ways of living that express and embody them.

Yet we now need to reflect on a question that many will see as essential to any discussion of beliefs, particularly religious beliefs – namely, how can these be evaluated? If a belief is something that cannot be *proved* to be true, what evidence can be set out in its support? We shall explore these questions further in the next chapter.

Chapter 4

Making Judgements:
Belief, Explanation and Interpretation

The *Oxford Dictionaries* 'Word of the Year' for 2016 was a new arrival, symptomatic of yet another shift within the public rationality of western culture – 'post-truth', defined as 'relating to or denoting circumstances in which objective facts are less influential in shaping public opinion than appeals to emotion and personal belief.'

The iconic cover of the April 1966 number of *Time* magazine posed a question, highlighted in red against a stark black background, that cut to the heart of the cultural debates of that age: *Is God dead?* Its March 2017 counterpart mimicked this dramatic style in posing the new question lying at the core of American public life: *Is Truth dead?* Do we live in an age of aggressively asserted private beliefs, rather than evidenced public truths? Was the sociologist and cultural critic Philip Rieff right in characterising the history of human civilisation as a shift from 'fate' to 'faith' – and finally to 'fiction'?[1] Why are objective facts now less influential in shaping public opinion than appeals to subjective emotion and personal belief? Is this just some transient form of generational narcissism, or is it the shape of the future?

In such an environment, personal belief – that is, something that cannot be proved to be true but is believed to be reasonable – flourishes; the problem is that it is recategorised as 'truth'. While some speak about a rejection of authority in western culture, we are really seeing a *relocation* of authority within individual private experience that leads to people becoming trapped in their own personal versions of reality, refusing to accept external referents that might call these into question.

Many are alarmed at these developments, feeling that such an emphasis on context, discourse and history has led to a neglect of traditional concerns for truth and a responsible attempt to grasp a reality which ultimately lies beyond our control and to which we can be held accountable. We are caught up in a battle of ideas in which there is no criterion of adjudication accepted by both parties. Some claim that knowledge is *independent* of history, power and perspective, and others that knowledge is *determined* by history, power and perspective.

A Post-Truth World: Conspiracy Theories and Wish-Fulfilment

One of the most important manifestations of a post-truth culture is the surge in contemporary conspiracy theories. Dan Brown's highly successful novel *The Da Vinci Code* (2002) fictionalised some controversial theories regarding early Christian history, arguing that the Catholic Church kept secret Jesus Christ's marriage to Mary Magdalene, from which sprang a 'holy lineage' protected by a secret organisation known as the 'Priory of Sion.'[2] Despite its obvious evidential deficits – and the fact it is conceived as fiction – this theory achieved a huge following. It was what a lot of people wanted to believe.

Some conspiracy theories are religious – for example, the idea that American government agencies have been infiltrated by Satanists. Others are anti-religious – such as the sensational theory that COVID-19 was a synthesised form of cobra venom that was intentionally being spread via drinking water and vaccines, possibly as part of a plot by the Catholic Church to turn everyone into a 'hybrid of Satan'.[3] Most, however, are based on cultural and political beliefs – such as an alleged London paedophile ring run by political elites, or the 'Great Replacement Theory' which holds that an indigenous white European population is being replaced by non-European immigrants. These theories often function as rallying points for social groups, especially minorities that are perceived or treated as marginalised outsiders. The rise of the Internet has led to uncontrolled dissemination of such conspiracy theories, which, on account of their 'ubiquity and repetition on the net, have assumed a veracity divorced from reality.'[4]

As might be expected, these theories have attracted a lot of academic attention. Why do so-called 'free thinkers' believe such weird things? Although these were initially seen as pathological, perhaps resulting from 'brainwashing',[5] more recent studies have seen them as indicative of neglected aspects of human reasoning that illuminate how people arrive at beliefs, and enact these in their lives. Such theories tend to attract people looking for simple explanations for complex phenomena, and who are unwilling or unable to think critically.[6] Studies of followers of the 'Da Vinci Code' theory, for example, suggest that they were unable or reluctant to consider alternatives, or engage the evidence suggesting it might be a fake. Once they believed it, they couldn't be swayed.

A dispassionate observer of conspiracy theories might suggest that they indicate the danger of belief – people see logic where there is none and then refute anything that contradicts their views, sometimes to dangerous and violent ends. Conspiracy theories are certainly indicators of gullibility, the disturbing capacity of human beings to believe weird things.[7] Yet the best way to counter this is not to suppress belief as a general category, but to foster the emergence of a *critical* belief – that is to say, a belief that is affirmed knowing its vulnerabilities, in the light of an individual's critical judgement that this represents the best way of making sense of things in comparison with a range of possibilities.

The rise of a post-truth world has exposed a major concern – the public assertion of ideas that people *want* to be true, and retrospectively developing arguments in their support. As the satirist Hasan Minhaj observed, 'emotional truth is first. The factual truth is secondary.'[8] If you want to believe something, you will find ways of rationalising that belief and persuading yourself that it is true.

Aldous Huxley, the author of *Brave New World* (1932), anticipates this form of thinking that has become so influential in a post-truth world: identify your preferred conclusion, persuade yourself this is a self-evident truth, cherry-pick the evidence, and declare this conclusion to be the only option for a thinking person. 'I had motives for not wanting the world to have a meaning; consequently assumed that it had none, and was able without any difficulty to find satisfying reasons for this assumption.'[9]

Sigmund Freud saw this need-driven form of argument as typical of religion, which proposed God as a human 'wish-fulfilment' offering a false consolation in the face of a meaningless world. Yet Freud failed to be consistent here: we are all – whether religious or secular – prone to create an imagined world which corresponds to our desires, and retrospectively develop arguments for its validation. Some secular humanists, for example, assert the fundamental goodness of humanity. It is a noble aspiration, which is called into question by the formidable moral challenge posed by the brutality of human history. As John Gray points out, 'genocide is as human as art or prayer'. The easiest way of coping with this is by denying the problem through a highly selective reading of our history. A more realistic approach recognises that we are indeed a flawed species with a remarkable capacity for self-deception.[10] At least this helps us to figure out how we might come to terms with this problem. Can we cope with human evil if we define humanity as fundamentally good? Happily, most humanists are fully aware of this problem, and are rightly cautious in asserting human goodness as a fundamental article of faith.

Atheism can be argued to represent another example of the reification of a desire for total autonomy and unaccountability. The philosopher Thomas Nagel illustrates this point well. Nagel's own account of the origins of and motivation for his atheism suggests that it is a *post hoc* rationalisation of something more fundamental – his *desire* for a godless universe. 'I hope there is no God! I don't want there to be a God; I don't want the universe to be like that.'[11]

In a post-truth age, it seems reasonable to claim experiential or emotional privilege for our beliefs and desires – 'it's true for me.' This self-referential position allows the individual thinker absolute authority in matters of their own beliefs; given their dismissal of external perspectives or adjudications, there would seem to be no way of disproving what they assert in terms that they would consider to be valid.

Yet even in a world in which there is a widening fissure between public truth and private belief, most still agree that beliefs need to be examined and assessed. The New Testament's advice that Christians should 'test everything, and hold fast to what is good' exemplifies the critical spirit that intelligent religious faith demands, deserves and regularly – though sadly not invariably – exhibits.[12] Pope Francis speaks for the Christian tradition as a whole when he points out that faith must be grounded in truth; if it does not it is simply 'a beautiful story, the projection of our deep yearning for happiness, something capable of satisfying us to the extent that we are willing to deceive ourselves.'[13]

As Plato suggested, an 'unexamined life' is not a meaningful form of existence. We need to think critically about what we believe – both in terms of what we affirm, and what we exclude. We cannot live authentically through affirming publicly what we know to be false privately. Yet as an educationalist, I have come to the reluctant conclusion that an alarming number of people don't want to think about their core beliefs or values, whether secular or religious, fearing that these might be exposed as inadequate or delusional.

I remember a conversation with a retired politician in Belfast many years ago, when I queried him on this point. How, I asked him, could he publicly defend an idea that was (at least in my view) ridiculous. His answer? 'Practice, dear boy. Lots of practice.' We need to have a serious conversation about these matters. The denial of reality may be a convenient political stratagem, but it is hardly a basis for a sustainable worldview. Can we live a meaningful life if we suspect that we may have based our identities on something false?

A good place to start is the science fiction writer Philip K. Dick's 1978 speech 'How to build a universe that doesn't fall apart two days later', in which he reflected on the nature of reality, and our generally hopeless attempts to resist the lure of fake realities.[14] We live in a society in which 'spurious realities are manufactured by the media, by governments, by big corporations, by religious groups, political groups – and the electronic hardware exists by which to deliver these pseudo-worlds right into the heads of the reader, the viewer, the listener.' But there is a problem here that goes right to the heart of human identity: 'Fake realities will create fake humans.' Human authenticity depends on experiencing and encountering reality which challenges and excites us, not some fake reality designed to advance someone's agenda. We need a centre to our lives that will hold firm and shelter us.

For Dick, human beings seem to be hardwired to construct 'universes of the mind'. We are brilliant at constructing throwaway worldviews, understandings of our universe and our place within it which are a response to a transient cultural mood or a pressing personal need. When the cultural wind changes direction, the worldview is quietly sidelined once it has ceased to be fashionable. Dick's analysis confirms the importance of a way of thinking that has been tried and tested over an extended period of time, having been both thought through and lived out. Its virtues lie not in its novelty, but in its perceived real-life relevance and reliability.

The German poet Hermann Hesse identified this problem in Germany during the period of the Weimar Republic in the 1920s. He despaired that what passed as 'critical thinking' back then was little more than a loose aggregation of 'intellectual fashions' and the 'transitory values of the day'.[15] To Hesse, it seemed that Weimar culture was little more than a superficial intellectual formalisation of 'intellectual mediocrity, of surface glitter, smug comfort, sham conventionality, and foolish optimism.'[16] The historian Peter Gay concurs with this analysis: in his view, the cultural mood of Weimar Germany was driven by a suspension of critical thinking, an exaltation of irrationality, and a romanticised yearning for the order and stability of the old German Empire which paved the way for Hitler's rise to power.[17]

Hesse concluded that many in Germany, dissatisfied with flaky cultural superficialities, were coming to long for a world-view that was anchored in the depths of reality. As we've seen, Germany in 1920s and 1930s, dominated by 'spurious realities', ended up lacking the intellectual and cultural resources to resist the more robust ideology of the age: Nazism. And so Martin Heidegger, that doyen of German philosophy, declared in 1933: 'The Führer alone is the present and future German reality and its law. Learn to know ever more deeply: that from now on every single thing demands decision, and every action responsibility. Heil Hitler!'

What is reality? For Dick, the answer could be stated in a single sentence: 'Reality is that which, when you stop believing in it, doesn't go away.' Reality does not depend on us for its existence. It is not a social construction or cultural invention, something that we control or create, but is rather something that stands in distinction to – though not necessarily *against* – us, which can ground, inform and enrich our social, cultural and spiritual existence. Dick's analysis raises numerous questions that need to be explored, including whether classical worldviews which have a much longer history of mental inhabitation, existential testing, and practical implementation might provide more resilient and fulfilling ways of living than their short-lived modern counterparts.

In what follows, we shall reflect on how we believe we might gain access to reality. To begin with, we shall reach into the past, and consider some formative reflections on these themes from classic Greek philosophy.

Plato and Aristotle on Theory

The word 'theory' is now widely used to refer to a 'system of ideas intended to explain something' or a 'rational type of abstract thinking about a phenomenon'. It has overtones of detachment and abstraction, allowing the observer to stand over and against the observed. Yet the modern English word 'theory' offers an impoverished and attenuated account of a more complex and comprehensive idea, which has been adapted for the specific technical needs of the natural sciences.

For classic Greek philosophers, a theory is not primarily an abstract set of ideas; it is fundamentally a way of beholding and inhabiting reality. Where modern understandings of theory, for understandable reasons, reduce it to an intellectual desiccation or a rational abstraction, the Greek term *theōria* offers us a richer vision of how we envisage our world, sensitive to our need to see or imagine things as they really are, and work out how we fit into the picture that it discloses.[18] We are not passive and disinterested spectators of an external reality, but are active and informed participants in its processes.

Plato used the term *theōria* to designate a way of seeing and grasping reality that lay at the heart of philosophy.[19] The philosopher is someone who has caught a grand vision of reality, or experienced a transformative beholding of the world, and is able to communicate this to others so that they might capture its vision and live accordingly. Plato draws on the metaphor of a shadowy cave, within which humanity is confined; the philosopher is someone who has seen the greater world beyond this cave, is transformed by this vision, and tries to articulate this to those who remain within the cave.

To 'theorise' was thus not about developing abstract ideas, but was rather about discovering and then actively participating in a vision of some greater reality that was best expressed using visual metaphors (such as 'seeing'). As Pierre Hadot has emphasised, many forms of ancient philosophy did not focus on abstract reflection, but on developing intellectually defensible and existentially viable 'ways of living' that *embodied* this transformative vision of humanity and the cosmos. A good philosophy is something that we can embody, not merely teach or explain.

In some ways, the classical understanding of 'theory' is thus closer to the modern idea of a worldview – a way of *framing* or *imagining* the world that both discloses its intrinsic rationality and interconnectedness, while at the same time providing a framework for the creation of meaning and moral values, enabling the human agent to act properly within the world. Early Christianity grasped the importance of this idea, speaking of a *bios theōretikos* – not an abstract and analytical approach to existence, but rather a 'contemplative life' in which individuals grasped how they were meant to fit into a greater scheme of things, and could act authentically within this framework. This *bios theōretikos* was not so much a set of ideas as a template for personal transformation.

This, however, does not detract from the importance of *theōria* as a means of explaining our world and illuminating our place and role within it. This naturally raises the question of how such 'theories' are developed, and how their reliability can be assessed. Let's begin to explore this question, starting with the natural sciences, widely regarded as providing the most reliable forms of knowledge outside the realms of logic and mathematics.

Explanation in Science

How do we move from observing the world to proposing and evaluating scientific explanations of the world? The reasoning process now known as 'Inference to the Best Explanation' (formally stated in the 1960s, but which was already widely used under other names) aims to identify possible explanations of observations of nature (a 'logic of discovery') before determining which of these is the 'best' (a 'logic of justification'), using criteria such as the degree of 'empirical fit' (how well the theory accommodates the evidence), and non-empirical criteria such as simplicity, elegance, predictability and comprehensiveness.[20] Not all of these criteria can be used in every situation; as Karl Popper pointed out, while Darwin's theory of natural selection offered a persuasive explanation of the history of the biosphere, it had limited predictive capacity.

Yet the identification of the *best* explanation currently available does not amount to a proof or demonstration that this explanation is *true*. Declaring that something has been 'scientifically proven' is potentially misleading. Science is about questioning everything in the quest for a better understanding of our universe and being willing to adopt a new perspective or theory if the evidence seems to demand it. If a scientist is 'certain' about her beliefs, she will be reluctant to challenge or criticise them, let alone abandon them. An openness to theory change is essential for scientific progress. Science depends on being willing to challenge the existing consensus, to doubt the allegedly certain, and open up new vistas of investigation.

In the bygone days of scientific positivism, it was widely assumed that data could *prove* theories. Today, the language has shifted in the light of changing theoretical models; the challenge is now to find the 'best of the available competing explanations', knowing that 'best' doesn't necessarily mean 'true' (it's just our best shot at the moment, and we may find something better later).

This helps explain why Thomas H. Huxley, an enthusiastic Victorian advocate of Darwin's account of evolution, refused to allow that Darwin's theory was 'factual' or that it counted as 'knowledge'. Huxley insisted that Darwin's theory was a most compelling and 'ingenious' hypothesis, with greater explanatory power than its rivals. Yet this judgement was comparative, not absolute. The relative superiority of Darwin's theory over other explanatory frameworks did not necessarily mean it was true.[21]

There is thus an inevitable provisionality to scientific theorising. Certain things can clearly be proved scientifically – for example, that the chemical formula of water is H_2O. But many others remain frustratingly elusive and uncertain – not because of any *failure* of the scientific method, but because of the *limits* that arise from its specific nature. As the scientific method is historically situated, it is necessarily provisional in some of its conclusions, in that it is restricted by the evidence that is available at that moment in time.

This is not a problem; it's just the way things are. With most serious forms of human understanding we must appreciate that our knowledge is located at a particular moment in history, and that the passing of time will bring new pressures – such as theoretical advance or the availability of new evidence – that require us to adjust our ideas in their light. The real problem is that we don't know what the future will hold, and thus cannot predict *how* our ideas will change.

What may seem to be epistemically secure today may thus be abandoned in the future, in the light of the emergence of new evidence and more sophisticated theoretical reflection. The bleak imagery of Arthur Koestler's narrative of scientific progress highlights the need to recognise the unpredictability of science: 'The progress of science is strewn, like an ancient desert trail, with the bleached skeletons of discarded theories which once seemed to possess eternal life.'[22] The phlogiston hypothesis is a good example of such a 'discarded theory'. 'Phlogiston' was proposed during the late seventeenth century as a fire-like element contained within combustible bodies which was released during the process of burning. The discovery of oxygen by Joseph Priestley in the 1770s led to the abandonment of this hypothesis. Phlogiston was thus a stepping stone on the way to a firmer grasp of reality, which we have now left behind in the relentless march of scientific progress. We need to be ready to let go of a theory if something better comes along in the future – no matter how secure it may appear at the time.

As the philosopher Michael Polanyi suggests in *Personal Knowledge*, science is on a journey, and we have no way of knowing where it will go and what it will leave behind in the future. Many scientific theories that once commanded widespread support have now been displaced by alternatives. So, what will happen to these new theories in the future? They might be *better* than those they had supplanted; but are they *right*? Might they simply be transient staging-posts to something else, at present unknown, rather than final resting places?

These reflections point to the need to speak, cautiously but legitimately, about scientific 'beliefs'. For example, most scientists today *believe* that the age of the universe is 13.77 billion years. They certainly have good reasons for doing so, but they don't *know* this. Nobody started a stopwatch when the universe began. It is a provisional inference from the best scientific observations of our universe in the light of the presently dominant Lambda-CDM model of the Big Bang. But there are alternative models already competing for attention, and modifications may need to be made to core aspects of this model in the future. And if that happens, our estimates of the age of the universe can also be expected to change.

Explanation in Religion

Explanation, then, is a significant aspect of the natural sciences. What about other areas of human belief, such as religion? In his influential *Golden Bough* (1890), James Frazer suggested that religion was a failed primitive version of science, offering explanations of the world and human society that have now been both discredited and displaced by modern scientific discourse. Yet despite Frazer's overstatement of the explanatory role of religion, many continue to argue that while the *primary* role of religion is not explanatory in the scientific sense of the term, it nevertheless provides a broad framework for making sense of our world and our lives.

The philosopher Richard Swinburne, for example, argued that God is the best explanation for the complex patterns of phenomena that we observe in the natural world – above all, the capacity of the natural sciences to make sense of our universe. 'I am postulating a God to explain what science explains; I do not deny that science explains, but I postulate God to explain why science explains.'[23] The existence of God may, Swinburne argues, be inferred from what is observed in the world – and once this idea of God is articulated, it can explain what we experience around us.

As we noted earlier, G. K. Chesterton popularised the idea of religion as a 'big picture', which was to be judged by its ability to make sense of multiple aspects of human experience. After a period of agnosticism during the 1890s, Chesterton returned to Christianity because he believed that it offered a coherent, intelligible and testable picture of the world.

In his famous 1903 essay 'The Return of the Angels', Chesterton pointed out that it is the Christian vision of reality *as a whole* – rather than any of its individual components – that proves compelling. Chesterton claimed to be adopting the scientific 'method of the hypothesis'.[24] Like a scientific theory, Christianity was to be tested in terms of the overall sense it made of observation and experience. Individual observations of nature, Chesterton declared, do not 'prove' Christianity to be true; rather, Christianity validates itself by its ability to make overall sense of those observations. 'The phenomenon does not prove religion, but religion explains the phenomenon.'

For Chesterton, a good theory – whether scientific, ideological or religious – is to be judged by its capacity *as a whole* to accommodate what we see in the world around us and experience within us. Chesterton's language echoes Plato's view of philosophy as a *theōria*, an illuminating imaginative framework: 'With this idea once inside our heads, a million things become transparent as if a lamp were lit behind them.' Chesterton explained this point as follows:

> Numbers of us have returned to this belief; and we have returned to it, not because of this argument or that argument, but because the theory, when it is adopted, works out everywhere; because the coat, when it is tried on, fits in every crease… We put on the theory, like a magic hat, and history becomes translucent like a house of glass.

Chesterton argued that Christianity, when seen as a complete 'spiritual theory', was able to offer a better account of the coherence of human history and experience than its rivals. On being asked why he was a Christian, Chesterton replied: 'Because I perceive life to be logical and workable with these beliefs and illogical and unworkable without them.'[25] We see here Chesterton articulating a *participatory* approach to theory – namely, that it creates a conceptual space within which people can generate meaning and value.

Religion is primarily a way of *interpreting* life, creating the possibility of existential meaning and moral values. An interpretation of human existence involves trying to answer questions of meaning – who we are and why we matter. As the German philosopher Walther Dilthey once remarked, 'we *explain* nature, but we *understand* the life of the soul.'[26] Within what story shall I locate myself? How shall I live? Who am I, and what am I meant to be doing? We therefore turn to reflect on the role of interpretation in religion and in science, focusing on Darwin's theory of natural selection.

Scientific Interpretation: What Does Darwin's Theory of Evolution Mean?

Theories about how our world *functions* can be tested by the application of the scientific method; those dealing with what it *means* cannot. Rabbi Jonathan Sacks, whose doctoral research was supervised by the philosopher Bernard Williams, made this point with particular clarity.

> We cannot prove that life is meaningful and that God exists. But neither can we prove that love is better than hate, altruism than selfishness, forgiveness than the desire for revenge ... Almost none of the truths by which we live are provable, and the desire to prove them is based on a monumental confusion between explanation and interpretation. Explanations can be proved, interpretations cannot.[27]

Scientific theories explain what we observe and discover in the world. Yet these also need to be *interpreted*.[28] Perhaps the most contested case of scientific interpretation concerns Darwin's theory of evolution. What does this *mean*? What are its moral and spiritual *commitments*?

Darwin's task was to make sense of a series of observations about the natural world, some of which were already well known, and others which he had accumulated while serving as naturalist on HMS *Beagle* during the five years of its voyage round the world (1831–6). How could he account for the observation of evolutionary change in the biological realm? Darwin's explanation of his observations, eventually published as *The Origin of Species* (1859), rested on a proposed mechanism of 'natural selection', paralleling the 'artificial selection' familiar to animal and pigeon breeders. Evolution arises initially through the emergence of variation in each generation, and subsequently through the differential survival of individuals. Those who have characteristics which increase their probability of survival will have a greater likelihood of survival and reproduction, thus passing these variations to the next generation.

Darwin's theory offered a plausible explanation of what was known about the biological world that was better than the alternatives then available – such as various forms of creationism, or the 'transformist' evolutionary theories of the French naturalists Georges-Louis Leclerc or Jean-Baptiste Lamarck. It was able to offer a better explanation, for example, of the persistence of vestigial structures and the distinctive characteristics of the flora and fauna of remote islands. Darwin did, however, face some difficulties, most notably his lack of a viable genetic theory which would allow the undiluted transmission of biological variations – something that was provided by Gregor Mendel's vital (yet initially neglected) 1866 paper on 'Experiments on Plant Hybridization'. Darwin's theory was placed on a more rigorous foundation in the twentieth century, particularly following the discovery of the gene.

Then what does Darwin's theory *mean*? How is it to be *interpreted*? For example, given that Darwin had clarified the mechanism of evolution, did this mean that it was now possible for humans to take control of this process, and direct it towards certain social or political goals? Some have argued that Darwin advocated what later came to be known as 'social Darwinism', which flourished in Britain and elsewhere in the 1920s, and came to be linked with eugenics as a means of limiting the capacity of certain social groups to reproduce. Though there are hints of such an attitude in some of Darwin's correspondence, this is better seen as a later interpretation of the significance of his theory, rather than something that Darwin himself recognised or advocated.

Some suggest that Darwin's understanding of evolution can be interpreted as the basis for a universal ethic. In a lecture of 1943, the evolutionary biologist and eugenicist Julian Huxley argued that Darwin's theory, when rightly interpreted, allows for a normative ethic, and not simply an explanation of how ethics might have evolved or become significant in human evolution. Huxley is a little obscure in explaining how we might move from value-free observation to value-determining prescription.[29] Yet Huxley was responding to a lecture on the same topic, delivered at Oxford in 1893, by his grandfather, Thomas H. Huxley. In that earlier lecture, Huxley argued that Darwin's evolutionary theory was ethically barren, incapable of informing human ethical reflection. 'Cosmic evolution may teach us how the good and the evil tendencies of man may have come about; but, in itself, it is incompetent to furnish any better reason why what we call good is preferable to what we call evil than we had before.'[30]

So which Huxley is right? We can't say. Both Huxleys offer *interpretations* of Darwin's theory. Even if we could ascertain that one of them represented a closer approximation to Darwin's own views, this would not make this right; it would simply count as a better interpretation of Darwin, rather than the right answer to the great ethical question under discussion.

Finally, does Darwin's theory entail atheism? Many populist atheist writers have taken it as self-evident that this is the case, despite Darwin's own statements that he did not consider his own theory to mandate atheism, in that it was compatible with conventional religious belief. It is certainly true to say that 'natural selection' contradicts, or at least presents difficulties for, certain religious understandings of creation; yet there is a significant intellectual distance between calling for a review of such doctrines of creation and proving atheism. After all, Augustine of Hippo set out an interpretation of the book of Genesis in 401 which held that God created the world in an instant, and then set in place an extended process of development through which the created order changed over time. Perhaps the time has come to retrieve this older theory.

Although I welcome and value the capacity of scientific theories to provide explanations for the workings of our universe, I am sceptical regarding their religious, metaphysical, or ethical interpretations. While Darwin's theory of natural selection effectively explained the observational evidence available to him at that time, the moral and spiritual implications of his theory are still ambiguous and subject to debate.

While scientific theories and explanations are grounded in evidence and are subject to empirical testing, our interpretations of their implications for human existence and self-understanding lack the same level of credibility and authority. In the end, they are opinions, not facts. They are beliefs about the implications of Darwin's theory for human morality and meaning. This is not a problem; it's just the way things are. But it can easily become a problem if these interpretations of scientific theories are mistakenly given the same authority as empirically-tested explanations of reality.

This naturally raises the question of whether interpretations, scientific or religious, lie beyond critical assessment. Are we free to choose any interpretation of our world that we like, without the need for reasoned consideration? What if the evidence is not adequate to compel us to adopt a particular position? This suggests we need to consider the relation of agnosticism and belief.

Agnosticism: A Better Way?

What happens when we are confronted with a situation in which the evidence is not sufficient to allow us to reach a secure conclusion? This problem arises regularly in everyday life – within the legal system, as juries struggle to make sense of a body of evidence; within the scientific community, where researchers often find the evidence is open to multiple (and inconsistent) conclusions; and in metaphysical and religious debates about 'ultimate reality' or God. We regularly make judgements, rather than draw necessary conclusions – judgements that rest on interconnected webs of personal beliefs, themselves open to challenge and critique.

We have already engaged the influential Victorian scientist Thomas H. Huxley – often known as 'Darwin's bulldog' – in this chapter. Huxley considered respect for evidence to be both an intellectual and moral virtue. However, not every aspect of a scientific way of thinking could be proved with the available evidence. Some fundamental scientific beliefs lay beyond proof, even if their reliability was widely assumed. Though often presented in populist atheist tracts as advocating the conflict of science and religion, Huxley's position was far more complex and nuanced than this, as this important reflection makes clear:

> True science and true religion are twin-sisters, and the
> separation of either from the other is sure to prove the
> death of both. Science prospers exactly in proportion
> as it is religious; and religion flourishes in exact propor-
> tion to the scientific depth and firmness of its basis.[31]

Huxley was critical of the dogmatism of theologians whose pronouncements, in his view, exceeded their evidential basis; he made the same criticism, however, of dogmatic atheists.

In a lecture of 1885, Huxley declared that science rests on a fundamental act of faith – 'the confession of the universality of order and of the absolute validity in all times and under all circumstances, of the law of causation'. Why was this confession of the uniformity of nature an 'act of faith'? Huxley was quite clear: 'because, by the nature of the case, the truth of such propositions is not susceptible of proof.'[32] This point is widely conceded. As Bertrand Russell observed, 'belief in the uniformity of nature' is a principle that 'cannot, without circularity, be inferred from observed uniformities, since it is required to justify any such inference.'[33]

Yet while scientists are aware of the problem of circularity in believing in the uniformity of nature, this is not seen as causing any significant difficulties. It constitutes a framing and grounding belief which undergirds the natural sciences; although it cannot be proved to be true, many consider that the ongoing explanatory and predictive successes of the sciences are an adequate (if purely pragmatic) confirmation of its reliability.

One of Huxley's more significant achievements was the introduction of the word 'agnostic' to characterise the scientific method. Huxley was clear that 'agnosticism is not, and cannot be, a creed';[34] it is fundamentally a *method*. Although the term 'agnostic' is now taken to refer solely or chiefly to religious belief, Huxley developed it specifically to characterise the methods of the natural sciences, while recognising that it could be applied more widely. In 1884, Huxley summarised his views on agnosticism in the form of two creedal statements:

> 1. Agnosticism is of the essence of science, whether ancient or modern. It simply means that a man shall not say he knows or believes that which he has no scientific grounds for professing to know or believe.

> 2. Consequently Agnosticism puts aside not only the greater part of popular theology, but also the greater part of anti-theology. On the whole, the 'bosh' of heterodoxy is more offensive to me than that of orthodoxy, because heterodoxy professes to be guided by reason and science, and orthodoxy does not.[35]

What of agnosticism today? The term is now used primarily in a religious sense, to refer to someone who declines to make a judgement on the existence or non-existence of God. While this is often presented simply as a personal stance of disengagement, it usually represents a reluctant pragmatic judgement that human reason is incapable of providing sufficient rational grounds to justify either believing that God exists or that God does not exist. The philosopher Anthony Kenny is an excellent example of a scholar to take this position:

> I do not myself know of any argument for the existence of God which I find convincing; in all of them I think I can find flaws. Equally, I do not know of any argument against the existence of God which is totally convincing; in the arguments I know against the existence of God I can equally find flaws. So that my own position on the existence of God is agnostic.[36]

These kinds of considerations led the Australian atheist philosopher Graham Oppy to argue that atheism, agnosticism and theism are all 'rationally permissible', in terms of their evidence base. Oppy defends his own preference (atheism) by arguing that this represents, in his view, the 'best evaluation' of all the relevant considerations, while making it clear that this is not intellectually compelling. Not all 'sufficiently thoughtful, intelligent, and well-informed people' will agree with his conclusion, he concedes, in that the evidence base for this belief is inadequate. 'When we consider the best cases for atheism, agnosticism and theism, there are many, many points where we are required to make judgements; and it is the accumulation of those many, many judgements that feeds into our overall assessment.'[37] In reaching his judgement, Oppy is obliged to rely on criteria that are of his own choosing and his perceptions of the weight of evidence for various options. His atheism is thus a belief, not a certainty.

My own view is that agnosticism is inevitable and proper if we agree to limit our beliefs to what the evidence clearly mandates – which is the working method of the natural sciences. The problem, as we have seen, is that beliefs about meaning and morality lie beyond the evidential confirmation that is the hallmark of *explanations* in the natural sciences. It is hard to be a moral agnostic in today's world, confronted with injustice on every side. While many would affirm that moral agnosticism is a legitimate intellectual option, most would concede that it is existentially unsatisfying and pragmatically irresponsible in today's world.

We shall reflect further on these issues in the following chapter as we turn to consider to the question of what difference belief makes to life.

Chapter 5

What Difference Does Believing Make?

The lingering influence of Freud in the twentieth century has until recently discouraged attempts to study the phenomenon of belief empirically, or to try to understand 'normal' belief, as opposed to its 'pathological' manifestations in various psychiatric disorders.[1]

Many have noted that psychology's past preoccupation with disorder and dysfunction led it to ignore the 'normal', and as a result failed to provide a reliable account of human potential. A focus on what causes 'abnormal' belief has led to a neglect of research into the grounds and consequences of non-pathological beliefs.

In his 1954 work *Motivation and Personality*, Abraham Maslow coined the term 'positive psychology' to highlight the contrast between the approach that he proposed and the traditional focus on 'abnormal psychology'. Martin Seligman and others introduced the discipline of 'positive psychology' in 1998, seeing this as a 'science of human flourishing' which could counter the dominance of psychopathology in the field.[2]

When viewed as 'normal', belief can be seen as significant to human functioning and wellbeing at several levels. We hold certain beliefs to be true and reliable, and see these as providing a basis for us to understand the world and act within it. Beliefs – individually, or more usually in the form of belief systems – provide the 'mental scaffolding' that human beings need if they are to appraise the environment, explain new observations and experiences, and construct a shared meaning of the world.[3]

While we regularly speak of human 'reason', 'emotions', or 'imagination', it is important to realise that these three are interconnected within the sense-making apparatus of the human brain.[4] It may be helpful to distinguish them for some purposes; yet in reality they cannot be separated.

A further misunderstanding, which has unfortunately marred research on human believing, is that belief is something distinctly religious or spiritual, and thus is of no interest or relevance to people who are nonreligious or generically secular. Astonishingly, these people have often been assumed to have no beliefs. Happily, such misunderstandings are now largely behind us. It is now widely appreciated that both the human act of believing and its outcomes are of importance for everyday human existence.

While some forms of belief are purely cognitive (for example, the average distance of the moon from the earth is 238,855 miles or 384,400 km), others straddle the boundaries between the realms of the cognitive and affective. Recent innovations in brain research have called into question views of emotion and cognition that treat them as noninteracting and isolated silos. 'Emotional information not only engages the whole brain during an emotional experience but also tunes what we see of the world and helps determine how and what we learn and remember.'[5]

The philosopher John Cottingham has argued that the specific nature of religious belief allows it to provide a 'conceptual home' that can accommodate and interpret human experiences such as awe and thankfulness in which value and significance are already implicit. For Cottingham, religious conversion often appears to involve some degree of emotional upheaval as well as cognitive realignment.[6] Yet similar patterns can be observed in other areas of human existence, such as the dynamics of persuasion in political beliefs, in which emotional and rational considerations both play prominent roles.[7]

'Belief' is now seen as relevant for both secular and religious domains, encompassing a rich spectrum of possibilities. Religious belief may be distinct in certain ways, but all human beings are 'believers' in some sense of the term. Both atheists and religious people can have 'crises of meaning' in their lives.[8] The study of the process of believing is of wide and general interest, especially in understanding human flourishing.

So why do we believe? The anthropologist Agustín Fuentes suggests that it is a bit like asking why human beings have five fingers. We just do. It is the way we are. It is part of the human condition, and it needs to be affirmed and embraced.

> We believe because we are human. Just like our large and complex brains, our ability to walk on our hind legs, our nimble fingers and hands, and our ability to make tools, the capacity for belief is part of our distinctive evolutionary history. To be human is to be able to believe.[9]

While nobody is really sure, we can certainly explore how both the act of believing and specific beliefs help to shape and

influence the distinctive ways in which individual human beings engage with each other and the wider world. Belief is an
ability to make connections that are not directly given in our
observations, which open up a grander vision of our world, or
to learn to see through the eyes of others, and thus extend the
range of possibilities at our disposal.

It is important to make a distinction between *believing* and
beliefs. Believing is a human mental *process*; beliefs are the
outcome of this process, often developing and changing over
time, through interaction with others and exploration of our
surroundings. Although we can 'articulate' – to use Charles
Taylor's helpful term – the intellectual content of our beliefs,
they are not restricted to the realm of human reason.

Beliefs actively shape the way in which we see and experience
the world, and the way in which we enact our lives.[10] Once a
belief is acquired, a process of reflection and adjustment sets
in, as the believer explores how this belief shapes their lives,
often in dialogue with others who already share this belief, and
have acquired a settled understanding of its implications and
consequences. Let's begin to explore the difference that belief
makes to our understanding of reality, our modes of experiencing reality, and our way of living.

We start by considering an aspect of believing highlighted in
Colin McGinn's stimulating study of 'mindsight' – the ability
of certain beliefs to refocus the 'mind's eye', enabling us to see
the world in a new way.[11]

Re-Imagining Reality: Seeing Things in a New Way
Hannah Arendt is one of many philosophers to note that
thinking has often been thought of in terms of *seeing*. Recent

studies have suggested that the human ability to see things in a new way is important to our evolutionary development, allowing us to solve problems through imagining alternative ways of thinking or acting.[12] The western scientific, religious, philosophical and literary tradition draws extensively on our experience of sight and vision for its metaphors of truth and meaning.[13] As we saw earlier, the modern term 'theory' derives from the Greek *theōria*, which means 'beholding'.

The writer Henry Miller, reflecting on the development of his own thought as he wandered through exotic landscapes, once remarked that he found his destination was 'never a place, but rather a new way of looking at things.'[14] Miller's comment points to the fact that we inherit or acquire, often without realising it, certain ways of 'seeing' the world which we treat as fixed or self-evidently true. Philosophers of science speak of 'theory-laden observation', meaning that what we think is a 'natural' understanding of the world is often informed and to some extent predetermined by an assumed or presupposed theory.[15] Scientific advance often proceeds by demolishing these assumptions, and replacing them with something more reliable. The first step in theoretical development is to identify our inherited or assumed theories, and subject them to critical examination.

Ideological enforcement, however, proceeds by imposing a 'sound' or 'rational' map that invalidates others, and allows us to see only what the ideologues want us to see, normalising what would once have been seen as strange and perplexing. Theories can too easily prevent us from seeing things fully, by declaring that only the deluded and irrational 'see' certain things, which wiser and more theoretically informed individuals know cannot exist, and thus discount any suggestion that they should be taken seriously. This crass intellectual condescension is perhaps an inevitable outcome of modernity's highly restrictive account of human rationality. We are only allowed to see what our theoretical precommitments permit – what our theoretical maps tell us.

The economist E. F. Schumacher highlighted this in his final work, reflecting on how his education constricted his grasp and appreciation of reality. 'All through school and university I had been given maps of life and knowledge on which there was hardly a trace of many of the things that I most cared about and that seemed to me to be of the greatest possible importance for the conduct of my life.' His moment of liberation arrived when he realised the solution to this impoverishment. 'I ceased to suspect the sanity of my perceptions and began, instead, to suspect the soundness of the maps.'[16]

Theories ought to be neutral; all too often they are not. Social conformity often influences us to use intellectual maps that were designed to control us, to limit us, to subjugate us – to persuade us that there is nothing more to reality or life than they allow. *Yet other maps are available.* One of the most important decisions we can make in life is which map we use to interpret the landscape, and guide us as we journey.

The map we use shapes our interpretation and evaluation of many aspects of our physical and social worlds. For example, consider religion. As Bernard Williams points out, from the standpoint of humanism, understood as 'a secularist and anti-religious movement', religion is a 'terrible thing'.[17] Those involved in the scientific study of religion, however, see it as an integral aspect of human identity and nature, that its study illuminates the complexity of human nature. And those who are religious see it as vitally important to their identity, wellbeing and self-understanding. So which map do we use?

Yet there is an obvious question here: do we *really* need to depend on a single map, becoming slaves to its limitations and hidden agendas? Earlier, we noted the work of the British public philosopher Mary Midgley, a trenchant critic of theory-driven reductionism. For Midgley, the solution to such cartographical privileging was to reject a single totalising map, and instead use a series of maps, each adapted to its specific domain of inquiry. No single map can show everything; to rely on a single map is thus to limit oneself to what it is intended to disclose.

By using a series of different maps, each grounded in a different intellectual discipline, Midgley argues that we can gain a deeper understanding of 'what the outside world is actually telling us'.[18] We need to avoid an imperialist map, which tries to colonise other disciplines, and instead find a way of bringing together the insights offered by multiple maps.

Science: The Importance of Paradigm Shifts

The philosophy of science highlights the importance of informing beliefs in determining how the natural world is seen and understood. Yet observation is not a neutral process, but is shaped by a set of beliefs, whether explicit or implicit, about *what* is being observed.

Most societies develop classifications of the natural world – such as birds, animals and fish – which are treated as universal, but are clearly culturally specific. European naturalists found their biological categorisations could not cope with the discovery of the platypus in Australia during the 1790s, which suggested that the category of mammals had to be expanded to allow that some might lay eggs instead of giving birth to live young. It was easier for leading British scientists of this period – such as the Scottish anatomist and ethnologist Robert Knox – to believe that the platypus was a 'freak imposture' created by some unscrupulous taxidermist than that the biological maps of their day might require revision.

Belief change arises when individuals find that their existing understandings are called into question – for example, through a reconsideration of their evidential basis, or increasing unease at their moral or existential implications. An inherited, imposed or apparently 'natural' belief is displaced by another, followed by a process of imaginative exploration of this new way of seeing things. In what follows, we shall look at some scientific, religious and philosophical examples of this process, and reflect on how they help us understand the role of beliefs.

In 1714 John Flamsteed, the British Astronomer Royal, observed a faint star in the constellation of Taurus, only just visible to the naked eye, which he catalogued as '34 Tauri'. In March 1781, however, the British astronomer William Herschel observed *the same object* through a telescope, and realised it was not a star; it was a *planet*, now known as Uranus.[19] Herschel realised it was a planet both on account of its faint disk, and its motion against the fixed stars in the short interval between his two observations. Neither its disk nor its slow motion could be discerned by the unaided human eye. Herschel was able to observe both because his more advanced telescope provided increased resolution of the night sky.

We see here the classic function of a good theory – to act as a lens which enables us to see things in a new way. What was once seen as a star was now seen as a planet – a new addition to the solar system, which had hitherto been assumed to end with Saturn as the outermost planet. The historian and philosopher of science Thomas Kuhn introduced the influential idea of a 'paradigm shift' to describe such radical re-imaginings of the natural world.

Kuhn's studies of the history of science suggested that there were two different types of scientific development. The first was gradual or incremental developments within the framework of what he described as 'normal science;' the second was the radical changes brought about by 'scientific revolutions', in which an accumulation of gradual changes bring about a tipping point – a changed way of thinking that Kuhn described as a 'paradigm shift' – such as Copernicus' theory of the solar system.

Before 1500, the scientific consensus held that the sun, moon and planets rotated around a fixed earth. Yet the more accurate observations of the sixteenth century suggested that this way of looking at things needed revision. The older geocentric model simply could not cope with the weight of this new information; a new model was clearly needed. Kuhn's point was that scientific progress cannot be thought of as a purely linear process of accumulating facts and observations. At times, these force radical shifts in the way in which we imagine reality, inaugurating a new phase of scientific understanding.

For Kuhn, a paradigm shift involves seeing the world through a new theoretical lens and appreciating the difference this makes to what we think we are seeing. A new theory allows us to imagine our world in a different way. Before Copernicus' theory, 'the sun and moon were planets, the earth was not.

After it, the earth was a planet, like Mars and Jupiter; the sun was a star; and the moon was a new sort of body, a satellite.'[20] Kuhn's point is that the phenomena were unchanged; they were, however, *seen* in a new way. What was physically seen did not change; the change took place within the mind of the observer, who interpreted what was seen in the light of this theory. A pre-Copernican observer might 'see' the sun rise and set; a post-Copernican would, however, 'see' the earth turning on its axis, leading to the *apparent* motion of the sun across the heavens.

Religion: The Role of Conversion

Many consider religious conversions to be one the most striking examples of how a new set of beliefs changes the way people see themselves and their world, often reflecting a growing disillusionment or dissatisfaction with an existing way of thinking that is found to be inadequate and unsatisfying. Consider the case of Paul Kalanithi (1977–2015), a promising Stanford neurosurgeon who died of metastatic lung cancer at the age of thirty-seven, before he was able to practice as a fully qualified surgeon. His bestseller *When Breath Becomes Air*, written during his advanced illness and published posthumously, tells how he became a neurosurgeon because he wanted to learn about 'what really matters in life' – only to discover that science failed to engage, and could not engage, the deep and urgent existential questions that mattered to him, and which became increasingly important as his illness progressed.

Science, Kalanithi concluded, might 'provide the most useful way to organize empirical, reproducible data, but its power to do so must be set against its inability to grasp the most central aspects of human life.'[21] This is no criticism of science; it is rather a penetrating diagnosis of what humans need, which lay behind Kalanithi's reappraisal of the importance of literature (especially Samuel Beckett and T. S. Eliot) in reflecting on meaning, and Christianity in providing it. His rediscovery of Christianity reflected his realisation of its capacity to engage these 'ultimate questions' in a time of crisis and need.

Kalanithi's moving narrative of reflection on how we cope with trauma and uncertainty also illuminates an issue that is of recurring importance to thinking about belief. How can we live on the basis of beliefs, when we crave certainties? Kalanithi found himself drawn to seven words of Samuel Beckett: 'I can't go on. I'll go on.'[22] We are caught in the insoluble enigma of the human situation. We can't reason our way to infallible truths that are existentially meaningful – but we can't live fully and authentically without such beliefs. Intellectually, we feel we can't go on; existentially, we know we have to go on.

Kalanithi found that his reaffirmation of a once-rejected Christianity gave him a new lens through which he could see his own situation. The Harvard psychologist William James, who recorded many personal accounts of religious transformation, noted how these often spoke of the world being experienced and encountered in a new way: 'everything looked new to me, the people, the fields, the cattle, the trees. I was like a new man in a new world.'[23] This is about more than a change of opinion about things; it is about the divine transformation of the perceiver – and hence of the appearance of the sensory world, and its practical inhabitation. The whole way of experiencing the world is transformed, affecting the observer's reason, imagination, emotions and actions.

In the case of Christianity, stepping into its 'big picture' radically alters our ways of thinking and imagining reality. The Greek word *metanoia*, used in the New Testament to refer to this re-imagination of reality, is often translated as 'repentance'. Yet it fundamentally means a rational and imaginative transformation in which we see things afresh in a new light, experience them in a new way, and reappraise them accordingly. '*Metanoia* calls for a fundamental change in human reality through a holistic "change of mind" ... a reshaping or "re-forming" of mental structures which is at the same time a new "form" or "shape" of a human life.'[24]

The New Testament uses a wide range of images relating to the human capacity to see to describe this change: people's eyes are healed, that they might see properly; a veil is removed to enable a fuller vision of God and the world. Developing this point, Augustine of Hippo wrote of 'healing the eyes of the heart in order that God may be seen.'[25]

In some important way *metanoia* designates what Kuhn designates as a 'paradigm shift'[26] – a new way of thinking, beholding and experiencing reality which is seen to offer a more satisfactory account of reality than its predecessors. Religious conversion often involves the setting aside of existing understandings of reality, displacing them with a new vision, and relocating the individual within this new imaginative framework which demands new habits of thought and theological visualisation. Perhaps these are best expressed poetically rather than analytically.

In her analysis of the theological poetry of George Herbert, Sophie Read points out that Herbert understands *metanoia* as 'a fundamental cognitive reorientation'[27] that is needed if we are to see and inhabit the world in a Christian manner. *Metanoia* thus denotes the 'reconceptualization on an intellectual as well as an emotional plane of an individual's relationship with God.' A 'natural' beholding of the world is inadequate to discern its spiritual aspects and significance; a new 'mindsight' is needed, adapted towards this end.

This process of visual or imaginative recalibration is explored in 'The Elixir', one of Herbert's best-known poems, which envisages *metanoia* as God's tutoring (or transforming) of natural human vision to enable the perception of the divine presence and activity within the natural order.

> Teach me, my God and King,
>   In all things Thee to see,
>   And what I do in anything
>   To do it as for Thee.[28]

Herbert's concern was that everyday human modes of engaging the world are trapped in a naturalistic mindset, which needs to be disrupted or reset to allow an alternative way of beholding and inhabiting this world. Conversion is about stepping into this new way of seeing reality, adopting a transforming paradigm through which things can be seen and interpreted afresh.

Moral Philosophy: Iris Murdoch on Attentiveness

The British moral philosopher Iris Murdoch held that any attempt to live properly and meaningfully within the world depended on the 'just and loving vision' of that world, and the people within it. Yet this vision is not passively received, but actively created. We do not simply look at our world; rather, we try to develop attentive and disciplined ways of intentionally seeing it, which lead us to redescribe and recategorise what we *think* we see, in order that we might see things *as they really are.*

Murdoch is acutely aware of the importance of responding properly to people in their different situations. She illustrates the process she has in mind through her example of a mother and her daughter-in-law. Although this analogy is rooted in the social realities of a bygone age, the point that Murdoch wants to make remains clear and significant.

> A mother, whom I shall call M, feels hostility to her daughter-in-law, whom I shall call D. M finds D quite a good-hearted girl, but while not exactly common yet certainly unpolished and lacking in dignity and refinement… However, the M of the example is an intelligent and well-intentioned person, capable of self-criticism, capable of giving careful and just attention to an object which confronts her. M tells herself: 'I am old-fashioned and conventional. I may be prejudiced and narrow-minded. I may be snobbish. I am certainly jealous. Let me look again.'[29]

Murdoch's point is that M realises that her initial attitude towards D (she believes her son 'married beneath him') is the outcome of her own prejudices, which skews her perceptions. She determines to reappraise D.

Murdoch argues that when M is 'just and loving' – in other words, when she *sees* justly and lovingly – 'she sees D as she really is.' As a result, 'D is discovered to be not vulgar but refreshingly simple, not undignified but spontaneous.'[30] The same empirical reality is observed, yet is interpreted – is *seen* – in a new way, thus leading to a transformed perception of D's value. Murdoch helps us grasp how self-criticism and self-exploration allows us to confront our initial prejudices, thus altering our perception of a person or situation.

These three examples from the worlds of science, religion and philosophy help us appreciate how beliefs shape the way we understand, envision and experience reality. Given the importance of the world of human subjectivity for many people and the growing interest in 'emotional intelligence', we need to reflect on how beliefs interact with feeling.

Beliefs and Feelings:
Connecting-up with Experience

The relation of belief and emotions has long been a subject of discussion, recently given added depth through a growing scientific interest in the relation between human emotion and thought.[31] For our purposes, the important point is to affirm the interconnection of beliefs and feelings. T. S. Eliot put his finger on the critical role of great poets in helping us to discover '*what it feels like* to hold certain beliefs.'[32] Poetry has the ability to allow us to access, perhaps even to intensify, our most profound emotions, Eliot argues, making us 'from time to time a little more aware of the deeper, unnamed feelings which form the substratum of our being, to which we rarely penetrate.'[33] Wordsworth earlier made this point in a much-quoted observation: 'Poetry is the spontaneous overflow of powerful feelings: it takes its origin from emotion recollected in tranquillity.' At times, poetry helps us to articulate certain ideas or feelings; at others, it *creates* them, offering us a new way of seeing and experiencing the world and our personal existence.

These themes are echoed in the rise of existentialism after the Second World War, responding to a perceived neglect of the inner world and a growing anxiety about humanity's meaninglessness. The rise of depersonalizing ideologies such as Marxism-Leninism in the 1930s and the brutality of the Second World War created a new passion for rediscovering and reaffirming the significance of the individual. During this 'existentialist moment', the French intellectual Jean-Paul Sartre led a wave of reaction against an excessive objectification of human beings.[34] Sartre's protest highlights the importance of human subjectivity in the quest for meaning and truth – and the intimate connection between our beliefs and our deepest desires. We are free to choose what we consider humanity ought to be, and create ourselves as we believe we really are.

Although this interaction is often presented as religious in nature, it seems clear that the importance of experience is appreciated in both spiritual and secular contexts. In October 1916, Bertrand Russell wrote to one of his lovers, the actress Constance Malleson, disclosing an inexplicable and seemingly meaningless sense of longing which haunted him.

> The centre of me is always and eternally a terrible pain, a curious, wild pain, a searching for something beyond what the world contains. Something transfigured and infinite. The beatific vision – God, I do not find it, I do not think it is to be found – but the love of it is my life. It the actual spring of life within me.[35]

Russell's intellectual motivation to discover the grounds of a powerful and indefinable experience of 'curious, wild pain' – something that seemed to point beyond 'what the world contains' – has parallels throughout human history. We might think of Isaac Newton's reflection, dating from late in his life, in which he imagined himself standing on the threshold of something that was signposted by this world, yet which tantalisingly lay beyond his reach:

> I seem to have been only like a small boy playing on the sea-shore, diverting myself in now and then finding a smoother pebble or a prettier shell than the ordinary, whilst the great ocean of truth lay all undiscovered before me.[36]

William Wordsworth expressed this idea in the phrase 'spots of time' – rare yet precious moments of profound feeling and imaginative strength, in which individuals sense that they have grasped something of ultimate significance within or beyond themselves. I can still recall vividly such an experience when, as an Oxford scientific researcher during the 1970s, I was travelling in the depths of a moonless night towards the Iranian city of Kermān on a dilapidated coach. Its sputtering engine finally failed, leaving the passengers to stroll around the ruins of an abandoned caravanserai while the coach driver tinkered with its fuel pump.

I saw the stars that night as I had never seen them before – a solemn and beautiful brilliance amid a dark and silent desert landscape. I experienced a 'rapturous amazement' (to borrow a phrase from Albert Einstein), an inexpressible sense of awe, the memory of which still sends shivers down my spine. I felt very small and insignificant that night in comparison with the untamed immensity of the heavens, experiencing a strange intimation of transcendence in the face of the overwhelming vastness of the natural world that I, as a scientist, had once hoped to master.

Richard Dawkins also recognises the importance of such experiences. 'The great religions have a place for awe, for ec-static transport at the wonder and beauty of creation. And it's exactly this feeling of spine-shivering, breath-catching awe – almost worship – this flooding of the chest with epiphanic wonder, that modern science can provide.'[37] Yet this experience is neither 'religious' nor 'scientific'; it is simply an experience, *until* and *unless* it is connected with a conceptual framework, a network of beliefs that illuminates its nature and endows it with meaning. Psychological accounts of the origins of an experience of awe can easily be given.[38] These, however, are simply explanations of how an experience of awe arises within the human consciousness; it does not explain how meaning might arise from it, or what that meaning might be.

In *The Varieties of Religious Experience* (1902), William James drew extensively on personal testimonies to the perceived sig-nificance of religious experiences, which he framed in terms of intense and brief 'privileged moments' that carry an 'enormous sense of inner authority and illumination', transfiguring the understanding of those who experience them, often taking the form of disclosures of 'new depths of truth unplumbed by the discursive intellect.'[39]

For James, it seemed as if there is 'in the human con-sciousness a sense of reality, a feeling of objective presence, a perception of what we may call "something there," more deep and more general than any of the special and particular "senses" by which the current psychology supposes existent realities to be originally revealed.'[40] Truth is something that needs to be *felt*, that needs to resonate with our experience of life.

Examples of these experiences would include the exquisite sense of longing for something undefined and apparently unattainable, often referred to using the German term *Sehnsucht*, which Matthew Arnold glossed as a 'wistful, soft, tearful longing'.[41] In his *Prelude*, Wordsworth similarly pointed to a 'dim and undetermined sense' of 'unknown modes of being.' These liminal experiences hint at a new world beyond a limiting threshold of human vision. Virginia Woolf once spoke of experiencing privileged 'moments of being', which seemed to her to be 'a token of some real thing behind appearances'[42] which constantly eluded her attempts to find and possess it.

More recently, the term 'epiphany' has come to be used for such moments of disclosure or insight – an 'overwhelming existentially significant manifestation of value in experience, often sudden and surprising,' which 'feels like it "comes from outside"' and allows us to grasp something new.'[43] While such epiphanies are not necessarily religious, they are often linked with what is usually described as 'religious experience'.

These experiences of 'partial and fleeting realisations' are seen as life-changing, possessing both weight and significance.[44] They are like 'bolts of lightning on a dark night that brilliantly illuminate everything in a single, instantaneous flash.'[45] These 'epiphanic' moments of disclosure illuminate what was once dark, obscure or out of focus, bringing a 'sense of clarification, which seems to allow us to understand things in their true nature'. Something of vast yet unassimilated significance seems to be *shown* to us in a dazzling moment of illumination – something that we proved unable to discover for ourselves by extended reflection and reason.

What, then, do such experiences mean? Is this deep sense of longing a genuine response to something that lies, dimly glimpsed and partially apprehended, beyond the world of appearances, or is it simply a trick of the mind that points to nothing – a cypher without a key? Might there be a conceptual scheme that can unlock its meaning?

Scientific study of such human experiences is often pre-determined by the decision to adopt the principle of the 'Methodological Exclusion of the Transcendent',[46] which presupposes a naturalist set of working assumptions, which inevitably focus on the mental mechanisms by which such experiences might arise, assuming that there is no transcendent referent for such experiences. The outcome of this is a premature foreclosure of a potentially important conversation, in which one possible explanation – some transcendent reality – is excluded in advance on methodological grounds. The parallels with J. B. S. Haldane's naturalist dilemma can hardly be overlooked: 'If my mental processes are determined wholly by the motions of atoms in my brain, I have no reason to suppose that my beliefs are true. They may be sound chemically, but that does not make them sound logically.'[47]

One influential interpretative framework originates within the Christian tradition, which proposes a dialectic between humanity being intended to relate to God, but presently being alienated from God. In consequence, human beings experience a general sense of longing which nothing seems able to satisfy, in that this both originates *from* God and is designed to lead *to* God.[48] The eleventh-century theologian Anselm of Canterbury expresses this interpretation in one of his meditations: 'Lord, give me what you have made me want. I praise and thank you for the desire that you have inspired. Perfect what you have begun, and grant me what you have made me long for.'[49]

Other interpretations of this sense of longing are, of course, available. Richard Dawkins suggests a 'general theory of religion as accidental by-product – a misfiring of something useful' within our evolutionary history, in which religious experience can be explained reductively by anyone with 'the slightest familiarity with the brain and its powerful workings.'[50] It is a fascinating hypothesis, although lacking evidential substantiation.

Yet Anselm's reflections show the importance of a specific belief in understanding both the origins and goal of what is otherwise an undirected and inchoate experience. The Christian tradition offers a unified philosophical frame of reference which enables these puzzling experiences to be interpreted, and seen within a broader context. While the Christian 'big picture' was developed for reasons other than engaging the world of experience, it proved capable of offering an interpretation of this otherwise puzzling experience, locating it within a 'landscape of desire'.

Human beings experience a sense of emptiness and restlessness in this life, perhaps reflecting an impaired or impoverished relationship with God – an idea expressed in Augustine of Hippo's fifth-century prayer: 'You have made us for yourself, and our heart is restless until it finds its rest in you.' This framework offers an interpretation of the origins and goal of this experience. It originates from God, takes the form of a 'homing instinct' for God within us, and is intended to prompt us to find our way back to God.

But what is the status of this line of reasoning? Let's be quite clear: this does not, and was not intended to, constitute a rational proof for God's existence. Perhaps C. S. Lewis's idea of a 'supposal' might be helpful here – a provisional assumption, proposed as a possible explanation of puzzling observations or experiences, which requires testing. Suppose there is a God, such as that which Christianity proposes. Does not this fit in well with our experience of reality? And is not this resonance indicative of the truth of the supposal?

The approach is clearly not compelling; it is rather *suggestive*, hinting that the best way of testing a worldview might not be to assess its individual components, but to step inside the larger vision of reality that it enfolds, and test its quality and depth.

One of the most important functions of a worldview is to inform and give stability to notions of meaning and purpose. In the next section, we shall consider how beliefs undergird these two important themes, which are of considerable importance to personal and social existence.

Meaning: On Finding Significance and Purpose

While some philosophers, such as Susan Wolf, appreciate the importance of the question of meaning, the most significant engagement in recent years with the pervasive human desire to find 'meaning in life' has come from psychology, which has sought to establish both what people understand by 'meaning' and the difference that this makes to their lives. The psychologists Login George and Crystal Park concluded that whether life is perceived as 'meaningful' or not is shaped by 'the extent to which one's life is experienced as making sense, as being directed and motivated by valued goals, and as mattering in the world.'[51]

Detailed surveys persistently indicate that human beings consider it to be important to have a perception of *coherence* in life allowing us to make sense of the world and our own personal existence; a sense of *purpose*, in which we discern core aims and aspirations for life; and a conviction of *significance*, in which our lives matter and are seen to have value.[52] A helpful distinction can be drawn between 'cognitive' and 'affective' aspects of meaning. The former is about making sense of one's experiences of life, while the latter concerns the feelings of satisfaction, fulfilment and happiness that result from our belief that we are living and acting meaningfully.[53]

Is this human longing for meaning in life a 'want' or a 'need'?[54] Is meaning something that some feel they would like, an optional extra that might add something to their existence? Or is it deeply rooted in our fundamental humanity, without which we cannot flourish – especially in the light of the 'existential nihilism of the scientific worldview'? While this debate continues, an excellent case can be made that this is something integral and essential to human actualisation.

Beliefs are important in grounding our frameworks of meaning – those complex webs of opinion that let us determine 'how things are in the world'. I experienced this when I was drawn to Marxism as a teenager. Looking back on that distant and bygone cultural world of the 1960s, I can now see that I was tuning into the three elements of meaning – comprehension, purpose and mattering – proposed by George and Park, without consciously framing my response to Marxism with those specific terms.

Marxism seemed to make sense of the complex and seemingly random flux of history; it gave me a sense of purpose as an agent of change who could end the oppression of the working classes, allowing me to feel I had significance in the grand scheme of history. I experienced both the 'cognitive' and 'affective' aspects of meaning, taking pleasure in being able to make intellectual sense of the world, and experiencing a sense of peace or fulfilment resulting from this perception of meaning and personal mattering.

How does this work in a religious context? How does the threefold account of meaning set out by George and Park work out in practice? Given the diversity of religious beliefs, I shall explore how a Christian might respond to this, and leave space for others to make their own connections.

1. *Comprehension.* We want to make sense of our world, grasping the oneness that lies behind the plurality of our experiences and weaves them into a coherent whole. Christianity has a deep belief in the fundamental interconnectedness of things in God, who is seen as the focal point of its threads of meaning (a major theme in Dante's *Divine Comedy*). The letter to the Colossians, a New Testament writing thought to date from around 60 CE, speaks of all things 'holding together', having a fundamental coherence grounded in the Christian faith (Colossians 1.17). No matter how fragmented our world of experience may at times seem, there is a half-glimpsed bigger picture which holds things together.

2. *Purpose*. A core theme in the outworking of Christianity is the idea of a 'calling'. This articulates the principle that doing something purposefully for God or for Christ invests the action with a deeper value that transcends – without diminishing – its utilitarian functions and benefits. The poet George Herbert engages this theme in his poem 'The Elixir':

> A servant with this clause
>   Makes drudgery divine:
> Who sweeps a room as for Thy laws,
>   Makes that and th' action fine.[55]

3. *Significance*. Many feel overwhelmed by the immensity of the universe and the depth of cosmic time, which seems to make human beings utterly insignificant. This point is explored by the novelist Marilynne Robinson, in a theologically engaged essay entitled 'Psalm Eight'. Robinson here explores the deep human feeling of insignificance in the face of the temporal and spatial vastness of the universe by drawing on the opening verses of this psalm:

> When I look at your heavens, the work of your fingers,
> the moon and the stars that you have established;
> what are human beings that you are mindful of them,
> mortals that you care for them? (Psalm 8:3–4).

Robinson suggests that the fact that this 'infinite distance between God and humankind' is intentionally and graciously bridged by God. In the act of incarnation – the distinctively

Christian idea that God enters and inhabits human history in
Christ – God 'visits' humanity, deeming us to be worthy of
such a divine act of humility and compassion.

> If the great heavens are the work of God's fingers, what
> is small and mortal man? The poem answers its own
> question this way: Man is crowned with honor and
> glory. He is in a singular sense what God has made him,
> because of the dignity God has conferred upon him.[56]

Beliefs shape our understanding of meaning, in a way that
bare facts do not. Each worldview will articulate significantly
different understandings of the nature and grounds of coherence, purpose and significance. The point is that beliefs can
make human existence existentially viable. Yet while some
beliefs liberate and ennoble, others enslave and impoverish.
Wittgenstein's dark broodings on the risk of being 'held captive
by a picture' express a genuine concern, which I shall consider
in the next chapter.

    Yet we need to move on to consider a further question: how
can we understand how beliefs are best enacted in life? What is
the most authentic or appropriate expression of certain beliefs?
If beliefs make possible certain ways of life, where can we find
models of such lives? What exemplars of embodied belief can be
identified, that help us grasp both the impact of beliefs on human
existence, and the forms of life that they inform and enable?

Saints and Sages: Exemplars and a Meaningful Life

In her important reflections on the growing importance
of moral exemplars in a postmodern context, the American

philosopher Edith Wyschogrod highlighted the importance of having someone we can observe or imagine who lives up to and lives out an ethical ideal, rather than simply being presented with an abstract theory that is detached from real life. 'To lead a moral life one does not need a theory about how one should live, but a flesh and blood existent.'[57]

Beliefs are not limited to the realm of the mind, but are capable of being lived out through the realities of a life which they both inform and enrich. An exemplar is someone who has internalised a way of thinking so that it becomes their way of living. Instead of telling us to be good, they *show* us what a good life can and should look like. We need a definition of goodness that is not framed in the language of ideas, but in terms of the character, and an exemplar shows us what goodness is like, rather than telling us how it is to be understood.

There is an important connection here with Pierre Hadot's account of some schools of ancient philosophy. While there is a degree of overstatement in Hadot's analysis,[58] he has clearly identified an aspect of earlier philosophical practice which has not found its proper counterpart in post-Enlightenment thought – the development of certain personal disciplines which help people assimilate and enact their vision of a good life. These transformed modes of seeing and being in the world were exemplified and lived out in the figure of the sage. In the ancient world, philosophy was eminently concerned with self-criticism and self-improvement. Plutarch spoke of 'weaving' or 'painting' our lives; Plotinus suggested we see ourselves as a sculptor, chipping away at a block of marble to allow the statue within to be seen. Philosophy is about seeing our potential, and guiding us as we try to achieve this, in company with appropriate mentors and exemplars.

While ancient schools of philosophy were concerned with the development of argument and reasoning, they also developed what Hadot calls 'spiritual exercises' as a means of enacting their ideas and values. Aristotle's discussion of the question of how we should live focuses on the idea of *eudaimonia*, a Greek term often translated as 'happiness', but which perhaps is better rendered as 'flourishing' or 'fulfilment'.

During the eighteenth century, the Enlightenment was seen as enfolding a single coherent manner of thought and life, valid for all places and times, so that its leading representatives might be regarded as sages – figures of wisdom with universal appeal and significance. Today, as the limitations of a purely rationalist worldview have become apparent, there is much greater interest in respecting the distinctiveness of different human understandings of rational and spiritual virtues, and retrieving older ways of thinking that had been sidelined during the Age of Reason.

British Enlightenment philosophers – most notably, John Locke and George Berkeley (and to a lesser extent, David Hume), have also been scrutinised and reappraised in the light of their involvement in the slave trade. This does not, in my view, discredit the philosophical beliefs of such leading representatives of the Enlightenment, although it certainly complicates attempts to present this as an emancipatory social movement, and raises some awkward questions about the connections between its philosophies and forms of life.

The diversity of belief systems is such that an exemplar of one philosophical or spiritual tradition may be viewed as deficient or unacceptable from the perspective of another such tradition. Edward Conze, a noted scholar of Buddhism, remarked that he did not think that any Buddhist could fully approve of the lives or teachings of Roman Catholic saints. 'They were bad Buddhists though good Christians.'

A 'saint' is best seen as an authentic embodiment and expression of the distinct manner of life and thought of a particular religious tradition. Although the popular sense of the term is that of a highly moral person, it is important to realise how moral values reflect the core themes of a tradition of belief. To ask that people should be 'good' is of little value without a lived example of a good life. We want to be *shown* a good life, not merely informed about an abstract idea of 'goodness'. Life is something that we want to *live*, not just talk about.

Christianity, as might be expected, has its own distinct take on the nature and means of achieving an authentic life. The primary source and focus of Christian identity-making is the person of Christ. For New Testament writers, Christ is both the ground of salvation and the model of the redeemed life. To be a Christian is to aim for 'Christlikeness', in that Christ is both the 'noble exemplar' of Christian existence and 'the very source which empowers the Christian to imitate the Lord.'[59] The New Testament encourages Christians to desire to emulate (and thus to imitate) Christ's behaviour and attitudes, especially in relation to how he treats other people.[60] Christ makes *visible* and makes *possible* the distinctively Christian understanding of a good life.

Linda Zagzebski notes that admiration often leads to emulation.[61] People are attracted to the quality of life exhibited by such exemplars, and are drawn to attempt its replication.

Encountering an exemplar may lead initially to eliciting admiration for them and subsequently to the enabling of emulation.[62] In effect, this leads to beliefs being assessed at least partly on account of their enactments and embodiments, rather than their purely intellectual virtues. 'I want to *be* like that' exists in a complex and multi-layered relationship with 'I want to *think* like that.'

This highlights the need to reflect further on human belief acquisition and formation. Too often, our evaluation of beliefs is presented in terms of the Age of Reason – as a rational calculation. Can it be justified by reason? Yet this represents a one-dimensional evaluation of belief. If someone's beliefs are rationally defensible, yet allow them to become involved with the slave trade, there are clearly some other questions that need to be asked of their beliefs.

It is little wonder than many philosophers are now using the language of virtue and character in discussing how beliefs are developed and enacted. Knowledge is not gained through a mechanised and impersonal process of rational calculation, but often involves making *judgements* in the absence of conclusive evidential warrant – judgements that ultimately reflect the character and wisdom of the thinker.

In this chapter, we have considered how beliefs shape individuals, and opened up new ways of seeing the world and behaving within it. Yet what happens when those beliefs appear to falter, or even to fail? What happens to those who hold them?

Chapter 6

When Beliefs Fail

In the previous chapter, we reflected on the difference that belief makes for individuals. But what happens when beliefs we hoped would offer a secure foundation for life fail us? When a belief we hoped would bring meaning turns out to be incapable of bearing this emotional and intellectual weight?

In his memoir *Immanuel*, Matthew McNaught reflects on his involvement with a Christian community founded in Southampton in the 1970s, which placed an emphasis on 'signs and wonders' and God's power to heal.[1] In 2002, the pastor of Immanuel was diagnosed with terminal cancer. The community prayed fervently for his recovery – but without success. The pastor then turned to the Synagogue Church of All Nations, a Nigerian megachurch with a healing ministry led by the charismatic preacher T. B. Joshua. Joshua prayed over the pastor and declared that he had been completely healed. The pastor was then instructed to refuse medication, as taking medicine for the illness would imply a lack of faith. Sadly, the pastor died shortly afterwards. Inevitably, this traumatic development caused some in Immanuel to question their belief about divine intervention in human lives. This core belief now seemed to some to have failed. What did that mean for their faith?

This story can easily be supplemented by other cases of failed beliefs – some religious, some political, some personal. What happens in the aftermath of such apparent failures, and the crises of faith that they so often precipitate? This process of re-evaluating individual belief systems is now generally described as 'deconstruction'. While this term was initially popularised by the French philosopher Jacques Derrida to describe the uncomfortable process of uncovering the hidden assumptions that influence our understanding of the world, it is now used in a broader context to refer to the deconstruction of belief systems. Deconstruction often begins when an individual encounters a troubling anomaly or inconsistency in their beliefs – such as a pastor who engages in abusive behaviour, harming instead of nourishing individuals' spiritual wellbeing, or a prominent male politician who publicly supports women's rights but whose private life reveals a *very* different outlook.

Some religious leaders consider any departure from or re-evaluation of what they define as 'orthodoxy' as amounting to a loss of faith. Yet this feels misguided – faith is dynamic rather than static, changing over time through an exploration of beliefs and the implications they have for our way of life. This process of growth inevitably involves reflection, reconsideration and adjustment.[2] In religious contexts, deconstruction often arises when beliefs are understood merely as strictures to be accepted, without exploring their emotional, moral and existential benefits. These forms of faith are emaciated and spiritually barren precisely because they have not been correlated and connected with the realities of life.

This is a particular concern for individuals whose religious beliefs have been inherited from previous generations within their family, rather than being a result of personal discovery or reflection. A static faith, some might argue, is a dead faith, inherited from the past like a mouldering family heirloom. It may ornament a room but makes no significant difference to the realities of life. It is a reminder of the past, rather than a resource for the present. What was meant to be a living reality thus becomes little more than an inert marker of familial identity.

Deconstruction initiates a process of dismantling the fundamental principles of a belief system, leading to its disintegration. While this process itself can lead to feelings of despair and a diminished sense of personal security, it does not necessarily lead to the abandonment of a belief system. Deconstruction can lead to reconstruction, in which an individual realises that their previous faith was immature or underdeveloped, and can be reimagined in a more profound and fulfilling manner.

The psychologist Kenneth Pargament has pointed out that religious belief allows people to respond to such crises of faith in two different ways. Religious faith offers resources through its teachings, rituals and narratives for both 'religious coping through *conservation*' (that is, assimilating these events into one's faith perspective and enriching it) and 'religious coping through *transformation*' (that is, accommodating one's faith perspective to these events, so that it is challenged and revised in their light).[3] Pargament's ideas can be helpfully correlated with New Testament insights, such as Paul's declaration that 'we know that suffering produces perseverance; perseverance, character; and character, hope.'[4]

Perhaps the most illuminating narratives of belief deconstruction are found in the political and religious domains – such as Arthur Koestler's disenchantment with Marxism-Leninism, or C. S. Lewis's experience of a partial fragmentation of his faith following the death of his wife – which we will consider later in this chapter. We begin, however, by reflecting on the significance of the rise of religious 'Nones'.

Losing My Religion: The Rise of Religious 'Nones'

One of the most interesting recent trends in modern American culture is the rise of religious 'Nones' – that is, individuals who define themselves as 'none of the above' in surveys inviting them to name their religious commitment from a standard checklist of possibilities, or who self-identify as having 'no religion'. Since 2013, Gallup has used this question to explore religious commitment: 'What is your religious preference – are you Protestant, Roman Catholic, Mormon, Jewish, Muslim, another religion or no religion?'

Gallup reports that the percentage of Nones measured in its surveys has risen from virtually zero during the 1950s to about twenty per cent of the American adult population today. In recent years, this appears to have stabilised: between 2017 and 2022, an average of twenty or twenty-one per cent of Americans defined themselves as Nones.[5] Similar patterns can be observed elsewhere in western culture. In the United Kingdom, for example, religious Nones have risen from twenty-five per cent in 2011 to thirty-seven per cent in 2021. It remains to be seen whether this is a plateau, or whether it will increase further in the future.

Who are these people, and what does the emergence of this phenomenon have to say about the future of belief? Sociologically, they are likely to be male, younger, higher educated, not married, without children and liberal in their opinions and values.[6] Among the factors that lead them to review or reject their religious commitments, the following appear to have been particularly influential: negative reactions against various forms of religious fundamentalism, a rejection of alliances between religion and politics, and intellectual disagreement with religious beliefs and practices. It is clear that Nones have a problem with religious institutions – many of them believe that religious organisations are excessively concerned with money and status, and are dangerously enmeshed with politics.

The rise of the Nones is sometimes interpreted to mean a growing absence of any religious beliefs in a significant section of the American population. This interpretation needs to be treated with caution.[7] People who choose not to self-identify using any specific religious category often hold beliefs about God or a 'supernatural' world, or take part in religious or spiritual activities. Indeed, many of those who move away from one set of religious beliefs often shift towards a *different* set of religious beliefs, rather than abandoning beliefs in general, or religious or spiritual beliefs in particular.

A recent study has pointed out that while Nones see themselves to be 'non-religious', they in fact endorse 'alternative supernatural beliefs' that are also driven by some of the 'same cognitive biases that underpin more conventional religious beliefs.'[8] This suggests that this group is defined more by their negative relationship with organised religions than by their 'intuitions about the supernatural'. As Fredrik deBoer remarked of modern American progressives: 'They're still religious; they're simply studying a different catechism.'[9]

An earlier survey by the Pew Research Center's Forum on Religion & Public Life found that many of America's 46 million unaffiliated adults were religious or spiritual in some way. For example, sixty-eight per cent reported that they believed in God, thirty-seven per cent identified themselves as 'spiritual but not religious', and twenty-one per cent reported that they prayed every day.

Yet despite these cautionary remarks, it is clear that the rise of religious Nones reflects concerns about the public *acceptability* of religious values or the public *credibility* of religious beliefs, leading them to develop 'alternative meaning systems'.[10] These adopted alternative systems themselves take the form of *beliefs*; the move is thus not away from *believing* in general, but from certain specific *beliefs* and tainted institutions.

What exactly leads people to question beliefs that might once have seemed stable and permanent?

Dissonance with Reality:
The Fragility of Human Goodness

In July 1944, Anne Frank wrote the following words in her diary as she and her family hid in Amsterdam from the Nazi authorities, who were in the process of deporting the city's Jewish population to extermination or concentration camps. Despite the weight of empirical evidence to the contrary surrounding her, what kept her going was belief in the goodness of human nature. The alternatives seemed unbearable to her:

> It's really a wonder that I haven't dropped all my ideals,
> because they seem so absurd and impossible to carry
> out. Yet I keep them, because in spite of everything, I
> still believe that people are really good at heart. I sim-
> ply can't build up my hopes on a foundation consisting
> of confusion, misery, and death.[11]

After their Secret Annex was discovered a month later, Anne
and her older sister Margot were deported to the Bergen-Belsen
concentration camp, where they are believed to have died in
February or March 1945.

Many share Anne's dogged determination to keep on believing in human goodness, even in the face of deliberate and
systematic suffering. Yet this belief in the goodness of human
nature is an *interpretation* of our situation. Other ways of
understanding human nature are available – some of which
are rather more negative. The eighteenth-century Italian
playwright Giuseppe Baretti, best known for his unevidenced
attribution of the words *eppur si muove* ('and still it moves')
to Galileo more than a century after his death, ridiculed the
idea of the fundamental goodness of humanity with a barbed
one-liner: 'I hate mankind, for I think myself one of the best
of them, and I know how bad I am.'[12] Or we might reflect on
the philosopher John Gray's view that 'humans are weapon-
making animals with an unquenchable fondness for killing.'[13]

Others might argue for a hybrid or more complex account
of human nature. One of the most interesting of these is the
Russian writer Aleksandr Solzhenitsyn, whose brutal experiences in Soviet labour camps from 1945 to 1953 led him to
conclude that the 'line dividing good and evil cuts through the

heart of every human being.'[14] Evil is not something that can be conveniently located in the 'other', people who we can designate 'evil' in a form of cultural Manichaeism. It is rather, and more disturbingly, a potential presence and possibility within all of us, elicited or activated through circumstances and situations. Although some suggest that Solzhenitsyn derives this insight from Russian Orthodoxy, it seems much more likely that it emerged from his life-experience which was subsequently correlated with Christian understandings of the ambiguities of human nature.[15]

My concern here, however, is not simply with the fragility of human conceptions of goodness, and their implications for those who want to lead a good life. What happens to someone when a core belief that gave them hope in the face of 'confusion, misery and death' turns out to be an illusion? In this section, I want to focus on the personal crises that the failure of our belief systems often precipitates through the psychological stress this creates – a process that has come to be known as 'cognitive dissonance'.[16]

Late in 1956, the American social psychologist Leon Festinger read a newspaper article about a group of people who believed that the United States was going to be annihilated by a cataclysmic flood on 21 December, 1955.[17] Everyone would die in this flood, apart from those who had privileged access to a prophecy from the people of the planet Clarion, transmitted by automatic writing to one of the members of this group, who would be able to board a flying saucer and evade this destruction.

Festinger realised that there were some excellent reasons for supposing that on 22 December, the members of this group

– which he called 'The Seekers' – would have to cope with the realisation that their belief system had spectacularly failed. The world ought to have come to an end the previous day; the Seekers would have to come up with an explanation for still being alive on earth. Festinger reckoned that the dissonance caused by this devastating disconfirmation of their belief would motivate them either to change their beliefs or seek strategies to reconfirm them. Festinger arranged for one of his research group to infiltrate the Seekers, and report on how the group responded to what he confidently expected to be a cosmic non-event.

As instructed, the Seekers gathered at midnight to await the spacecraft that would carry them to safety on the planet Clarion, making sure they removed all metal objects. As the hours passed, nothing happened – until one of the group suddenly received an additional message from Clarion by automatic writing at four in the morning. Because of their faithfulness to their instructions, the destruction of earth had been averted![18]

Festinger and his colleagues developed a theory of 'cognitive dissonance' which held that individuals experience mental discomfort when there is a tension between their beliefs and behaviour. The phenomenon is well known – think, for example, of animal lovers who eat meat, yet feel intense discomfort when they think about the processes by which this meat is produced. Unsurprisingly, they tend to avoid thinking about where meat comes from. How might this work out for someone who is convinced that people are fundamentally good, but is confronted with evidence of atrocities committed by human beings – such as genocides and other war crimes, often carried out by ordinary citizens?[19] Or the sexual and physical abuse of local populations in Africa by United Nation peacekeeping forces, who were supposed to protect them?

One option is to see these atrocities as an atypical response to a traumatic situation – the onset of war – which will cease to be a troubling issue when the situation has passed, and normal life resumes. C. S. Lewis, an atheist scholar of Renaissance English literature at Oxford University who converted to Christianity in 1931, argued that while optimistic views of human nature had been dealt a death blow by the horrors of the Second World War, humanity's capacity for self-deception and selective memory was so great that such lessons, learned at such cost, would simply be suppressed and forgotten once the war was over. Similar concerns were, of course, expressed after the First World War. Lewis was traumatised by the brutality of this conflict, initially blaming God for failing to prevent it, but gradually realising that the real target of his criticism ought to be human self-deception.

Another option is to block out the memory of troubling events or episodes that subvert the plausibility of individual beliefs or ensembles of beliefs – such as the goodness of humanity. The 'art of forgetting' plays a significant role in Renaissance literature, allowing 'those moments that threaten to destabilise – or even to shatter – identity' to be erased from an individual's memory, and thus cease to be a threat to a worldview that underlies existential wellbeing.[20]

Lewis himself bears witness to this construction of mental frontiers and imaginative barriers, as he sought to keep his traumatic memories of combat in the First World War at a safe distance. Some might see this as a 'flight from reality'. Lewis, however, chose to see this as 'a treaty with reality, the fixing of a frontier.'[21] Lewis realised that there were limits to the 'reality' that he could cope with, and had to draw a dividing line between what he wanted to remember and what he needed to forget.

A third option is to affirm individual human goodness, while suggesting that social forces give rise to pressures and stimuli that lead good people to do bad things. One of the most influential and thoughtful presentations of this approach is found in Reinhold Niebuhr's classic work of moral theology *Moral Man and Immoral Society* (1932). Niebuhr's prophetic essay recognises the 'constant and seemingly irreconcilable conflict between the needs of society and the imperatives of a sensitive conscience.'[22] The pure morality of the individual conscience is simply not transferable to the messy realities of collective human activity. It's a fair point. Yet others would object that 'society' is an aggregate of human beings, so that the problem of human goodness has simply been displaced, not resolved.

Held Captive by a Big Picture:
Wittgenstein the Therapist

In famously declaring that 'a *picture* held us captive',[23] making it difficult for us to liberate ourselves from its imaginative thrall, Ludwig Wittgenstein was pointing out how easily our understanding of our world can be controlled by an 'organizing myth'[24] – a worldview or metanarrative that has, whether we realise it or not, come to dominate our perception of our world, in effect predisposing us to interpret experience in certain manners as natural or self-evidentially correct, while blinding us to alternative ways of understanding it.

When you are trapped in a worldview, you need a philosophical therapist who can diagnose the problem and propose a solution. And that's why Wittgenstein is so important to our reflections. One way of making progress in philosophy, according to Wittgenstein, is to loosen and finally escape from 'the grip of simplifying "pictures" or conceptual templates that attempt to generalise beyond their contextually specific sphere of applicability.'[25]

How might this be done? One way of applying Wittgenstein's critical method is to look at the world through a series of potential informing 'pictures' or 'worldviews'. We cannot dispense with these pictures; we can, however, ask which is the most reliable and appropriate. For Wittgenstein, a 'picture' changes the ways in which we see things. We can look at reality through a range of such pictures, and ask which of them offers the best rendering of our world.

As Gordon Baker points out, Wittgenstein sets out 'a kind of homeopathy' in which 'pictures are to be treated with pictures'.[26] His philosophical therapy involves a willingness on our part to explore comparisons, leading to a 'conversion to a new way of seeing things'. How well does it make sense of what we observe? What does it tell us about ourselves, and other human beings? Does it promote fulfilment? Or does it trap us in a limited and limiting world, such as Max Weber's 'iron cage' of rationalism? The first step to securing freedom is to realise that alternative ways of seeing the world are available.

Wittgenstein's critical analysis is invaluable for those who find themselves shackled to a bad philosophical system or individual 'bad beliefs',[27] and want to break free from their thrall. As with the approach of Alcoholics Anonymous, Wittgenstein's first step is to force us to realise that we are 'captive' – that we have trapped ourselves within a limiting worldview, and need to break free from its constraints and distortions (Wittgenstein is particularly helpful to those recovering from the existential nihilism of scientism).

Some worldviews offer us reassurance that the world is coherent and existentially inhabitable. Yet others are often constructed to justify the marginalisation, exclusion or even persecution of others. The most familiar example of this is the dehumanising racial ideology of National Socialism, which treated Jews, Roma, Poles and Serbs as *Untermenschen* ('sub-humans').

However, similar racial ideologies became influential in the United States after the First World War. During the 1920s, William McDougall – chair of the Psychology Department at Harvard University – advocated disenfranchising blacks, re-stricting intermarriage between races and complete segregation of blacks from whites on 'scientific' grounds.[28] A decade later, Wallace Fard Muhammad, the founder of the 'Nation of Islam' in the United States, set out a creation narrative which claimed that blacks were 'God's Original People', and that 'whites were grafted into existence by Yakub, an evil black scientist, around 6,000 years ago.'[29]

Sadly, there is no shortage of ideologies which cause one set of human beings to regard others as representing a lower form of life – and hence as not entitled to the respect and rights afforded to proper human beings. Belief systems can easily lead to the construction of a moral framework that privileges some and legitimises discrimination and violence against oth-ers or gives a dangerous amount of normative or interpretative authority to a particular institution. The author and journalist Arthur Koestler learned this lesson the hard way.

Abandoning a Big Picture:
The Case of Arthur Koestler

As a campaigning journalist on the Republican side of the Spanish Civil war, Koestler had enthusiastically embraced Marxism-Leninism as a totalising theory of life and history which promoted justice and freedom. Yet Koestler's early infatuation with Marxism as an explanatory theory and political programme was shattered by events in the Soviet Union during the 1930s, especially Stalin's 'purges' of political opponents and other 'unreliables', which are estimated to have led to the execution of more than half a million people. Koestler decided the most powerful way of challenging Marxism-Leninism was through fictional narration rather than through factual analysis. His novel *Darkness at Noon* (1941) is a cautionary tale about the dangers of self-delusion, above all the belief that human beings can create and sustain a perfect society, exposing both the inner contradictions and inhumane outcomes of a totalitarian ideology.

The Russian Revolution promised to end the oppressive slaughters of the Tsarist era. Yet somehow, Koestler remarked, every Russian revolutionary discovered that they had 'to become a slaughterer, in order to abolish slaughtering', whipping 'the groaning masses of the country towards a theoretical future happiness.'[30] As Koestler later explained in *The Invisible Writing* (1954), he found that he simply could not cope with the cognitive dissonance between theory and reality. 'I went to Communism as one goes to a spring of fresh water, and

I left Communism as one clambers out of a poisoned river strewn with the wreckage of flooded cities and the corpses of the drowned.'[31]

What *exactly* was the problem? For Koestler, Marxism-Leninism may have originated as a purely theoretical account of historical process; it ended up, however, as an ideology that justified and served the interests of the Soviet Communist Party, which proclaimed itself sole interpreter of Marxist theory, enforcing its authority by force. Isaiah Berlin tracked the origins of this authoritarianism back to Marx himself, who interpreted the world 'in terms of a single, clear, passionately held principle, denouncing and destroying all that conflicts with it.'[32]

Koestler's most fundamental point remains valid and significant. A worldview may be both 'rational' and 'evidenced', attractive and compelling to its audience – yet despite these obvious merits, it can still lead to the suppression of human dignity, value and freedom. Koestler reminds us that we should not judge a worldview simply by its intellectual credentials; we must ask what it *does* to people. Rationalist critics may feel that 'liveability' seems a poor criterion to use in making such judgements, but Koestler's experience points us in a very different direction, and forces us to ask whether the effect a belief has on individuals and communities should be a reason to affirm – or reject – it.

Koestler helps us see that the core of any oppressive system is a *belief* – a conviction that one group is somehow superior to another. For example, many believe that women are physically weaker than men. What matters, however, is how this belief is applied – such as excluding women from certain social roles, or subordinating them to men. Oppressed groups internalise the ideology of inferiority, seeing themselves through a dominant social or cultural lens, rather than challenging the legitimacy of this lens.

Koestler is an important witness to how individual beliefs or a 'big picture' can entrap individuals, allowing them to oppress others in the fight against oppression, and to tell lies in the fight for truth – while at the same time anointing these beliefs with an ideological balm that somehow makes them appear true, noble and inevitable.

Yet Koestler's realisation of the illusory promise of Marxism-Leninism ultimately led him to question the reliability of any such 'big picture'. Where many abandoned one worldview to embrace another, Koestler became suspicious of the overreach of worldviews and metanarratives in general. Where he once regarded the universe as an 'open book', he now saw it as a 'text written in invisible ink', allowing us at most to 'decipher a small fragment' of its complexity.[33] Big pictures could only cope with the density and disorder of human history by simplifying and distorting it, offering a 'specious clarity'. That is why Marxist theory 'had frozen to a dogmatic cult, with a simplified, easily graspable catechism.'[34] All the questions had been answered correctly and authoritatively; there was no need for further reflection, merely to learn and repeat the right answers.

The outcome of Koestler's dramatic abandonment of Communism was thus not the adoption of another worldview, but rather a dawning realisation that no such big picture could be trusted. We live in a twilight world of shadows, in which there are no certainties. A throwaway line at the end of

Darkness at Noon, as Rubashov waits in his cell for the arrival of his executioners, is significant here. 'Perhaps reason alone was a defective compass, which led one on such a winding twisted course that the goal finally disappeared in the mist.'[35] There were limits to human reason, which might lead us astray if pressed too far.

For Koestler, Marxism was an example of such an overreach of reason; so, perhaps, were all other attempts to rationalise the complexities of nature or social reality. The political writer Rafael Behr makes this point neatly: 'every aspiration to contain human experience in a unified theory, every urge to order mankind in neat rows, every codified system of belief that despises dissent, involves some inward violence.'[36]

Our two examples of beliefs that seem to totter on the brink of failure under relentless pressure from the world of observation and experience have focused on the difficulties in speaking of human goodness and the deeply problematic link between a worldview and the institution that embodies, interprets and enforces it. For many observers, Koestler's problem lay primarily with an authoritarian institution, and secondarily on the ideology on which it was based. The Marxist theorist Antonio Gramsci certainly thought so, and argued the need for a new kind of radical intellectual if Communism was to gain in strength in his native Italy – not someone who parroted the views of the Soviet Communist Party, but rather an 'organic intellectual' who understood Marxism, and could explain and defend this to ordinary people.[37] Marxism had to focus on its intellectual and political appeal, and avoid appealing to the institutional authority of the Soviet Union as the basis of its credibility.

Although I have focused on the relationship between Marxism and the Soviet Communist Party, the same pattern of a problematic relation between *beliefs* and *institutions* can be observed elsewhere. For example, Galileo's problems were not with Christianity as such (one of the great myths of the late nineteenth century, by the way), but with the centralised authority of the Pope as an interpreter of the Bible. Where Galileo was in correspondence with the Catholic biblical scholar Paolo Antonio Foscarini about late Renaissance biblical hermeneutics, Pope Urban VIII feared that these new theories might weaken the authority of the Catholic church in the face of the rising threat from Protestantism.[38] The best defence of the Church's institutional authority seemed to be a reiteration of its past interpretations of the Bible – a judgement that most now consider to be flawed.

While some Christian theologians or apologists see themselves as defending the institution of the church and affirming its teachings, others (such as C. S. Lewis) see themselves as commending the basic ideas of a consensual Christianity – what Lewis termed 'mere Christianity', which was denominationally open-ended. Lewis thus defended Christian ideas, not a Christian institution.

This neatly brings us to consider an explanatory difficulty of religious belief. While every worldview experiences some degree of discomfort at its interfaces with the world of observation and human experience, it is widely agreed that Christianity experiences a particular challenge on account of the existence of suffering and pain in the world. If God is good, why is there suffering in the world? Surely God ought to be doing something about that? If there is a God, that is.

Christianity and the Problem of Suffering:
Setting the Scene

Suffering is a universal human experience, framed in different ways by a variety of worldviews. Most consider suffering not as an intellectual riddle that we can *hope* or *need* to solve; it is rather something that has to be *endured*, raising the issue of how we can cope with both its pain and the deeper existential distress that it so often causes.[39]

This insight was characteristic of classic Greek philosophy and literature, which were much more concerned with cultivating the art of right living than their modern counterparts.[40] Greek tragedy thus shunned simplistic intellectual resolutions of complex questions, focusing instead on narrating how people learned to deal with suffering. The American philosopher Martha Nussbaum highlights the educative role of suffering in Greek tragedy, in that it helps us to grasp what it means to be human through an explicit 'acknowledgement of difficult human realities'.[41]

Whether suffering is seen as an intellectual problem or not depends on the specific theoretical lens through which it is interpreted. For reasons that we shall explore, the Enlightenment's emphasis on rational explanation has led to a new emphasis on *explaining* or *rationalising* suffering, and particularly on demonstrating the consistency of a philosophical worldview that affirms both the goodness of God on the one hand, and the reality of suffering on the other. As Charles Taylor has argued, this seems to have created the expectation that every aspect of the universe is completely accessible to human reason, so that we are able to comprehend everything rationally.

Yet the problem goes much deeper than our unattainable longing to see things with total clarity; we seem to think that a meaningful life is about the evasion of pain. We feel we are entitled to avoid suffering and see its existence as an intellectual scandal. Yet this is an inadequate modern response to an age-old problem. More reliable alternatives are available, as the psychologist Robert Emmons points out:

> 'The good life' is not one that is achieved through momentary pleasures or defensive illusions, but through meeting suffering head on and transforming it into opportunities for meaning, wisdom, and growth, with the ultimate objective being the development of the person into a fully functioning mature being. On this formula for happiness, age-old wisdom and modern science are in agreement.

A good example of such older approaches to this riddle of human suffering is found in early Christianity. The New Testament, for example, recognises suffering as a 'given', something that was an everyday aspect of life, yet which had been given new dignity and significance through the suffering and death of Christ. The New Testament does not offer any *explanations* for suffering or see it as necessary to do so. The letters of Paul, which offer the most substantial engagement with suffering, consider suffering to be an integral aspect of existence in the 'new age' within which the 'old age' still remains an active presence.[42] Paul's concerns include reassuring his readers that to suffer does not mean that they have been abandoned or rejected by God; that Christ suffered *before* them, and *for* them;

and that they may look ahead to the hope of a new order, of which they will be part.[43]

These views remained central to Christian thinking for the next thousand years. Although many Christian theologians – such as Augustine of Hippo – felt it important to reflect on how suffering was to be understood,[44] the dominant theme within Christian spirituality was that reflection on Christ's sufferings enabled believers to cope better with suffering in their own lives, and to grow through this. Suffering was a fact of life and was not to be seen as a disconfirmation of religious belief. Yet this changed during the 'Age of Reason' as a new philosophical emphasis on the perfection of God framed the existence of evil and suffering in the world as a contradiction. Hopes subsequently grew of eliminating suffering through medical advances, making its persistence an increasing personal concern.

The term 'theodicy' was invented by the philosopher Leibniz in 1710 to refer to the kind of impersonal theoretical rationalisations of the problem of evil that we are familiar with today. Yet there is a growing realisation that this enterprise of 'theodicy' is problematically linked with the rationalising concerns of the Age of Reason. Though suffering and evil have been around since the dawn of civilisation, earlier generations of philosophers and theologians do not appear to have seen these as calling the existence of God into question; if anything, it made clinging to God all the more important in difficult times.

The belief that suffering is a problem for believing in God is a relatively new idea, reflecting a new confidence in the capacity of human reason to comprehend our universe. Charles Taylor, one of the most perceptive analysts of the rise of modern secularism, points out that the writers of the Age of Reason too often assumed that human beings have complete access to the structures of the universe and the nature of human life, and can answer every 'why' question – including why suffering and evil exist.

The result is that many modern Christian writers offer detached and disengaged rationalisations of the existence of suffering in the world, rather than showing how it is possible to live meaningfully in the presence of suffering. The philosopher James K. A. Smith argues that many philosophers have 'bought into the spectatorish "world picture" of the new modern order', which makes us think we are 'positioned to see everything' and hence can – and should – 'expect an answer to whatever puzzles us, including the problem of evil.'[45] As Stephen Wykstra cautions, drawing on his principle of 'Reasonable Epistemic Access', we need to be sceptical of those who declare that we can take a 'God's eye' view of the world, being able to see everything in its totality and grasp its full significance.[46]

C. S. Lewis made this point in his *Problem of Pain* (1940), in which he wrestled with the questions raised by the human experience of pain and suffering. Lewis here suggests that we cannot see things clearly from our human perspective and will always see things darkly and incompletely. Drawing on an analogy that would have been familiar to his British readers at this time during the Second World War, Lewis suggests that the life of faith is like walking around during the Blackout – the periods of enforced darkness, devoid of any artificial light, designed to prevent German bombers from having visual sight of their ground targets.

Lewis used this analogy to suggest that we don't see everything clearly. There isn't enough light. But 'the blackout is not quite complete. There are chinks.'[47] For Lewis, we must learn to live and work with the partial apprehension of a complex and ambivalent world, in which pain does not fit easily with some core Christian themes – yet does not contradict them either.

This, then, is the context within which discussion of God and suffering is now set in western culture. Yet this is a recent (and, in my view, *reversible*) development, which is increasingly being subjected to criticism on account of – to mention only a few concerns – its intellectual over-reach; its under-evidenced notions of God, goodness and human freedom; and its abstract and impersonal framing of issues that might be suitable for a college seminar room, but fails to connect with the deeper questions of everyday life.

With these points in mind, we turn to reflect on the challenges that suffering causes for belief in God in the contemporary world, focusing on C. S. Lewis's reflections following the death of his wife from cancer.

Suffering: C. S. Lewis and the
Reconstruction of Belief

One of the surprise bestsellers of 2007 was William Paul Young's *The Shack*, a twenty-first century re-imagining of the book of Job published by Windblown Media, a Californian company that nobody had ever heard of.[48] The book sold twenty million copies. As if that wasn't enough, ten years later the novel was made into a Hollywood blockbuster that grossed over $96 million globally. Some critics of the movie complained about its 'pontificating'[49] which they felt blunted the imaginative power and dramatic force of the novel. Yet the remarkable popular success of both book and movie made it clear that many today remain intensely engaged with the issue of suffering, yet are dissatisfied with the abstract and inaccessible philosophical rationalisations which are routinely presented as solutions to these enigmas.

The problem is that philosophical theories that aim to make sense of suffering are often presented in immensely dull and technical ways, that treat suffering as a rational problem demanding an intellectual solution, often involving arcane definitions and distinctions that baffle their readers, leaving them drowning in a glutinous alphabet soup. The success of *The Shack* made it clear that what people were looking for was a meaningful and accessible engagement with the problem of suffering which they did not find in self-help manuals, traditional spiritual comfort food, and least of all in an abstract rational analysis based on generic notions of divinity which failed to engage the emotional aspects of suffering and pain.

This is a real problem. The American philosopher of religion Nicholas Wolterstorff found himself unable to read academic works on theodicy following the death of his son in a climbing accident in 1983. They just didn't connect with his situation. 'I cannot fit these pieces together. I am at a loss. I have read the theodicies produced to justify the ways of God to man. I find them unconvincing. To the most agonised question I have ever asked I do not know the answer.'[50] When it enters our lives, we are overwhelmed by the immensity of the question of suffering. As Johann Baptist Metz remarks, this is 'a question that can neither be answered nor forgotten, a question for which we, from our side, have no answer; it is the question of "too much.'"[51]

Wolterstorff is one of many Christian writers to explore the question of whether the painful presence of suffering in the world negates Christian belief. C. S. Lewis, now a canonical Christian writer, found the devastation of World War One so troubling that he doubled down on his teenage atheism.

Shortly after the end of the war, Lewis published a collection of poems entitled *Spirits in Bondage* in March 1919 under the pseudonym 'Clive Hamilton'.[52] Lewis's 'Ode for New Year's Day', written when under fire from German artillery near the French town of Arras in January 1918, protests against a silent uncaring heaven, a disinterested spectator of the carnage of the war. The existence of evil and suffering in the world was a moral outrage that would lead any intelligent person to reject belief in God.

This is an influential argument, and many have experienced its force. David Hume, for example, argued that the world we know and experience is so clearly inadequate that it could only have been made by an 'infant deity', or some elderly deity in his dotage, who urgently needed to be retired from duty.

Yet there is a problem with this argument. *How can Hume reach this conclusion?* He has no knowledge of any other universe, so cannot make a comparative judgement. His belief that this world of suffering and pain is inadequate or substandard seems to rest on an *intuition*, a *feeling* that there must surely be a better universe than the one we know.

It is important to pause here, and note how much influence emotions, feelings and intuitions have on human reasoning. As the psychologist Jonathan Haidt points out, many of our supposedly 'rational' moral arguments reflect emotional stances; moral reasoning is usually a post hoc construction, generated after a judgement has been reached on other grounds.[53]

Hume himself argued that moral judgements, like aesthetic judgements, derive from sentiment rather than reason, so that we achieve moral knowledge by 'immediate feeling' rather than by a 'chain of argument'.[54] Steven Wykstra points to the problem that emerges here: the way we *feel* about our world does not count as *evidence*. Most of us, he notes,

> have at some times in our lives felt instances of suffering
> in this world to be evidence against theism, according
> to which the universe is the creation of a wholly good
> Being who loves his creatures, and who lacks nothing
> in wisdom and power. If it has proven hard to turn this
> feeling into a good argument, it has, perhaps, proven
> just as hard to get rid of it.[55]

Lewis – who initially studied and taught philosophy at Oxford – was aware of Hume's argument. Yet he came to see this as a vulnerable line of reasoning, dependent on unacknowledged prior beliefs which could not be proved to be true, and might simply amount to matters of personal taste.

> My argument against God was that the universe
> seemed so cruel and unjust. But how had I got this
> idea of just and unjust? A man does not call a line
> crooked unless he has some idea of a straight line.
> What was I comparing this universe with when I
> called it unjust?[56]

The force of the argument from the injustice of evil and suffering depends upon the strong conviction that 'the world was really unjust, not simply that it did not happen to please my fancies.' Yet Lewis found he could not articulate a meaningful notion of 'justice' without grounding this *transcendentally* in something that lay beyond his own personal beliefs or those of the community to which he belonged. It was a classic example of the difficulties faced by thinkers of the Age of Reason – having to judge one belief in terms of another belief. In the end, Lewis set his atheism to one side, and reaffirmed faith in God.

Thirty years later, however, Lewis found that the experience of the slow death of his wife, Joy Davidman, from cancer in 1960 reopened the question of pain and suffering for him emotionally, not simply intellectually. Lewis wrote *A Grief Observed* (1961), one of his rawest and most challenging books, as a way of recording and reflecting on his thoughts and experiences as he grieved. Suffering is portrayed as relentlessly opaque, resisting rational explanation.

> Where is God? … Go to him when your need is desperate, when all other help is vain, and what do you find? A door slammed in your face, and a sound of bolting and double-bolting on the inside. After that, silence.[57]

Lewis's journal for this difficult period records his thoughts, no matter how incoherent, as he explored every intellectual option open to him. Lewis was determined to confront and engage with each of them, experiencing the emotional distress and cognitive dissonance they each evoked. Maybe God was a tyrant. Maybe there wasn't a God.

So, was this the end of Lewis's Christian faith? Was the suffering and death of his wife such a blatant contradiction of Lewis's core beliefs that his only option was to abandon them? Was the cognitive dissonance unbearable for him? That is certainly the impression created by the movie *Shadowlands* (1993), which suggests that Lewis's faith collapsed after Davidman's illness and death, leading him into some undemanding form of Stoic humanism.

Yet here, as so often, movies offer their own version of history. In reality Lewis's faith recovered. *A Grief Observed* describes what Lewis regarded as a process of testing – not a testing *of God*, but a testing *of Lewis*. 'God has not been trying an experiment on my faith or love in order to find out their quality. He knew it already. It was I who didn't.'[58] In a letter written a few weeks before his death, Lewis remarked that while *A Grief Observed* 'ends with faith', it nevertheless 'raises all the blackest doubts *en route*'.[59] It was, nevertheless, a *reconstructed* faith, more attentive to the raw emotions caused by suffering and doubt in the life of faith.

In the end, Lewis held his faith together, not so much by a rational argument or logical analysis, but rather through a controlling image that captured his imagination, and gave him imaginative space to hold multiple themes together – namely, the image of the crucified Christ.[60] Lewis here draws on a long-standing Christian devotional practice which generally takes the form of affective contemplation of the sufferings of Christ, generally mediated through reflections on the passion narratives and images of the crucified Christ.[61] Such a devotional reflection on the suffering and death of Christ engages the emotions and imagination, allowing the believer to step into the scene of Christ's crucifixion and experience the sense of awe, bewilderment and distress that this so clearly evoked on those who saw it happen – and then correlate this with their own situation.

As Lewis found, the intellectual issues may not be resolved; yet they are no longer seen as posing an existential threat to faith. Rather, this refocusing on a person (rather than an idea) allows a believer to find a way of envisaging life in a suffering world, and make it meaningful by living it out.

This point is brought out by the novelist Francis Spufford in his *Unapologetic*, one of the finest recent explorations of the capacity of a Christian worldview to make emotional sense of things. Spufford suggests that a fixation on over-intellectualised accounts of suffering is 'a phase in the early history of our belief' that tries to 'abolish the mystery' of suffering. Instead, we need to face up to something that *nobody* can explain, and learn the wisdom of coping with it.

> We take the cruelties of the world as a given, as the known and familiar data of experience, and instead of anguishing about why the world is as it is, we look for comfort in coping with it as it is. We don't ask for a creator who can explain Himself. We ask for a friend in a time of grief ... We *don't* say that God's in His heaven and all's well with the world; not deep down. We say: all is not well with the world, but at least God is here in it, with us.[62]

Coping with Trauma and Suffering:
Viktor Frankl and Jordan Peterson

This leads us into the move from the intellectualisation of suffering to living meaningfully in a world of suffering. Meaning-making is not a purely cognitive matter; it is also about *enactment*, living in certain ways. In their different ways, both Judaism and Christianity offer 'present suffering as part of a broader story of redemption. In complicated ways, each tradition depicts catastrophe as a path forward.'[63] Both experienced trauma – Judaism through the Babylonian deportation and exile, and Christianity through the crucifixion of Christ – and both developed the strength and flexibility to endure in the face of present and future disaster.

The question of finding meaning through suffering surged in significance during the traumas of the First and Second World Wars. Yet it has been given a new importance with the increase in human lifespan in western culture, which often involves living with suffering over extended periods. As early as 1958, the psychologist Edith Weisskopf-Joelson noticed that American culture seemed intolerant of suffering, and reluctant to help people to find belief systems to cope with this. 'The incurable sufferer is given very little opportunity to be proud of his suffering and to consider it ennobling rather than degrading.'[64]

So how can this be done? In an important reflection on means of coping with suffering, Sarah Bachelard suggests that it is helpful to distinguish 'resigning ourselves to the inevitable' in relation to a crisis or suffering, and 'giving ourselves' into this crisis or suffering,[65] allowing this to challenge our preconceptions about what the world ought to be like and learn to live within it as it is. We insert ourselves into the world, and create meaning through the things we encounter, rather than those we expected or hoped to find, not least by allowing what we find to be seen as a means of growth.

Perhaps the best-known engagement with this issue arises from the work of Viktor Frankl, whose experiences in Nazi concentration and extermination camps during the Second World War helped him to appreciate the importance of discerning meaning in spite of traumatic situations.[66] Frankl argued that survival in concentration camps depended on maintaining the will to live, which involved finding meaning and purpose in demoralising or traumatic situations. Those who coped best were those who had developed frameworks of meaning that enabled them to fit their experiences into these mental maps, and allowed them to interpret and experience them as times of personal growth and development. In exploring this point, Frankl often cited Friedrich Nietzsche's famous one-liner, 'If someone knows the "why" of life, then the "how" can look after itself.'[67]

More recently, the psychologist Jordan Peterson has insisted we recognise the fragility of human existence and recognise the pervasiveness of suffering. 'Pain and suffering define the world.' They are givens, not options.

> We can be damaged, even broken, emotionally and physically, and we are all subject to the depredations of aging and loss. This is a dismal set of facts, and it is reasonable to wonder how we can expect to thrive and be happy (or even to want to exist, sometimes) under such conditions.[68]

While Peterson's approach to suffering is opaque and controversial, his willingness to engage this pervasive phenomenon
and explore its existential threat has secured him a substantial
readership.

Frankl and Peterson share some common themes: both recognise the depth of human suffering and the challenges it poses
for religious belief – yet paradoxically both consider a spiritual
worldview that recognises the existence of God and a transcen-
dental reality to hold the key to living well in a suffering world.
To live a 'good life' is not about self-satisfaction, but rather
living responsibly, facing up to a suffering world, and finding
meaning and opportunities for service within it. Suffering is
not something we are asked to comprehend; it is something we
must confront, and create meaning in doing so. Beliefs help us
cope with times of darkness.

But what if those beliefs themselves cause darkness?

Chapter 7

The Dark Side of Believing: Tensions, Intolerance and Violence

One of the most common criticisms of beliefs is that they are divisive. It is a valid concern – beliefs can indeed lead to violence. Yet the human condition is such that we refuse to confine ourselves to what is demonstrably true, and reach beyond this limited and restrictive domain to offer sometimes shallow, sometimes deep, and always *unprovable* answers to the great questions of life.

Unfortunately many have failed to master the art of learning through disagreement. In a recent discussion, the head of one of Britain's public service broadcasters suggested that many younger people seemed to lack the skills to discuss alternative viewpoints in terms other than outright rejection. Research points to the emergence of 'Young Illiberal Progressives' who 'have very little tolerance for people with beliefs that they disagree with'.[1] Their exposure to short form content (such as online videos) and ideological online echo chambers seems to create an incapacity for critical reflection and unwillingness even to consider, let alone to discuss, ideas that they find challenging.

No exploration of 'believing' can therefore avoid discussing how perceived conflicts and tensions arising from this basic human instinct and practice can be mitigated, or perhaps even redirected in a creative and constructive manner. How can we create a social space within which other peoples' beliefs can be explored intelligently and responsibly, free from external pressure and influence?

Tensions: Traditional and Modern Beliefs

A classic case of conflicts of beliefs involves a perceived tension between traditional belief systems and their modern equivalents. A good example of this can be seen from early twentieth-century China. After a long period of occupation by colonial powers, China was able to begin to regain its sense of national identity following the collapse of the Qing dynasty in 1912 and the end of the First World War in 1918. Chinese nationalists called for a rejection of traditional values – such as those of Confucianism – and the adoption of western cultural values as the best way of modernising the bruised nation.[2] Gradually western science came to be seen not simply as an instrument or a technique for achieving cultural and social change, but as an ideology – a way of determining values and meaning, which inevitably eroded traditional Chinese values. Western science was seen as progressive; Confucianism as regressive.

In the late 1950s, however, 'Neo-Confucianism' emerged as a means of maintaining continuity with older and distinctively Chinese understandings of the natural world, and offering answers to important questions that could not be answered on the basis of science alone.[3] Neo-Confucianism did not deny the usefulness of scientific discourse, but rather emphasised the importance of complementing its 'objective logical causal mode of thinking' with an approach which could offer 'a subjective, direct, and empathic comprehension of the world.' This development was consolidated through the widespread revival of Confucianism in contemporary China, following the ending of Mao Zedong's abortive 'Cultural Revolution' (1966–76).[4] Neo-Confucianism allowed an account of the world which was attentive to both its objective and subjective dimensions, rooted in traditional Chinese understandings of the natural world.

The perception of a significant tension between traditional belief systems and their modern western equivalents has become particularly significant through the rise of post-colonial criticism of the imposition of western cultural norms and values on indigenous cultures in the Americas, Africa, Asia and Polynesia. What happens when traditional beliefs, often held as identity-giving by indigenous peoples, are not so much disparaged as suppressed? To illustrate the difficulties that arise, we shall consider issues relating to the role of indigenous belief systems in modern science education in New Zealand.

In recent decades, *mātauranga Māori* (Māori 'ways of knowing') has been included in the teaching of science in New Zealand.[5] This has been criticised by some within the western scientific community, such as the American geneticist Jerry A. Coyne.[6] While Coyne concedes that *mātauranga Māori* 'contains "practical knowledge," like how to catch eels, that could conceivably be inserted into science courses,' the natural sciences are universal, and not limited to or determined by any national or tribal identity. It made no sense to Coyne that contemporary scientific understandings of the origins of the universe were being depicted as a western 'creation myth' and placed on an equal level with its 'indigenous' alternatives in New Zealand. *Mātauranga Māori* is important to an understanding of the cultural history of New Zealand and ought therefore to be taught in anthropology or sociology courses – but not in science.

Coyne makes an entirely fair point in stressing that the fundamental method of the natural sciences is universal. In one sense, 'scientific' knowledge is defined by the manner of its acquisition and validation, not the social, tribal, religious, cultural or gendered identity of scientific practitioners. To be a natural scientist is to step inside this specific understanding of human knowledge production. Yet there is a deeply problematic historical dimension to this matter which seems to have been overlooked here – namely, the role of the natural sciences in the British colonial endeavour.

To appreciate the problem, let us consider a lecture delivered to the Anthropological Society in London on 1 March 1864 by Charles Darwin's colleague (and occasional rival) Alfred Russel Wallace. Alluding to the subtitle of Darwin's *Origin of Species* (1859),[7] Wallace made the following statement:

> It is the same great law of 'the preservation of favoured races in the struggle for life,' which leads to the inevitable extinction of all those low and mentally undeveloped populations with which Europeans come in contact. The red Indian in North America, and in Brazil; the Tasmanian, Australian and New Zealander in the southern hemisphere, die out, not from any

one special cause, but from the inevitable effects of an unequal mental and physical struggle. The intellectual and moral, as well as the physical qualities of the European are superior; the same powers and capacities which have made him rise in a few centuries from the condition of the wandering savage with a scanty and stationary population to his present state of culture and advancement, with a greater average longevity, a greater average strength, and a capacity of more rapid increase, – enable him when in contact with the savage man, to conquer in the struggle for existence, and to increase at his expense.[8]

This statement raises difficult and disturbing questions about how Darwin's evolutionary ideas were interpreted within British colonial thinking and practice concerning the role of 'favoured races' in Australia and New Zealand. Wallace concluded his lecture with some significant reflections on where accepting 'natural selection' as a biological and cultural metanarrative pointed, including his suggestion that 'it must inevitably follow that the higher – the more intellectual and moral – must displace the lower and more degraded races.'[9] Wallace's lecture creates the impression that there is scientific justification for the historical inevitability of the triumph of intellectually and morally superior Europeans over 'mentally undeveloped populations' or 'savages,'[10] thus improving the human condition.

Darwin himself entertained similar ideas. In a letter of 1862 to Charles Kingsley – to which the Darwin Correspondence Project wisely attaches a 'Content Warning' on account of the unsettling views it expressed – Darwin concurs with Kingsley's remarks (which appear to have been widespread in educated British circles of this period) that in 500 years 'the Anglo-saxon race will have spread & exterminated whole nations; & in consequence how much the Human race, viewed as a unit, will have risen in rank.'[11]

Most evolutionary biologists today would reject these historically specific interpretations and applications of Darwin's evolutionary theory. It is, however, important to note the intellectual plausibility and cultural prominence of these interpretations in the 1860s and 1870s, and the perception that they created or encouraged – namely, that colonialism would lead to the improvement of the human race. Wallace's specific (and demeaning) references to 'the Tasmanian, Australian and New Zealander' can hardly be overlooked.

What can be learned from this? For Coyne, the integrity of the natural sciences is at stake; for others, there is a real problem arising from the abiding historical memory of the way in which science was deployed as a legitimating resource by British colonial administrators and educationalists to suppress indigenous beliefs and peoples in New Zealand (and elsewhere) in the late nineteenth century. Anyone concerned with the public understanding of science needs to confront the ways it has been exploited, abused and distorted in the service of political and social agendas. To indigenous populations, Darwinism turned out to be yet another aspect of the western colonial attempt to deny or eliminate 'the knowledge and cultures of these populations, their memories and ancestral links and their manner of relating to others and to nature.'[12]

For these people, *mātauranga Māori* was identity-giving, essential to their future survival and flourishing, and part of their self-understanding as a distinct people group. It is not a 'fixed' form of detached knowledge, but is a form of embodied knowledge, understanding, wisdom and practices which is intergenerational, being expanded as it is passed on. Yet there are clear possibilities for dialogue with other approaches here – for example, in the emerging discipline of 'ethnoastronomy', which allows dialogue between the ancestral Polynesian astronomical knowledge systems and their western counterparts.[13]

Wisdom: Holding Beliefs in Creative Tension

How can we integrate the multiple elements of human understanding? Edward O. Wilson's *Consilience* (1998) is an important, though flawed, attempt to offer a unified account of human knowledge, which sets out to make connections across disciplines in the quest for meaning and a proper understanding of the human situation. 'We are drowning in information, while starving for wisdom.'[14] Stephen Jay Gould argues that while the differences between the sciences and humanities must be respected, they have a genuine potential for synergy. Why should we not acknowledge and respect the differences between these disciplines, and at the same time 'find some meaningful order in the totality?'[15] Both Wilson and Gould point to the concept of 'wisdom' as a means of coordinating and holding together a rich and diverse range of insights. So, what are we to understand by 'wisdom'?

Recent empirical studies of the nature of human wisdom suggests that one of its core capabilities is to hold potentially conflicting ways of thinking together in a creative tension.[16] While there is no consensual definition of wisdom, it is clear that a common theme is a deep knowledge base that enables meaningful living, particularly coping with complexity and ambiguity.[17] Where some would see diversity of beliefs as intrinsically incoherent and self-contradictory, a wise person recognises that have to learn to see our world and frame our experiences from multiple perspectives, rather than from within a single limiting perspective or controlling paradigm.

At the very least, we need to be able to create a map of insights that we cherish, whether we can integrate them or not. A patchwork quilt of beliefs and values can begin to form building blocks of wisdom, even if the question of how they are to be coordinated remains open. In my view, Socrates was right in suggesting that a wise person is aware of their own ignorance, and thus is open to learning from others; who has realised that reality is complicated, and does not try to force everything into a preconceived mould; and who has conceded the finite capacity of the human mind, and does not limit reality to what we can rationally demonstrate.

Acceptance of 'divergent perspectives', which entails the virtue of intellectual empathy and willingness to embrace and learn from others,[18] is now regularly cited as a key aspect of wisdom. So how might this be correlated with beliefs? A key point here is that intellectual empathy enables us to gain insight into other people's emotions and beliefs – to understand why they believe certain things, the difference that this makes to their lives, and whether this belief, when properly understood, is something that we might wish to appropriate and incorporate into our own ways of thinking.[19] Wisdom requires humility, realising our own perspective is not the only one, and coming to understand how much we do not know. It is by engaging rival perspectives and worldviews that we arrive at wise judgements about how best to make sense of this world and live accordingly.

The issue here is being willing to see things in a new way and explore the quality of the intellectual vision that this alternative belief system enables. C. S. Lewis is one of many writers to note how literature opens our eyes, offering us new perspectives on things that we can evaluate and adopt. 'My own eyes are not enough for me, I will see through those of others... In reading great literature, I become a thousand men and yet remain myself. Like the night sky in the Greek poem, I see with a myriad eyes, but it is still I who see.'[20] Reading literature, Lewis suggests, enables us 'to see with other eyes, to imagine with other imaginations, to feel with other hearts, as well as our own.'[21] In using this image of multiple eyes, Lewis is urging us to learn from others, who may have seen something that we have missed. We expand our own vision of reality through borrowing someone else's eyes and trying to grasp what they have seen.

The Problem of Dogmatism

Charles Taylor once remarked that 'understanding the "other" will pose the twenty-first century's greatest social challenge.' I think he is right. Yet one of the biggest challenges facing this manifesto of understanding is a disturbing human personality trait – dogmatism.[22] While the term 'dogmatism' can be defined variously, its two central themes are an excessive confidence in a belief or belief system which is not adequately grounded in the evidence, and an authoritarian style of discourse that is used in the defence of such beliefs or systems.

The term 'dogma' has a neutral sense of a belief that is seen as being of critical importance for a belief system or scientific theory. Early Christianity, for example, recognised two such dogmas – the two natures of Christ, and the Trinity – which gave Christianity its coherence and focus. This terminology is also regularly used in the natural sciences. The 'central dogma' of molecular biology, for example, concerns the asymmetry between genomes and enzymes: informational asymmetry, in that information flows from genomes to enzymes but not from enzymes to genomes; and catalytic asymmetry, in that enzymes provide chemical catalysis, but genomes do not.[23]

Dogmatism, however, designates a different category of discourse, which can be framed as a tendency to regard the beliefs and principles of a specific individual or community as objectively and self-evidently correct, despite their deficient evidential foundations and the existence of viable alternatives. Whereas 'good thinking' leads to a confidence that is proportional to the evidence available, dogmatic beliefs are held and asserted with a confidence that masks their being grounded on inadequate or biased thinking. Although some suggest that dogmatism is characteristic of religious people or beliefs, the evidence clearly indicates that it is linked with a wide range of domains, situations, topics and issues – particularly politics.[24]

While the Enlightenment project of the eighteenth century emphasised the importance of open-mindedness and the destructive nature of dogmatism, the twentieth century witnessed the emergence of a new authoritarianism, made tangible in the rise of Fascism and the cult of submission to strongmen such as Mussolini, Hitler or Stalin.[25]

Our concern, however, is not so much with an 'authoritarian personality' (someone who prefers a social system with a strong ruler)[26] as with dogmatic beliefs or hardened belief systems – ideas that clearly cannot be shown to be true, but which are asserted and enforced as if they were absolute certainties. A dogma is a belief which commands acquiescence and assent as a matter of obedience to a charismatic individual or a controlling community – such as the Soviet Communist Party during the 1930s and 1940s. Though having the epistemic status of a belief or opinion, a dogma is treated as a truth whose denial constituted irrationality or mental illness. It is worth recalling that *Pravda* (the Russian word for 'truth') was the official organ of the Communist Party of the Soviet Union from 1918 to 1991, which informed its readers what they ought to think. This was the 'truth' that Party members were required to acknowledge.

The psychologist Judy K. Johnson argues that dogmatism is 'the arrogant voice of certainty that closes the mind, damages relationships and threatens peaceful coexistence on this planet.'[27] For the philosophers Richard C. Roberts and W. Jay Wood, dogmatism represents a 'disposition to respond irrationally to oppositions' to certain tenets of their beliefs,[28] often leading to ridicule rather than engagement, evasion rather than discussion. Dogmatism can be seen as an epistemically unjustified certainty arising from the confluence of cognitive, emotional and behavioural characteristics that lead to prejudicial closed-minded belief systems. A 'dogmatic' person is likely to be intolerant of ambiguity, to encourage an in-group vilification of out-groups, and to develop a form of mental compartmentalisation which protectively encloses its own declarations in barbed wire, while sealing off contradictory beliefs in such a way that they do not pose a threat.

Such people tend to think in highly polarised terms, preferring reductive simplifications over acknowledging the complexity of the world and life, and adopting an 'arrogant, dismissive communication style', talking *at* others rather than *with* others, and preferring personal disparagement to serious engagement with the issues – precisely because such an engagement is seen as threatening. As Johnson points out, this sort of 'defensive cognitive closure' leads to rival or conflicting ideas being judged immediately and automatically as 'ridiculous'. People holding rival views are not simply wrong; they are often denigrated as 'stupid' as well.

What can be done about this? My training as an academic immediately suggests a set of solutions. Go where the evidence takes you – and be honest if you are going beyond it. Be willing to confront ambiguity and live with uncertainty. Talk to people with opposing views, partly to ensure you have grasped their positions, and partly because of the importance of maintaining personal relationships in the face of disagreements. As a scholar, I make a point of reading works advocating alternative perspectives and talking to those who hold such views, partly to ensure I have understood them properly – but more importantly, to ensure I can hold my own views with integrity in the face of rival beliefs.

But this won't work in the face of dogmatism because the problem is ultimately psychological, not evidential. The issue is an 'intolerance of ambiguity',[29] which leads certain individuals to perceive an ambiguous situation 'rigidly in black or white', often leading to rapid evaluations and unreliable foreclosures of complex issues – such as medical diagnosis.[30] An ability to tolerate ambiguity is increasingly being linked with wellbeing. Perhaps we shall see more research on how to confront and cope with dogmatism in the future, as a way to help us understand others and achieve greater social cohesion.

When Worlds Collide: Believing and Violence

Growing up in Belfast during the late 1960s, I was surrounded by sectarian tensions arising from Ireland's complex and troubled political history, which often involved religion. It was not difficult for me to frame these persuasively within my early atheist worldview: if there was no religion, there would be no religious violence.

I never gave much thought to the consequences of my emerging teenage belief that religion was evil, and thus ought to be eliminated or excluded from society. The idea that this might violate human rights never entered my head, partly because I was inclined to think that a religion-free world was itself a basic human right. Where some argued for freedom of religion, it seemed obvious to me that an ideal world involved freedom from religion.

I would have been shocked to read of what I now know happened in the Soviet Union during the 1920s as a state-sponsored programme of the suppression of religion took place, using execution squads, prison camps and protracted social violence to create a religion-free world. Because religion was evil, its elimination justified any means that this required.

At Oxford, I discovered Isaiah Berlin and the intensely serious tradition of reflection on diversity and its implications that his writings stimulated. For Berlin, individuals, communities and nations have divergent visions of what is good and right. Back in the 1960s, some visionaries dreamed of diverse communities of individuals who each pursued their own goals and visions of personal fulfilment independently and harmlessly. Today, we are perhaps more realistic, recognising that one community's exercise of freedom may impact on another's identity, wellbeing or freedom – and thus lead to conflict and the possibility of violence.

In this section, we shall consider the ways in which the human propensity for belief can create tensions and violence, and reflect on its implications for our understanding of the place of belief in life. I have no doubt that religion can generate tensions and violence. But it's not alone in this. As writers as diverse as Aristotle and Jean-Jacques Rousseau make clear, viable accounts of the origins of division and conflict can be offered that neither require nor exclude a significant religious element.[31] Racial and political ideologies are human belief systems with a particular propensity for violence and extermination. In Latin America, millions of people seem to have 'disappeared' in ruthless campaigns of violence by right-wing politicians and their militias. In Cambodia, Pol Pot eliminated millions in his relentless pursuit of an elusive communist paradise.

Any form of ideological exclusivism inevitably leads to social and intellectual tensions, in that it divides the world into in-groups and out-groups – 'friends and enemies', 'good and evil', 'us and them', 'human and subhuman', or 'enlightened and irrational'.[32] All these value-laden categorisations provide an impetus to demonise and dehumanise the 'other' which can lead to discrimination, hostility and violence. The Nazi ideological recategorisation of certain human communities as *Untermenschen* (sub-humans) allowed their elimination to be framed as socially therapeutic and morally unproblematic.

Violence against women is widespread, with extensive research suggesting that men's controlling attitudes and behaviour towards women often rest on underlying traditional gender norms – a set of beliefs about the place and roles of men and women in society, such as ideologies of hegemonic masculinity which are internalised as normative by both men and women. This framing ideology leads women to blame themselves for being the victims of violence by men, so that they are less likely to disclose it or seek legal support.[33]

Overcoming such traditional beliefs and ideologies is not easy, not least on account of the social pressures to conform to dominant local accounts of human identity. It is, however, necessary to challenge certain understandings of being human and the illusions that are employed to sustain them. It is helpful to remember that an ideology is a human construction, not some eternal truth characterised by a mathematical or logical certainty which demands our assent.

And what of religion? Surely religion is implicated in the violent history of human culture? Of course it is. But things are more complicated than its critics suggest – not least because religion is not a catch-all. For a start, some secularist critiques of religion are highly selective, presenting religions as a monolithically violent and oppressive reality, and failing to respect its complexity and depth, which makes such generalisations questionable.

Michael Shermer, President of the Skeptics Society, made the significant point that while religions were implicated in some human tragedies, such as holy wars, there is clearly a significant positive side to religion that has to be acknowledged:

> However, for every one of these grand tragedies there
> are ten thousand acts of personal kindness and social
> good that go unreported... Religion, like all social institutions of such historical depth and cultural impact,
> cannot be reduced to an unambiguous good or evil.[34]

Shermer's point is given added weight by atheist violence against religion. Some New Atheist writers insist that there is no evidence that atheism systematically influences people to do bad things.[35] Others might beg to differ, noting that neither the Bolsheviks nor New Atheists consider atheism to be the mere absence of belief in God, but make a normative judgement that religious faith is evil. Following the Bolshevik seizure of power in 1917, the forcible elimination of religious belief came to be an increasingly important element of their revolutionary programme. Religion was believed to be evil and counter-revolutionary, and hence had to be neutralised. In their efforts to enforce this atheist ideology, the Soviet authorities systematically destroyed and eliminated large numbers of churches and priests during the period 1918–41.

As Bertrand Russell noted in his remarkably perceptive 1920 account of the Soviet Union, Bolshevism 'is to be reckoned as a religion, not as an ordinary political movement.'[36] Why? Because it transcendentalised its ideals, leading to the Soviet state and its institutions being seen as God-surrogates. Recognising the need for a religious revival within Russia after the catastrophe of the First World War, Bolshevism presented itself as a new religion – a 'combination of the characteristics of the French Revolution with those of the rise of Islam.'

What matters here is that worldviews and their associated institutions are demonstrably prone to intolerance, violence and dogmatism. It is pointless to argue for the elimination of individual beliefs or extended belief systems, which are part of the human condition. It is, however, entirely right to ask what can be done about mitigating the risks of beliefs leading to violence. Some might suggest that the obvious way ahead is to criminalise what are seen as dangerous beliefs, given that these cannot be proved to be true and can be the cause of social tension and personal distress. Belief in God is often singled out as an especially appropriate target for suppression.

Yet when a society rejects the idea of God, it tends to transcendentalise secular alternatives and allow them to function as alternative gods. Emilio Gentile's studies on fascism and totalitarianism show how worldviews emerge which, though secular in their outlooks and foundations, nevertheless take the form of 'a more or less developed system of beliefs, myths, rituals, and symbols that create an aura of sacredness around an entity belonging to this world and turn it into a cult and an object of worship and devotion.'[37]

A good example of this phenomenon can be seen in a later phase of the French Revolution. Doctrinaire disputes between the Jacobins and Girondins claimed thousands of lives through mass executions of 'enemies of the revolution' in one year. Safeguarding the Revolution justified whatever means were deemed necessary to this end. Marie-Jeanne Roland, a Girondist revolutionary activist who now found herself out of favour, was brought to the guillotine in 1793, where she spoke her famous final words: 'liberty, what crimes are committed in your name.' Liberty had been transcendentalised, becoming a sacred entity which justified such extreme violence in its defence.

The historian Martin Marty identified five 'features' that he holds to be characteristic of religion; all five, he pointed out, are equally characteristic of political movements.[38] Politics thus often morph into forms of *religion*, claiming the right to define the fundamental purpose and meaning of human life. The result is inevitable – a tendency towards intolerance and violence when these secular 'objects of worship and devotion' are challenged or threatened. Ontologically, they are secular; functionally, they are divine – and divisive.

On Coping with Difference

I noted earlier Charles Taylor's remark that 'understanding the "other"' is the greatest social challenge that we face today. While I think he's right, I'm not sure he offers us a solution to this problem – more a way of understanding how it arises, and how we might learn to live with it. It's better than nothing. But dare we hope for more?

The central problem is this: our defining beliefs – especially about ultimate questions, such as the nature of justice or the question of meaning in life – remain obstinately resistant to philosophical or scientific justification. There is no Archimedean point from which such beliefs can be evaluated. The modern period has witnessed a surge of alternative beliefs (often carefully packaged and presented as reliable certainties), rather than a solution to how we live with a plurality of informing and controlling beliefs, and cope with the social tensions that inevitably arise from this.

Belief systems are often an extension or an essential component of what Hélène Cixous describes as 'the battle for mastery' that rages everywhere between social classes and people groups. Paradoxically, many of those who challenge their social, political or intellectual 'masters' simply propose an overcoming of those specific masters and their replacement with alternatives – a process that Julietta Singh describes as 'an overcoming, a mastering of that which masters'.[39] Singh's concern is that this appears to concede 'the inescapability of mastery as a way of life'.

A similar pattern underlies critiques of beliefs. The problem, we are told, is that we have the wrong set of beliefs; once we adopt the right set, everything will be just fine. For reasons we have explored, there are good reasons for accepting the 'inescapability of belief as a way of life'. Yet this does not resolve the question of how we cope with such diversity and learn to live with the ensuing uncertainty.

Individuals often find a sense of intellectual achievement and inner stability when they feel that they have found a way of holding together multiple aspects of their lives and when they can accept the tensions between their and others' views. Yet when confronted by the fact of an irreducible plurality of beliefs, a liberal society needs to navigate a set of shared public values. Or so John Rawls argued in his impressive manifesto of egalitarian liberalism *A Theory of Justice* (1971), demanding that we find and impose principles of fairness that are independent of people's different and contestable conceptions of what is 'good'.

Rawls explicitly recognises the concern we have been exploring throughout this chapter – that free societies are necessarily divided by 'reasonable but incompatible comprehensive doctrines'.[40] Rawls argued that each individual citizen has a distinct and reasonable 'comprehensive doctrine' – such as a religious faith, or some other way of thinking about God, the nature of life, what is right and what is wrong. Yet they are unwilling to impose these 'comprehensive doctrines' on other people, and instead are willing to find mutually agreeable rules that permit fairness in public life.

Rawls suggests that while each citizen may believe they hold reasonable political and moral views, they will not wish to impose these on others.[41] A negotiated settlement of the role of individual beliefs in public life is needed, which will be publicly accepted as fair and right. The issue is thus not the intellectual resolution of a plurality of beliefs, but their political accommodation in the public square by adopting 'principles of justice that are neutral among competing conceptions of the good life'. Rawls advocates adopting a 'freestanding' political conception of justice that does not itself depend upon any particular 'comprehensive doctrine'.

Yet Rawls' appeal to such neutral principles has been criticised by Michael Sandel as 'a hollow view of the world, one that refuses to take up discussions of the best way to live.' While Rawls conceded that 'comprehensive doctrines, religious or nonreligious, may be introduced in public political discussion at any time', he did not see these as foundational to this discussion. Sandel's concern is that Rawls offers a strategy of accommodation rather than a serious discussion about the nature of 'good', and particularly 'the public good'. The focus is on what is fair, rather than what might be true.

While Sandel makes a fair point, Rawls nevertheless gives us a workable framework for engaging the concerns highlighted in this chapter. Rawls uses the notion of a 'reasonable comprehensive doctrine' to organise and arrange our beliefs so that they can 'express an intelligible view of the world', which involves the recognition of judgement in balancing conflicting values.[42] The political task is to work out a conception of justice that 'a plurality of reasonable comprehensive doctrines' are able to endorse and support,[43] while recognising that many of the 'comprehensive doctrines' are incompatible with each other. Disagreement over beliefs is not necessarily a barrier to agreement about social and political outcomes.

Yet the studied neutrality of Rawls' analysis raises difficult questions. One difficulty concerns the increasingly polarised nature of American political discourse since the 1970s. An ideological polarisation, resulting from divergent viewpoints, is increasingly being supplemented with an affective polarisation, expressing distaste and dislike for the people holding these views.[44] It is not simply that American culture has become more polarised; the nature of that polarisation has become more complex, involving often trenchant views about the morality, intelligence and integrity of those who hold alternative viewpoints. It remains unclear whether Rawls' views regarding finding agreement about fair outcomes can be sustained when there is such personal distrust within and across the political spectrum.

Beyond the difference that believing makes to individuals, we have begun to contemplate how these shape public life and debate. In the next chapter, we shall focus on the question of the relation of beliefs and communities, focusing particularly on how 'communities of belief' come into being, function, and are prone to losing their way.

Chapter 8

Beliefs and Communities

According to the World Population Review of 2022, some eighty-five per cent of people on this planet claim adherence to a faith. In earlier chapters, we considered some ways in which beliefs affect the outlooks and lives of individuals, while occasionally touching on their more communal aspects. We now need to focus on the interaction of beliefs and communities, why they arise and the purpose they serve.

A 'community' arises in response to many factors, including the need for social interaction, a sense of solidarity, shared interests and views of the world, and collective action.[1] Some of these communities have a territorial basis, in that they are restricted to or focused on a geographical space around which a boundary can be drawn – for example, a local place-based community, such as a rural sports club. Other communities, however, are spatially dispersed, focusing on more general issues that are not specifically linked with a geographical location – such as political, philosophical or religious beliefs.

Communities of belief can take both forms. In the case of Christianity, we might think of local parish churches (embedded in a specific place) or dispersed communities in which individuals gather with belief-based agendas and interests, rather than with specific local issues in mind. In recent years, there has been a dramatic increase in online gatherings, whether these take the form of territorial meetings with an extended range (for example, a parish church or cathedral which reaches thousands of people for their online services), or spatially dispersed gatherings which choose to increase their reach online.

In a socially and ideologically fractured age, communities play an important role in maintaining the fabric of a culture which might otherwise unravel. It is well understood that communities of belief have an important integrative function, individually and socially, which has been particularly well studied in the case of religious communities.[2] Yet such communities are about more than socialisation and solidarity; the dynamics of belief in a community involves a complex interaction of 'believing' and 'belonging'.

Some believe and are drawn to communities of belief as a social expression of their beliefs. Others are drawn to these communities for social reasons, and gradually come to appreciate and appropriate their belief systems. Religious narratives, rites and rituals form a system of symbols, which is of critical importance for creating and maintaining a sense of 'belonging' or 'togetherness', thus serving as the nucleus of a community shaped by these values.[3]

A 'community of believers' offers reinforcement of the plausibility of the beliefs of what Peter Berger refers to as a 'cognitive minority' – a 'group formed around a body of deviant knowledge', whose view of the world 'differs significantly from the one generally taken for granted in their society.'[4] Berger's notion of 'plausibility structures' offers an important lens through which we can understand the role of communities of belief, which offer both social and cultural support to their members through inhabiting a common framework of meaning and the sense of belonging that arises from it.

Community and Human Sociality

Aristotle declared that we are social animals. This communal aspect of human identity is not unique; most animals show substantially the same types of social behaviour such as affiliation and aggression, the use of rituals, or the establishment of hierarchy and territoriality. Biological organisms function in groups, in which cooperation is key to survival. This cooperation can take many forms – such as the collective intelligence of a colony of ants or a school of fish, or human beings constructing cities in Mesopotamia. Groups survive; isolated individuals don't.

It is thus not difficult to explain why human beings are social, but this does not account for the emergence of 'communities of beliefs', in which the organising principles are not specifically linked to biological survival, but to the fostering, inhabiting and study of ways of understanding our world. These communities are cultural, rather than biological, in their origins.

At one level, culture is not a uniquely human phenomenon, if this is understood in terms of learning new patterns of behaviour that are acquired and shared by other members of the group, and then passed down to the next generation. A well-known example is the sweet potato-washing monkeys (*macaca fuscata*) on the Japanese island of Koshima. In the 1950s, researchers left some sweet potatoes on the island's beach, and noticed one of the monkeys washed the sand off the potato with sea water before eating it. Why? Perhaps the potatoes tasted better when they were salted? But for whatever reason, over a period of five years this practice was universally adopted within this animal community and was then passed down to succeeding generations.

Back in 1971, the primatologist Hans Kummer noted that species seemed to adapt to their environment mainly through two processes: *phylogenetic adaptation*, which takes the form of a gradual evolution of the species at the genetic level; and *adaptive modification*, in which individual members of the species adapt to their specific present environment. The gradual emergence of a new way of treating and eating sweet potatoes on Koshima is a good example of this second process.

Yet some cultural changes appear to emerge internally within the group, rather than in response to external environmental change. In 1999, Jane Goodall and her colleagues highlighted thirty-nine unusual forms of behaviour specific to certain chimpanzee populations – such as patterns of tool usage or grooming and courtship rituals – where the catalyst appeared to be social in origin rather than some form of adaptation to the environment.[5] Goodall witnessed chimpanzees embracing each other as human beings do to comfort those in mourning. Yet she also observed chimpanzees exhibiting more disturbingly human-like behaviour, such as waging war on rival groups and killing members of their own species.

One of the most important things that seems to distinguish human communities from those of other animals is the role of beliefs in sustaining personal existence, creating public norms of behaviour, and distinguishing one human community from another. The transmission of these beliefs, whether tradition-al or newly minted, is a core element of human culture. And when those beliefs undergo radical change – as in the rise of the Protestant Reformation in western Europe during the sixteenth century, or Marxism in the twentieth century – they can significantly impact the visible forms of human culture.

The Italian Renaissance, for example, witnessed a revival of interest in classical forms of architecture, leading to a radical change in the cityscapes of northern Italy. There seems to be no direct equivalent to these ideologically directed changes within colonies of ants and schools of fish, which tend to respond directly to stimuli from their environments. Human culture involves one generation being able to pass its wisdom on to its successors through language and writing – by putting into words their core beliefs and values.

C. S. Lewis captured this point in reflecting on the role of literature: 'Humanity does not pass through phases as a train passes though stations: being alive, it has the privilege of al-ways moving yet never leaving anything behind. Whatever we have been, in some sort we still are.'[6] Lewis here points to the cumulative capacity of human beings to retain the wisdom of the past, while ensuring that its subsequent development and enhancement is passed on to future generations. Communities of beliefs can thus be grounded in the inherited wisdom of the past, and see this as generating strategies for dealing with the future.

Communities of Belief as Places of Safety

I have deliberately spoken of '*communities* of beliefs'. There is no universal, indubitable foundation for human knowledge, no set of grounding or informing beliefs that is shared by all human beings. What we find empirically is a diversity of beliefs across history and human culture – beliefs that are not universally perceived as intellectually self-evident. This naturally leads people to gravitate towards communities that share their beliefs, partly for intellectual and cultural security (beliefs can easily lead to discrimination or social conflict), but also to enable them to flourish within this tradition of belief by exploring its implications for an appropriate way of living. Communities of belief arise due to the observable diversity of human beliefs and the intellectual and social needs that this diversity raises.

In western culture, communities of belief – irrespective of the genre of those beliefs – can be seen as playing two significant roles: as places of *safety* and *reflection*. Human communities emerged primarily as 'safe places' to enable physical survival, allowing individuals within those communities to feed and defend themselves, and ensure their futures through reproduction. The nomadic lifestyles of hunters and gatherers gradually gave way to more settled forms of existence. Cities emerged, capable of sustaining their existence through agriculture in Mesopotamia, and along the Nile in Egypt, the Indus in Asia, and the Huang (Yellow) River in China.

Within those cities, social stratification took place at several levels. At least three different forms of monarchy are known to have emerged in ancient Mesopotamia, whose authority was often associated with (and perhaps even dependent) on each city-state's patron deity. In ancient Egypt, the king was seen as both the chosen representative and servant of the gods. To be a member of these communities was to be entangled within their founding myths, social norms and beliefs. Although these were often expressed in state or civic festivals, many of them took place at the level of households, where rituals relating to family events were celebrated.[7]

In the ancient world, the 'city' designated a *polis*, a community of citizens united by common origins and sharing common concerns. The core identity of the city – what was transmitted from one generation to another – rested in its citizens and their beliefs, not its physical structures. As Catherine Morgan points out, one of the key questions about ancient Greek cities concerns 'the extent to which cities served as statements of community identity', particularly through 'ideological institutions such as communal cults.'[8] Cities were understood to be cohesive corporate entities, rather than aggregates of individuals, shaped by a set of beliefs and values, which in turn influenced the personal belief systems of their members.

Our concern here, however, is primarily with the situation today, particularly in the western world, in which communities increasingly arise around specific beliefs or values – whether these are political, social, religious, cultural or recreational. Many people today belong to several such communities, seeing each as engaging, informing or sustaining an integral aspect of their personal identities, providing them with a richer quality of life. Let us first consider how communities act as safe places.

In the ancient world, cities were above all places of security against external threats. Their gates and walls protected their populations against their enemies, whether these took the form of marauding wild animals or invading armies. One of the great prayers of ancient Israel was that there should be no breaches in the walls of the city of Jerusalem (Psalm 144: 14). The security of the city's population depended on the integrity of its walls, towers and gates. Early Christian communities met in secret during the second and third centuries, as their refusal to conform to the imperial cult marked them out as potentially seditious to the Roman authorities.

Communities of belief are social spaces where believers meet to socialise, as well as to receive ideological support, encouragement and affirmation from fellow believers. In most cases, such communities take the form of physical gatherings of believers. Yet online communities are playing an increasingly important role in creating and sustaining a sense of community identity, partly by reassuring groups who consider themselves to be marginalised or under threat to experience a sense of solidarity.

The general human need to seek out and socialise with like-minded people is mirrored widely in the cultural and religious domains. People want to meet those they feel at home with and with whom they can share their experiences and concerns in an affirming manner – rather than be ridiculed, abused or dismissed. People feel the need to feel valued and supported – irrespective of their beliefs. This is particularly important in nations in which state criticism of religion, or one specific religion, causes some religious individuals to feel insecure, threatened or unwelcome.[9] For example, the public visibility and activity of Christianity is limited within the highly restrictive political context of China. Chinese Christians have adapted to this context by using social media apps such Weixin and Weibo to develop a sense of community and provide religious teaching and news through regular online publications.[10]

As noted earlier in this chapter, an important function of a community of belief is to affirm the plausibility of these beliefs, especially in the case of a 'cognitive minority' – a group whose view of the world does not conform to, or deviates from, those that are taken for granted in the wider culture. Confronted with a culture which is, or is perceived to be, antagonistic to certain beliefs, communities of faith provide a context within which these beliefs are treated as both normal and significant, rather than being seen as weird. No apology is required for holding them within these communities, nor are they seen as embarrassing.

Berger's sociological analysis highlights the importance of 'plausibility structures' that are embedded within a trustworthy community. 'The plausibility, in the sense of what people find credible, of views of reality depends upon the social support these receive. Put more simply, we obtain our notions about the world originally from other human beings, and these notions continue to be plausible to us in a very large measure because others continue to affirm them.'[11]

Berger points out that communities of belief often hold to forms of 'deviant knowledge' that are out of tune with the mainstream of the wider culture. Yet this perception of 'deviance' is historically situated, determined by the dominant ideologies of a particular age and location. What is 'deviant' today might have been acceptable or even normal in the past, and may become so again.

An atheist might feel they belong to a 'cognitive minority' in the United States, which is largely Christian; yet Christians felt they belonged to a 'cognitive minority' in the Soviet Union for much of its history. No community of belief is intrinsically a 'cognitive minority' or 'deviant'; it may *become* so, however, on account of its changing social context, rather than its fundamental beliefs.

Communities of Belief as Places of Reflection

A second significant role of communities of faith is that they
are places of *reflection*, in which beliefs are incubated and enabled to grow and mature within a supportive environment.
The community of belief sustains and catalyses a process of
learning about the intellectual and social world that these beliefs create. It is about exploring the landscape of faith, and
learning to inhabit this new set of perspectives and relationships. To believe is to occupy the same physical landscape as
everyone else, but to *see* it and *experience* it in a new and distinctive manner. The community of belief helps us to expand
our vision of this landscape, and encourages us to go 'further
up and further in' (C. S. Lewis) to this way of thinking and
living.

Communities of faith provide an environment in which
their underlying beliefs – again, whether political, religious
or cultural – can be studied, internalised and appropriated.
Particularly in religious communities – such as churches, syna-
gogues and mosques – education is seen as integral to achieving
a mature faith, capable of engaging the world and sustaining
a meaningful life. This typically takes the form of explaining
the core beliefs and defining practices of a community and
pointing to exemplars who are able to enact and model the
community's distinctive ethos.

There is now a growing awareness of the need to prepare
communities of belief for the challenges of living in a pluralist
western context, in which there are no universally accepted
norms of truth, justice or goodness, and in which nobody is
seen as having privilege in matters of belief. While some communities of belief are trying to find an appropriate place and

voice within wider culture, re-reading their histories to see if the past might help them navigate the stormy seas of the present, others isolate themselves from the complexities of our social world to maintain the myth of their totalising truths.

This isolationism is a source of concern because it detaches such communities from the cultural mainstream, often leading to the perception that they are at war with, or threatened by, wider society. This can easily lead to alienation or even radicalisation within these communities, which result in political or religious extremism. Some Islamic communities in secular France or alt-right networks in Germany provide illuminating examples of this problem, for which there appears to be no obvious solution.

Charles Taylor noted the 'fragilisation' of belief in the modern period, which was catalysed by a growing awareness of alternative possibilities. The emergence of a pluralist culture 'fragilises' belief systems – whether religious or atheist – by undermining their self-evident correctness. 'If my view of the world is right, why do other views exist?' The hostility of certain forms of secular atheism to continuing religious belief in a supposedly secular culture is partly a response to the threat that they pose to its plausibility, heightened by the growth and enhanced visibility of religious immigrant communities in many western nations. 'If my theory is right, religion ought not to exist.' Peter Berger concurs: 'The appearance of an alternative symbolic universe poses a threat because its very existence demonstrates empirically that one's own universe is less than inevitable.'[12]

Communities of belief thus serve an important role in maintaining the plausibility of their own position in the face of

a cultural milieu that suggests that their views are not as secure
and self-evident as they might like to believe they are. The challenges posed to traditional cultural or religious values by rapid
social changes in the West illustrate this concern well.[13] While
some see these as the bedrock of their communities of belief,
other such communities see them as backward looking and
oppressive. The outcome is that the existence of a plurality of
communities of belief leads to a sense of anxiety and hostility,
in that one's own beliefs are not seen as respected, but as something that others believe ought to be rejected and overthrown.

This means that communities of belief must also learn how
to reflect on how they can survive and adapt in the present,
alongside other communities with divergent views. Can their
traditional beliefs simply be reasserted? Or do they need to
be translated into a new social language? How can a community's past, particularly if considered to be problematic, be
repurposed, refocused or reconfigured to meet new situations
and challenges? This very often involves asking hard questions
about the core vision of a community. To take a political example, what exactly is the essence of being a Conservative in
Britain? Or a Democrat in the United States? Which of the
competing visions of these political movements is most authentic and translates into electability?

Holding Communities Together:
Narratives and Rituals

Foundational narratives are essential to building a sense of
community and explaining not simply how a community
came into being, but *why*. What core themes and concerns
were hardwired into its emergence? Abraham Lincoln, one of

America's most admired presidents, did much to consolidate the emergence of American identity, particularly in the aftermath of the Civil War. His Gettysburg Address of November 1863 sought to consolidate the idea that America was 'a new nation, conceived in Liberty, and dedicated to the proposition that all men are created equal.' Lincoln's address set out a new foundational narrative for a United States *without slavery*, thus distancing himself from the views of the Founding Fathers, many of whom (such as Thomas Jefferson, author of the 'Declaration of Independence' and third President of the United States) had been slave-owners.

The identity of what is now known as the European Union is shaped by a series of foundational narratives explaining the decision of the original six nations – Belgium, France, Italy, Luxembourg, the Netherlands and West Germany – to work together collaboratively.[14] Four distinct foundational narratives were constructed to account for the formation of this union, and to give its members a sense of identity and direction for the future. This was essential at the time, given that it 'was largely an elite-led project', lacking a core vision. Perhaps the most important function of these narratives was to create a shared vision for this new political community, and depict it as offering a new way ahead, allowing these six nations to move on from a troubled past.

On this account, the European Union was essentially a 'peace project in which nation-states learned from the atrocities of World War II and bound themselves together in peaceful co-operation in its aftermath.' This created a powerful grounding and defining narrative of the European Union as a necessary consequence of the destructiveness of the Second World War, instrumental in restoring Europe to its rightful cultural and economic place. The historical accuracy of this narrative is, of course, somewhat questionable. Critics observed that it was not 'nation-states that kicked off the process of European integration, it was fading empires, exhausted by their colonial efforts.'[15] The failures of Belgian, Dutch and French colonial projects demanded a recasting of their national identities and a reshaping of their futures.

We have already seen that it is natural for humans to form communities; it is becoming increasingly accepted that it is also natural for us to tell stories. The sociologist Christian Smith makes the point that we are story-telling animals, who 'understand what reality is, who we are, and how we ought to live by locating ourselves within the larger narratives and metanarratives that we hear and tell, and that constitute what is for us real and significant.'[16] As Ursula K. Le Guin once pointed out, there have been 'great societies that did not use the wheel, but there have been no societies that did not tell stories.'[17] Why do we do this? One reason is to tell the story of how our community came into being, and the values it embodies.

Narratives lie at the heart of many of the world's great religions, possessing a remarkable ability to capture the imagination and at the same time to convey ideas and values. For C. S. Lewis, stories shape our thought, not by a cold dialectic of logic, but by an imaginative captivation. They somehow seem to have a capacity to enchant us, to shape our thinking by *showing* us another world, by inviting us to step into another landscape, and reflect on what we find and how it may force reconsideration and recalibration of our ideas. The most compelling worldviews are thus often *narrated*, rather than merely *articulated*.

J. R. R. Tolkien suggested that the natural human inclination and capacity to create stories (such as his own great fantasy epic *The Lord of the Rings*) is the result of bearing God's image and likeness. We find ourselves motivated to tell such stories, and construct our identities in narrative terms and forms. 'We make in our measure and in our derivative mode, because we are made: and not only made, but made in the image and likeness of a Maker.'[18]

The Christian theologian Stanley Hauerwas is one of many writers to emphasise the importance of these foundational narratives for personal growth in faith and communal participation. Christianity is about seeing the world in a certain way, and acting in accordance with this vision of reality. But how does this way of seeing the world come about? Hauerwas points to the need to be 'trained to see' the world in a Christian manner. 'We do not come to see just by looking, but by disciplined skills developed through initiation into a narrative.'[19] We see ourselves as part of this ongoing narrative. It is not just *a* narrative, but *our* story as a community – a narrative that we allow to enfold and inform our life story.

For C. S. Lewis, the Christian narrative is primary; Christian creeds are secondary. The narrative invites participation; the creeds invite reflection. Creeds articulate the core themes of this narrative and describe the framework of beliefs that it conveys; yet they cannot convey either its imaginative appeal or its subjective impact. For Lewis, it is important to step inside this narrative and inhabit it.

Both Judaism and Christianity (which, despite their significant divergences, share many important points of connection), see themselves as communities grounded in identity-giving stories, which are retold within the community to affirm their distinct identities, recall their histories, and to give them hope for the future.

Take the story of the exodus of the people of Israel from Egypt, which plays a particularly important role in shaping the sense of distinctiveness and identity of Jewish communities. This narrative set out the origins of Israel as a people, explained their distinctiveness, and offered hope. While the historical details of the exodus remain unclear and are at points contested, its cultural memory and perceived significance for Judaism are affirmed and consolidated through the annual Passover Seder. Yet this foundational narrative is not simply something that is told again and again, as if it were merely a favourite family story. This story is expressed *ritually* in an annual meal, which adds depth, detail and imaginative engagement to a narrative performance.

Human beings are not simply social creatures, nor are they simply story-telling creatures; they are also creatures who use rituals as ways of creating, expressing and internalising meaning. As the anthropologist Dimitris Xygalatas points out, rituals are 'seemingly senseless acts' that end up making life worth living.[20] Outsiders may find the rituals of a community puzzling, even unintelligible. Yet the logic of a ritual is embedded within a community of belief, which can see and make the vital connections that an outsider would find puzzling, irrational, or alienating (think of E. M. Forster's 'othering' of the ritual celebrating the birth of Krishna in the Hindu village of Mau in his novel *A Passage to India*).

The participants in the Friday evening ritual meal are encouraged to feel as if they are leaving the captivity of Egypt. A centrepiece of the meal is the following question, traditionally asked by a child: 'Why is this night different from all other nights?' The remainder of the meal explains why, using various foods – such as bitter herbs and unleavened bread – as symbols to evoke the memory of Israel's exodus from bondage. Each element of the meal evokes the memory of this historical event, at which none of the participants in the Seder meal were physically present – and yet which defines and constitutes their identity.

Rituals do not change the external world; their impact lies on the internal world of the believer – someone who inhabits a community of beliefs. As Xygalatas points out, while rituals have no impact on the physical world, they help human beings cope *subjectively* with a complex and sometimes senseless world. They enable us to 'connect, find meaning and discover who we are'. Rituals are acts through which we create meaning and facilitate social connection to others. Some rituals are highly individual and idiosyncratic – such as Rafael Nadal's complex preparations for tennis matches.[21] Perhaps the most famous of these involves water bottles. 'I put my two bottles down at my feet, in front of my chair to my left, one neatly behind the other, diagonally aimed at the court.' Nadal dismisses any suggestion this is some form of superstition. 'It's a way of placing myself in a match, ordering my surroundings to match the order I seek in my head.'[22]

Yet most rituals are communal and social, involving people gathering together. The disruption of these and many other forms of social gatherings by the COVID pandemic of

2020–22 clearly demonstrated the social importance of these rituals. For religious communities, online worship services proved an inadequate substitute for face-to-face encounters, not least because of loss of the social support that is known to be important for human wellbeing.

Communities and Traditions of Rationality

In the ancient world, various schools of philosophy emerged, some of which anticipated aspects of what we now know as the 'natural sciences'. Each of these philosophical communities developed its own distinct mode of thinking, alongside practising an understanding of how to live authentically that was grounded in those ideas. In classical Greece, Platonist, Aristotelian, Stoic, Epicurean and Sceptical schools of thought emerged, each attracting followers to their visions of the good life. A similar pattern can be seen in China, with the emergence of the 'three teachings' of Buddhism, Daoism and Confucianism.

In each of these cases, reflecting on how best to understand our world and live meaningfully within it was carried out within a community of belief, developing often quite sophisticated accounts of the acquisition of wisdom and its implementation in real life. Some might be drawn to these schools or traditions on account of their intellectual appeal; others because they were attracted by the quality of life that these philosophical communities seemed to enable or inform.

A similar recognition of the importance of communities of enquiry and beliefs can be seen within the modern academic world, especially within the natural and social sciences. The phrase 'the scientific method' does not imply a single normative way of gaining knowledge; it rather articulates the general criteria of attention to evidence and critical and consistent thought that are typical of individual natural sciences, yet which are implemented in different ways within each scientific disciplinary community that they consider to be appropriate to their subject matter.

Each of these disciplinary communities developed its own distinct research methods and criteria of adjudication, based on their specific fields of engagement. This is reflected in the concept of an 'epistemic community', developed in the late twentieth century to help make sense of the complex inter-action between professional communities, in particular their epistemic values and their rationalities. Such communities hold their own distinct set of normative and principled beliefs, based on 'internally defined criteria for weighing and validating knowledge in the domain of their expertise.'[23]

To use the analogy of a map, favoured by Mary Midgley, we are not talking about an empire which enfolds a series of distinct subordinate territories, each of which operates under centralised control. Rather, we are dealing with a series of loosely confederated territories, each of which is independent, while at the same time is willing and able to contribute to the wider field of human knowledge and understanding.

Instead of the monolithic approach to knowledge demanded from some rationalists of the late eighteenth century, the recovery of a broader sense of rationality has enabled a more diverse and richer approach to human knowledge and wisdom. This suggests that the landscape of human knowledge production can be likened to a patchwork quilt of communities of reflection and investigation, each exploring its own chosen area of expertise with the tools it has developed and adapted for those purposes. Each has its own identity and integrity, its own contribution to make to human society.

Perhaps the Enlightenment's tendency to think of reasoning as a form of impersonal rationalist mechanical calculus led to a disregard for the moral qualities of thinkers. A growing realisation that thinkers are human beings, subject to and limited by the many fallibilities of human nature, has led to a reconsideration of this viewpoint. Recent scholarship has explored the importance of what is now known as 'character epistemology', characterised by certain 'epistemic virtues' and 'epistemic vices'. The important point is that the knower, or the seeker after knowledge, should be an epistemically *moral* person. For Linda Zagzebski, a philosophical pioneer in this field, such 'epistemic virtues' would include intellectual humility, diligence and open-mindedness.[24]

Although traditional Aristotelian character ethics tended to focus on individual agents as the primary embodiments of virtues and vices, more recent studies of human character have drawn attention to the importance of *collective* epistemic virtues and vices.[25] Groups and communities can be seen as acting as epistemic agents, with their own distinct virtues and vices. One of the latter is 'epistemic arrogance', the tendency of an individual or community to believe that their self-declared intellectual or social superiority entitles them to have privileged status in the public arena and exclude or marginalise others.[26]

Individual thinkers or communities of beliefs have often been deliberately excluded or treated as inferior or insignificant in mainstream discourse – an act of discrimination and repression that is increasingly discussed in terms of 'epistemic injustice.'[27] This practice continues to this day, both in the forms of denigrating certain epistemic groups, or privileging others. Certain groups of people have historically been discounted or marginalised as the bearers or interpreters of truth – particularly women and people of colour. Many religious traditions, for example, clearly treat women as having lesser status as witnesses to truth, teachers, or exemplars.[28] A growing awareness of the historical use of the Bible to perpetuate and justify racism and abusive male dominance has led to a closer reading of this text to understand how these interpretations arose in the first place, and might be challenged in the second.

Yet while religious communities are certainly guilty of some forms of discrimination, they are also discriminated against, particularly in the epistemic domain – think, for example, of the imperious dismissal of religious believers as evil, stupid or mentally ill by some rationalist writers. Yet this epistemic arrogance is not specifically linked with a criticism of religion. It is now widely encountered within western culture, with the potential to increase its fragmentation and polarisation. For example, the growth of online 'echo chambers' providing selectively curated information that is consistent with an in-group's ideology or identity is not merely heightening cultural tensions; it is making it increasingly difficult to mediate between factions and tribes, who see the perpetuation of their favoured stereotypes as simply articulating 'their truth'.

As noted earlier, this problem is becoming especially significant within the political domain, as an increasingly toxic culture emerges, particularly in the United States. Fewer politicians are willing to socialise across party lines, or even partner with opponents in a variety of other activities. Ideological distance, based on what people *believe*, is now being supplemented by personal antagonism, based on how people *feel* about members of other communities.

If we are to rebuild social cohesion and mitigate the negative social impact of 'affective polarisation' in western culture,[29] there is a clear need for public intellectuals to become diplomats, explaining one specific community's idea without condemning or ridiculing others. In view of the importance of this issue, we shall reflect more on the role of 'public intellectuals' in mediating between communities of belief.

Communal Mediation:
The Role of the Public Intellectual

So how do communities of belief communicate with a wider culture? Or with other communities of belief? As human knowledge expands, making it increasingly difficult for individuals to know what else is going on in the world of thought, how can these communities ensure that their ideas or perspectives are known to and appreciated by their peers in the world at large? The answer seems to lie, at least in part, in the idea of a public intellectual – a term that was first used in 1987 to explore the changing role of intellectuals in American public life. For Russell Jacoby, the term referred to 'writers and thinkers who address a general and educated audience.'[30]

It has since taken on a number of meanings, including the justification of the academic life to a sceptical public, the defence of a specific discipline in the face of its critics (who wants to study classics in a scientific age?), or an individual without academic affiliation who speaks and writes intelligibly and engagingly on issues of public importance (such as Jonathan

Sacks, the former Chief Rabbi of the United Kingdom, or Naomi Klein, before her appointment as professor at the University of British Columbia in 2021).

I shall use the term more or less as Jacoby intended it, to refer to an individual intellectual, embedded within an academic community and credentialised by that community – perhaps an intellectual discipline within the natural sciences or humanities, or a political or religious community – who aims to make developments, debates or discussions within these communities intelligible and accessible to a broader audience (think of Brian Cox or Carlo Rovelli in the field of physics, or Mary Beard in the field of classics). This involves both communication, correction and correlation – being able to explain ideas, correct misunderstandings, and 'tease out some of the links between their own discipline and the wider context beyond it'.[31]

It is widely considered that the 'public intellectual' is of major importance in enhancing and correcting public perceptions of communities of belief or practice. At points, certain public intellectuals feel that they are able to speak about a 'range of public issues outside the discipline in which they have earned their academic stripes'. As the case of New Atheist writers makes clear, this is intellectually risky, in that it often involves accidental or intentional academic over-reach, misunderstanding and misrepresentation. The problem, of course, is that audiences often assume that an individual's competence and prominence in one intellectual discipline amounts to a transferable character trait, allowing their pronouncements in unrelated fields of knowledge to be treated as authoritative and reliable.

Yet when rightly understood and enacted, a public intellectual represents a vital bridge of contact between communities of belief, offering an informed and empathetic account of how insights from one community might be relevant to another, resolving misunderstandings, and creating personal relationships which can mitigate suspicions and enable dialogue. Unsurprisingly, those who advocate such dialogues are often abused by those wanting to maintain a 'cold war' between communities of beliefs or academic disciplines. Yet the increasingly polarised nature of western culture means that we need bridge-builders, who are able to explain the ideas and values of their communities *dispassionately* without censuring or misrepresenting others.

Schism: When Communities of Belief Split

Communities split over time – and beliefs often lie at the heart of these fractures. While some suggest this demonstrates that beliefs are fundamentally divisive, it is too easy to overlook the fact that beliefs created these communities in the first place, providing them with their grounds of unity and coherence. Communities of belief gather around the narratives and rituals which express their fundamental identity.

While the formal statement of beliefs – for example, in creeds – may create the impression that these are fixed and static, the human act of believing takes place in the flux of history, involving constant reflection and review as communities of faith face new challenges, opportunities and issues. The concept of 'living tradition' expresses the idea that communities of belief change over time, as they evolve in their self-understanding – but see this development as an ongoing exploration of their fundamental identity. Communities of belief aim for faithful continuity to the past, while being responsive to the challenges and concerns of the present.

Yet there comes a point at which communities of belief find themselves faced with internal tensions of such moment that it becomes impossible to continue in their present form. Often the causes of such divisions and ruptures within a community are responses to changes in their environments, which seem to call for new ways of implementing a traditional belief system, or changing its focus or manner of application. Sometimes movements fragment; sometimes a majority expels a minority, who form a new community with appropriate adjustments to their beliefs.

Although these fragmentations take many forms, the most significant schisms are generally thought to be religious in nature, focusing on the identity of a religious community, and the implementation of its core vision. A good example is found in the 'parting of the ways' between Judaism and Christianity. This fissure took place over an extended period, and was not centrally directed, taking different forms in local contexts. Judaism and Christianity coexisted for a while, with local variations in how the two communities related to each other. By the second century, however, a permanent separation had emerged.

Recent scholarship has shown how two theological issues were of importance in creating tensions between early Christianity and Judaism – namely, how to understand the identity and significance of Jesus Christ, and the correct way of interpreting Israel's sacred scriptures.[32] Christianity regarded these sacred writings as important to its own identity, but framed them in a way that differed significantly from traditional Jewish readings of the same texts. For example, Christians do not consider the cultic regulations of Israel's sacred texts to apply to them, and thus do not observe its food laws or its requirement that males should be circumcised

Within Islam, an unhealed division arose after the prophet Muhammad's death in 632. Muhammad had not stipulated who should succeed him as the political leader of the Muslim community. One group (the Shia) believed only someone from Muhammad's family should succeed him; most (the Sunni) felt that the community was free to choose from a wider range of candidates, and selected Muhammad's close friend Abu Bakr to become his successor (Arabic: *khalif*). The two groups seem to have coexisted in relative peace for many centuries. However, the 1979 Islamic Revolution in Iran gave rise to a more radical form of Shia Islam. Subsequent upheavals in the Middle East caused by two Gulf Wars, the Arab Spring of 2011, and the civil war in Syria have significantly increased polarisation between these two groups.[33]

Christianity has been significantly affected by two schisms or fragmentations. The first was the extended drifting apart of the Latin-speaking Christian West, focused on Rome, and the Greek-speaking Christian East, focusing on Constantinople. Several factors contributed to this Great Schism, generally re-garded as formalised in 1054 following a fierce dispute over a demand that Greek churches in southern Italy should conform to Latin practices.

The second is the movement generally known as the Protestant Reformation within western Christianity, which emerged following increasing demands for reform within the Church, particularly to the role of the Papacy, associated with leading Christian writers such as Erasmus of Rotterdam. What began as reforming movements in many sections of the Church (especially in France, Germany, Italy and Switzerland) gave way to the emergence of new alignments of churches, which no longer considered themselves to be under papal control.

The origins of this movement are complex, including the growing social power of the middle classes, the rise of self-governing urban communities, a demand to use the vernacular rather than Latin in preaching and worship, and a return to simpler and more biblical ways of Christian thinking. Eventually it led to the emergence of various forms of Protestantism, and the loss of unity within western Christianity. Many scholars feel that this fragmentation was not necessary, in that the difficulties could have been resolved.[34] While there is little chance that the situation will now be reversed, there is growing interest in rebuilding relationships across these denominational divides. Recent ecumenical dialogues between these communities of belief may not have led to their reunion, but have at least led to an increase in mutual understanding and lessening of tensions.

Yet the Reformation illustrates how beliefs can have social functions, serving as boundary markers between communities. The doctrine of justification by faith alone came to define the boundaries between Protestantism and Catholicism in the sixteenth century – a convenient theological litmus test which reduced these two complex and variegated religious communities to a set of binaries.[35] For Martin Luther, the 'article of justification' defined whether the Christian Church stood firm or fell apart. It thus was a point of coalescence for Protestantism, and a line of demarcation from Catholicism.

Why is this point important? Because it illustrates the dual function of beliefs – to unite people into communities on the one hand, and divide them on the other. Beliefs are not purely divisive; where they do lead to divisions, they were often responsible for the unity that existed beforehand. The challenge is for the wise to give thought to how these dual aspects of belief can be managed. It is natural for humans to believe and to form communities; this problem is located deep within the human condition, and is not going to go away.

While there is much more that needs to be said about the interplay of beliefs and communities, we need to bring our reflections on this theme to a close. I will conclude by considering the following: if belief is inevitable in life, how can we, whether as individuals or communities, be reassured that we have chosen wisely in what we believe, given that we cannot prove these beliefs?

Conclusion: Living in a World of Uncertainty

Who can we trust? *What* can we trust? These are among the most difficult and cognitively demanding tasks that we face in everyday life. We look for individuals who are smart, honest and dependable – just as we seek beliefs that are trustworthy and enable us to flourish. My argument in this book is that belief is natural, reasonable and has the potential for good. To deny it is simply to diminish us as human beings.

For some epistemic Puritans, we ought only to believe what we can prove. Logic and mathematics thus provide us with the norms that we should apply to everything in life. I share their admiration for these glittering peaks of human knowledge production. Yet these are singularities, areas of knowledge in which a degree of certainty is possible which distinguishes them from other domains of human understanding, rather than being representative of them.

We seem to be hard-wired to seek certainty, and so find uncertainty worrying and stressful.[1] Perhaps this helps us understand why many people impose rational and moral certainties, or find themselves drawn to populist orators offering a return to absolutist ideologies or a bygone, yet wistfully re-membered, social order with familiar and known values. Yet we should challenge our natural craving for certainty in all areas of our lives. It is a delusion.

The ideas I explore in this book are not new; in fact, they have a distinguished history in the long tradition of scientific and philosophical reflection and religious faith, which are deeply attuned to the problem of uncertainty, both as a cognitive and existential concern. Consider, for example, the personal credo of the Italian theoretical physicist and writer Carlo Rovelli:

> I believe in justice. I believe that the Earth is round. I believe that my name is Carlo and that my father's name was Franco. I believe that life is worth living. My beliefs are rooted in me. They define me. I hold them dear and I strenuously defend them against any challenge.
>
> *But I am not certain about them.*[2]

For Rovelli, we live in 'a vast intermediate space' located between 'full ignorance and total certainty'. That's an imagi-natively helpful way of describing the realm of belief or faith, which locates itself firmly within this domain of uncertainty – a domain within which human thought, action and life must and can take place. It is within this space that we frame our ideas of meaning, value and justice – all of which are critical to human distinctiveness on the one hand, and to meaningful human existence on the other. Like Odysseus, we have to learn to find a navigable channel between the Scylla of 'full igno-rance' and the Charybdis of 'total certainty'.

Certainty is simply not an option for any nuanced under-standing of the meaning of life, why we are here, or the nature of the good. These questions *matter* – but we can't answer them with the certainty we mistakenly believe is our intellectual birth-right. This does not condemn us to total ignorance; it simply opens our eyes to the complexity and ambiguity of many aspects of our world, and prompts us to question the assumption that we can expect certainty in relation to life's big questions. We have to learn to walk the poorly signposted and unpoliced line between certainty and doubt as we try to make sense of the chaos.

In a 1770 letter to Frederick II of Prussia, Voltaire com-plained that only charlatans offered certainty. 'While doubt is not a particularly pleasant state, certainty is a ridiculous state.'[3] Some would suggest that the Enlightenment is to blame for these unrealistic expectations for human knowledge, which suggested that a universal human reason could eliminate un-certainties and ambiguities. I think the problem lies much deeper than this – in human nature itself. The human craving for certainty is rooted deep within us. While we cannot elim-inate it, we can at least challenge it, and try to rise above it. We have to learn to live with it and resist the temptation to overstate the capacity of human reason.

Does this realism about reality prevent us trying to find a set of habitable beliefs, capable of sustaining meaningful life? No. But it allows us to understand why there have been so many false dawns, promising direct access to certainties that turned out to be contested opinions, imposed dogmas, or cul-tural fads. We seem to be drawn to people who exude certainty, perhaps assuming their attitude reflects a vastly superior grasp of reality than the rest of us.

Maybe that's why Forrest Gump gained such a following as he ran across the United States. People felt he had a personal authenticity, a certainty of purpose that they could share by running alongside him – before, of course, he declared he was tired and going home, leaving his frustrated followers to reluctantly figure things out for themselves.

In this book, I have argued for a retrieval of the more modest category of belief, which squares up to this disturbing human tendency to construct certainties when the evidence does not permit it. I have told you something about what I believe to illustrate some of the points that I have been making, but my own beliefs are of little relevance to this discussion.

My position is this: *believing is not only intellectually defensible but existentially necessary.* It is time to move on from movements and individuals who offer facile solutions in the face of life's endless ambiguities. We have to live with a degree of uncertainty about our lives, while realising that this does not need to overwhelm us with the feeling of confusion and disconnectedness that caused the poet John Donne such distress in 1611: ''Tis all in pieces, all coherence gone.'

Embracing Uncertainty in the
Face of Spurious Certainties

In his 2003 book *A Mathematician Plays the Stock Market*, John Allen Paulos channels the first century philosopher Pliny the Elder in setting out a guiding principle he had learned to trust in life: 'Uncertainty is the only certainty there is.' This powerful one-liner may sound bleak; yet its austerity simply reflects the reality of the human situation, and echoes the suppressed wisdom of the past, in which this insight was regularly acknowledged and lived out.

Provisional certainties often turn out to be the prevailing view of an age, before being discarded or surgically modified by its successors. We can't be sure about what the future holds, and whether it will discredit what some currently regard as secure knowledge – including many current scientific theories. As Carlo Rovelli observed, 'we have no other tool to guide us than our limited and always insufficient intelligence, no other reliable adviser than uncertainty.' For Rovelli, we are constantly tempted to eagerly embrace 'shiny new ideologies', each proclaiming its triumph over failed alternatives. Yet we live in an age of multiple temporary certainties, unsure what will come next, or how the future will judge what we consider to be secure. Our judgements are obstinately tainted and limited by our historical location.

A more literary exploration of this theme is found in Alexander Pope's *Essay on Man* (1733–34). This masterpiece of poetic philosophy acknowledges and affirms the human need to believe as we try to make sense of a seemingly chaotic and meaningless world, yet which seems to hint at a deeper orderliness. We might well wonder, Pope comments, why we are 'form'd so weak, so little, and so blind?'[4] We have to realise that we are 'darkly wise', in that we can only know incomplete truths, being able to grasp and understand only a small part of our universe.

Human beings, Pope declared, are 'born but to die, and reas'ning but to err',[5] trapped in an unsettling world of belief, when some would rather inhabit a secure realm of proved certainties. For Pope, humanity longs to find beliefs that can be trusted, despite evidential uncertainty and the limits of human reasoning. We are unable to see the big picture, but can only discern some of its parts: ''Tis but a part we see, and not a whole.'[6] We have to face up to the problem that the big questions in life cannot be answered with certainty.

Pope's analysis was prophetic. To understand the importance of beliefs in human life, we must confront our limitations and weaknesses. We aren't rational calculating machines who know and act perfectly and infallibly; we are limited by our natural cognitive endowments which appear to have emerged to enable us to survive, rather than achieve total coherent insight. The Cambridge philosopher Frank Ramsey's influential discussion of the relationship between truth and probability echoes Pope's language and his concerns. We too easily construct a philosophical ideal of certainty in the belief that it 'is more suited to God than to men',[7] and is unrealistic for human application.

For Ramsey, to act only on the basis of certainties 'is too high a standard to expect of mortal men, and we must agree that some degree of doubt or even of error may be humanly speaking justified.' Rather than crying for the moon, we have to be realistic about the limits of human beings and pragmatic about the forms of knowledge that we can achieve – and be willing to live accordingly. Beliefs offer us a map by which we might steer as we navigate an ocean of uncertainties.

Perhaps in an ideal world it might be possible to assemble convincing proofs for our fundamental beliefs, so that these convictions could be as certain as the proven truths of mathematics and logic. But we don't live in that kind of world. We have to get used to the limits of human reasoning, and face up to the kind of world we inhabit and the kind of creatures we really are.

The academic philosophical literature, despite its 'forests of depressingly oblique, hyper-technical and often deeply boring discussions',[8] at least helps us to develop a sense of realism about the dilemma that we face – namely, that neither our need to know nor our desire to be sure secures our ability to know with certainty. There is a tension between our expectations and their outcomes. We don't have access to methods and criteria that command universal rational assent and deliver secure and certain outcomes. There is no single method for gaining personal knowledge; beliefs can arise and be assessed in many ways.

Perhaps that's why many now speak of the *permissibility* of beliefs, reassuring us that it's OK to believe. As the psychologist William James pointed out, the reality of life is that we often need to give answers to our deepest existential questions which go beyond the evidence and what reason can deliver. That's why we keep on speaking about *believing*, and resist the fatal trap of fabricating certainties to make sense of our unrealistic expectations.

We need to be realistic about what we can hope for, while searching for an existentially habitable space of relative stability amid a troubled ocean of uncertainty. Rovelli's 'vast intermediate space' of ambiguity and uncertainty is not an unknown territory or an unexplored ocean; it has been recognised and inhabited by philosophers, theologians, artists and writers since the classical period, who have found ways of flourishing in its half-lights and coping with its ambiguities – and in doing so, demonstrated the ability of human beings to deal with a complex world. We can learn from them, and put their wisdom to good use today.

Most of us know the experience of a seemingly irrepressible drive to make sense of ourselves which can send us on 'dangerous voyages of exploration' (Bernard Lonergan).[9] The human mind roams the intellectual landscape in search of stable and meaningful beliefs, which might offer what the American philosopher Charles S. Peirce termed 'an ideal of life' or a 'thoroughly satisfactory explanation' of things that matter to us.

My argument throughout this work is that the big questions of life – such as the meaning of life, or the nature of the good – lie beyond rational or scientific proof. Like Isaiah Berlin, I am suspicious of those who claim to possess 'incorrigible knowledge about issues of fact or principle in any sphere of human behaviour'. I'm willing to accept my limitations – indeed, the limitations of the human race – when it comes to these questions. Like Alexander Pope, I have reluctantly come to accept the limited degrees of certainty that are associated with these 'ultimate questions' – not because I am weak minded, but because the evidence clearly points to this conclusion. Believing is a human stance to be embraced, not a liability that is to be eradicated. 'Faith' is the name we give to this commitment to living in line with what we believe to be true.

This does not, as I have emphasised throughout, permit us to 'believe anything we like'. We all need to give good reasons for what we believe, accepting responsibility for our beliefs, while realising that neither proof nor certainty are possible in dealing with 'ultimate questions'. We have to accept that others will disagree with us on these grand questions, not because they are stupid or evil, but because the questions simply cannot be answered with the precision and certainty that many would hope for.

Believing and Human Nature

Human beings are believing and meaning-seeking animals, with an imprinted instinct to make sense of what we experience. We can no more eliminate our propensity to believe than our tendency to be tribal – despite the difficulties this creates, not least the risk of genocide (think of Rwanda in 1994, which pitted Tutsi against Hutu), or the serious communal tensions that can arise between people groups in multicultural western cities. We have to work with human nature as it actually is, and confront the fact that 'tribal bias is a natural and nearly ineradicable feature of human cognition and that no group – not even one's own – is immune'.[10] Evolutionary pressures have 'sculpted human minds to be tribal', leading to the potential for social antagonism and violence. The New Atheism suggested that religion is the cause of toxic social division; a more reliable view is that our instinct for tribalism often seizes on religion for its own ends.

Like just about everything that human beings turn their hands to, this enterprise of believing can go wrong. As we have seen, beliefs can lead to discrimination, violence and prejudice. This, however, points to the need to be critical and reflective about those beliefs, and how they are enacted and embodied. We can't change who we are – but we can try to live ethically and peacefully. Paradoxically, it is the belief that we *should* live in these ways that allows us to subdue and redirect our more fundamental human instincts – a point emphasised by Thomas H. Huxley in his famous 1893 lecture 'Evolution and Ethics'. For Huxley, ethical values – which human beings create – can help suppress our more fundamental primitive tendency towards violence, rooted in a distant past.

The solution to toxic beliefs is not a crude abolition of the category of 'believing', but the search for better forms of believing that foster good lives, individually and communally. Much research has been carried out on the way in which belief systems are correlated with flourishing and resilience, at both the individual and communal level. This research often focuses on how beliefs help individuals cope with ageing, trauma and uncertainty; in recent times, its scope has been expanded to include indigenous communities, exploring how their beliefs and practices enable them to survive, particularly in the face of colonialism and the erosion of their traditional cultures.[11]

A recurrent theme to emerge from this research is that existentially disengaged beliefs do not seem to encourage human flourishing or create resilience. We care about beliefs that make a difference to us. I was fascinated by the 2006 debate which led to Pluto being reclassified as a 'dwarf planet' by the International Astronomical Union. But did it impact on me in any meaningful way? No. It was interesting in a detached sort of way. I also believe that the atomic weight of the chemical element chlorine is 35.453 – not because I've checked this out myself, having outsourced this matter to the scientific community at large. But if it turned out it was 35.467, I would shrug my shoulders. It would be interesting, but not personally relevant to me, even though it might be important to theoretical chemistry. Yet other beliefs make a profound difference to how we understand ourselves, and feel about our lives.

Human flourishing seems to rest on three broad pillars: truth, purpose and meaning.[12] To flourish is to live according to realities that are not of our own fabrication or invention; to live a life that is significant and leads to the advancement of what is good and just; and to know that we matter in life. 'Flourishing' includes good mental and physical health, but is also linked with happiness, life satisfaction, meaning, purpose, character, virtue and close social relationships. People flourish when they *believe* and *feel* they are part of something greater, as when individuals and communities locate themselves within 'Big Pictures'.

Flourishing in an Uncertain World

The poet John Keats coined the term 'negative capability' to refer to a willingness to accept and embrace 'being in uncertainties, mysteries, doubts. While some might hastily draw firm conclusions about the significance of an idea or event, Keats encouraged remaining in a state of openness, continuing to probe and reflect on a complex reality to gain a more comprehensive understanding of it. Keats grasped the importance of a respectful contemplative musing on an object – such as a Grecian urn – without feeling compelled to arrive at a definitive and conclusive interpretation of its meaning or prematurely shutting down the process of reflection. He was willing to inhabit a realm of uncertainties, mysteries and doubts, affirming and experiencing the complexity and depth of the world rather than trying to subjugate it with the precision of logical analysis.[13]

This book leaves readers in a similar position. My concern has been to describe the epistemic dilemma in which we find ourselves, and to caution against prematurely dismissing some of the most significant beliefs that have shaped human culture and civilization throughout history. We can prove shallow truths, but not the profound existential, moral and spiritual beliefs that bestow dignity and significance upon human life. Some individuals may find this profoundly uncomfortable and may wish to eliminate the category of belief, or convert their own beliefs into certainties. Yet for reasons that we have explored in this book, I do not consider this to be a defensible position.

Recognising that we live in a world of uncertainties, mysteries and doubts may be unsettling; however, this is surely preferable to constructing a world of imagined self-evident truths in response to our aversion to uncertainty. Though we live in a world that is existentially ambivalent and morally uninformative, beliefs make this is a profoundly habitable place by allowing us to see it (and ourselves) in a new way. Beliefs *involve* us, giving us the capacity to discern or create human meaning, purpose and significance, and live this out in community with others.

So why believe? Because we're human. Because it's normal. Because it's realistic. Belief is as natural to human beings as it is necessary for their wellbeing. We have to deal with humanity as it is, as 'moral believing animals',[14] shaped in ways we do not fully understand by our evolutionary past and cultural present, rather than as the universalised logical or rational calculating machines envisaged by the Age of Reason, which held what turned out to be a forlorn hope of clear and certain answers to our deepest questions.

This kind of algorithmic reasoning may work well in the domain of logic. Yet human existence demands engagement with aspects of life characterised by ambiguity, uncertainty and complexity – such as medical diagnosis and forensic examination.[15] Questions of meaning and moral value lie even further beyond the scope of mechanical reasoning, not least on account of their deeply subjective significance. Information, as Susan Sontag points out, is 'always, by definition, partial, incomplete, fragmentary'.[16] In both clinics and courts of law, human judgement is of critical importance in creating trustworthy syntheses of the partial and fragmentary – a judgement

that rests on wisdom, in the form of long experience and reflection in coping with such complex questions. The process of
reflection is an *art*, and its outcomes are *beliefs*.

In his *Dark Materials* trilogy, Philip Pullman develops one
of the most creative – though oblique – critiques of mechanical
models of human reasoning. Pullman introduces us to the 'alethiometer,' a complex rational calculating machine, 'very like
a clock, or a compass', which delivers secure readings of reality
once the symbols of its three wheels are correctly set to frame
the question being asked.

Yet the alethiometer can only be read correctly by a small
group of people who have developed the art of doing so – including the central character of the trilogy, Lyra Silvertongue,
who is initially able to use the device intuitively. Puzzled by the
device's behaviour, Lyra asks Farder Coram whether it is functioning properly. 'It's working all right, Lyra. What we don't
know is whether we're reading it right. That's a subtle art.'[17]
Answering life's great questions is indeed an art, a skill that has to
be acquired, transcending mechanistic and algorithmic ways of
thinking or understandings of human rationality, and alert to the
importance of interpretation and the inevitability of ambiguity.

How might we find such habitable beliefs? Bernard
Lonergan's 'dangerous voyage of exploration' and Carlo Rovelli's
'vast intermediate space' of ambiguity and uncertainty help us
imagine a voyage of exploration for an existentially habitable
island in a vast ocean of possibilities – a place of safety in which
we can hope to flourish and become the people we are meant
to be. Such islands already exist, and we do not need to invent
them. Some of them have been known and found to be habitable for thousands of years. Our task is to locate them, check

them out, and work out whether we can make them our home. Others have found them before us, often leaving us accounts of how this happened and assessments of the difference that this made to the quality of their lives.

And so, like the seafaring Polynesian navigators of old, we develop wayfaring skills and search strategies which allow us to locate even the most remote islands of beliefs that might allow us to flourish and live a good life of joy and wonder. I began my explorations by navigating my way to Marxism, and spent some time exploring its landscape and figuring out whether I could thrive there. Disillusioned, I began to island-hop, eventually alighting on Christianity, which proved much more resilient and engaging. It provided me with a stable refuge to weather life's challenges and a secure base from which I could comprehend and participate in our complex world. I'm still there, happily settled.

In the end, we are all believers, whether we like it or not, in that our lives and knowledge are grounded and shaped by assumptions and beliefs that lie beyond comprehensive empirical verification or rational proof. This is not a new idea; it has deep roots in ancient philosophy, and is now widely discussed in more pragmatic traditions of philosophy, building on Charles S. Peirce's recognition of the fallibility of knowledge and William James's reconstruction of belief in a world of uncertainty. Yet perhaps its moment has now come, as disillusionment with the alleged certainties and simplicities of the recent past gives way to a longing to reconstruct, move forward, and find beliefs that are stable, significant and supportive of a good life. Living in this vast space of ambiguity and uncertainty is an art, a skill that we have to learn. Happily, it can be done.

Acknowledgements

My thanks to Cecilia Stein, my editor at Oneworld Publications, for suggesting this book, and providing encouragement and criticism as it took shape over time. I also owe a considerable debt to academic colleagues and students at Oxford University over the last ten years, who have provided me with an intellectually hospitable yet critical environment in which to discuss the great questions that lie at the heart of this work. I am especially grateful for many conversations over the last ten years with Joanna Collicutt about the importance of belief for psychological wellbeing.

Notes

Introduction

1   Peter Slezak, 'Gods of the State: Atheism, Enlightenment and Barbarity'. In *Politics and Religion in the New Century: Philosophical Perspectives*, ed. Philip Andrew Quadrio and Carrol Besseling, pp. 42–72. Sydney: Sydney University Press, 2009.

2   Greg M. Epstein, 'Less Anti-Theism, More Humanism'. *Washington Post*, 1 October 2007.

3   Ashley Miller, 'Atheist tribalism poisons everything'. *The Orbit*, 2 October 2015, https://the-orbit.net/ashleyfmiller/tag/poisons-everything/.

4   Giovanni Tiso, 'With Religious Fervour'. *New Humanist*, 24 July 2019.

5   Doris Lessing, *Prisons We Choose to Live Inside*. London: Flamingo, 1998, pp. 48, 59.

6   Alister E. McGrath, *Natural Philosophy: On Retrieving a Lost Disciplinary Imaginary*. Oxford: Oxford University Press, 2022, 74–7.

7   Bertrand Russell, *A History of Western Philosophy*. London: 1950, p. 2.

8   Pew Research Center, December, 2023, 'Spirituality Among Americans', pp. 77, 76.

9   Neil Dagnall, Andrew Denovan, Kenneth Graham Drinkwater and Andrew Parker. 'An Evaluation of the Belief in Science

Scale'. *Frontiers in Psychology* 10 (2019). https://doi.org/10.3389/
fpsyg.2019.00861.

Chapter 1 – Believing: A Mental Experiment

1   Agustín Fuentes, *Why We Believe: Evolution and the Human Way of
    Being.* New Haven: Yale University Press, 2019, p. 116.
2   Fuentes, *Why We Believe*, pp. 3–30.
3   Rüdiger J. Seitz, 'Believing and Beliefs – Neurophysiological
    Underpinnings'. *Frontiers in Behavioral Neuroscience* 15 (2022).
    https://doi.org/https://doi.org/10.3389/fnbeh.2022.880504.
4   Rachel Pechey and Peter W. Halligan, 'Exploring the Folk
    Understanding of Belief: Identifying Key Dimensions Endorsed in
    the General Population'. *Journal of Cognition and Culture* 12, no. 1
    (2012): pp. 81–99.
5   Daniel Carey, *Locke, Shaftesbury, and Hutcheson: Contesting
    Diversity in the Enlightenment and Beyond.* Cambridge: Cambridge
    University Press, 2006, pp. 14–97. For the geographical diversity of
    rationalities, see Charles W. J. Withers, *Placing the Enlightenment:
    Thinking Geographically about the Age of Reason.* Chicago: University
    of Chicago Press, 2007.
6   Alasdair MacIntyre, *Whose Justice? Which Rationality?* London:
    Duckworth, 1988, p. 6.
7   For the philosophical background to this, see Lee Braver, *Groundless
    Ground: A Study of Wittgenstein and Heidegger.* Cambridge, MA:
    MIT Books, 2014.
8   For the development of this grounding belief, see William
    T. Cavanaugh, *The Myth of Religious Violence: Secular Ideology and
    the Roots of Modern Conflict.* Oxford: Oxford University Press,
    2009. For the opportunistic use of history in modern debates, see
    Borden W. Painter, *The New Atheist Denial of History: Hijacking
    the Past in the Name of Reason.* New York: Palgrave Macmillan,
    2014.
9   Karl R. Popper, 'Natural Selection and the Emergence of Mind'.
    Dialectica 32 (1978): 339–55; quote at p. 342.
10 Albert Einstein, *Ideas and Opinions.* New York: Crown Publishers,
    1954, pp. 41–9.

11 Sam Harris, *The Moral Landscape: How Science Can Determine Human Values*. New York: Free Press, 2010, pp. 189–90.

12 Alexander Rosenberg, *The Atheist's Guide to Reality: Enjoying Life without Illusions*. New York: W.W. Norton, 2011, pp. 7–8.

13 Michael Tomasello, *A Natural History of Human Morality*. Cambridge, MA: Harvard University Press, 2016.

14 David J. Chalmers, 'Why Isn't There More Progress in Philosophy?' *Philosophy* 90, no. 351 (2015): pp. 3–31, especially pp. 16–22.

15 Richard Fumerton, 'Why You Can't Trust a Philosopher', in *Disagreement*, edited by Richard Feldman and Ted A. Warfield, pp. 91–111. Oxford: Oxford University Press, 2010; quote at p. 110.

16 See especially Jonathan Haidt, *The Righteous Mind: Why Good People Are Divided by Politics and Religion*. New York: Pantheon Books, 2012.

17 Sam Harris, *The End of Faith: Religion, Terror, and the Future of Reason*. New York: W.W. Norton & Co., 2004, pp. 52–3.

18 Harris, *The End of Faith*, pp. 192–9.

19 For example, see Scott A. Anderson and Martha C. Nussbaum, eds. *Confronting Torture: Essays on the Ethics, Legality, History, and Psychology of Torture Today*. Chicago: University of Chicago Press, 2018.

20 Isaiah Berlin, *Concepts and Categories: Philosophical Essays*. 2nd edn. Princeton, NJ: Princeton University Press, 2013, pp. 4–5.

21 Isaiah Berlin, 'My Intellectual Path'. In *The Many Faces of Philosophy: Reflections from Plato to Arendt*, edited by Amélie Oksenberg Rorty, pp. 482–97. Oxford: Oxford University Press, 2004; quote at p. 489.

22 Isaiah Berlin, *The Proper Study of Mankind*. New York: Farrar, Straus and Giroux, New York, 1998, p. 5; 16.

23 Ludwig Wittgenstein, *On Certainty*. Oxford: Blackwell, 1974, p. 117.

24 For illuminating accounts of this point and its implications, see Anthony T. Kronman, *After Disbelief: On Disenchantment, Disappointment, Eternity, and Joy*. New Haven, CT: Yale University Press, 2022.

25 Login S. George and Crystal L. Park, 'Existential Mattering: Bringing Attention to a Neglected but Central Aspect of Meaning.' In *Meaning in Positive and Existential Psychology*, edited by

Alexander Batthyany and Pninit Russo-Netzer, pp. 39–51. New York: Springer, 2014.

26 Jeanette Winterson, *Why Be Happy When You Could Be Normal?* London: Vintage, 2012, p. 68.

27 Clifford Geertz, *The Interpretation of Cultures.* New York: Basic Books, 1973, p. 140.

28 Login S. George and Crystal L. Park, 'Meaning in Life as Comprehension, Purpose, and Mattering'. *Review of General Psychology* 20, no. 3 (2016): pp. 205–20.

29 William James, 'Is Life Worth Living?' *International Journal of Ethics* 6 (1895): pp. 1–24.

30 James, 'Is Life Worth Living?' p. 15.

31 Martin E. P. Seligman, *Flourish: A Visionary New Understanding of Happiness and Well-Being.* New York City, NY: Atria Books, 2011.

32 Charles Dickens, *Hard Times.* London: Wordsworth, 1995, p. 3.

33 Dickens, *Hard Times*, p. 11; 75.

34 Christopher Hitchens, *God Is Not Great: How Religion Poisons Everything.* New York: Twelve, 2007, p. 5.

Chapter 2 – Seeking a 'Big Picture'

1   Joseph Mileck, *Hermann Hesse and His Critics: The Criticism and Bibliography of Half a Century.* Chapel Hill, NC: University of North Carolina Press, 1958, p. 129.

2   For the history of this remarkable journal, see Tim Satterthwaite, *Modernist Magazines and the Social Ideal.* New York: Bloomsbury, 2020, pp. 75–200.

3   Hermann Hesse, 'Die Sehnsucht unser Zeit nach einer Weltanschauung', *UHU* 2 (1926): pp. 3–14.

4   John Moriarty, *Serious Sounds.* Dublin: Lilliput Press, 2007, pp. 58–62.

5   George Orwell, *New English Weekly*, March 21, 1940. Orwell also suggests that 'Fascism and Nazism are psychologically far sounder than any hedonistic conception of life.'

6   E. M. Forster 'What I Believe', in *Two Cheers for Democracy.* San Diego, CA: Harcourt Brace, 1951, pp. 67–76; quote at p. 67.

7   See, for example, Paul T. P. Wong, *The Human Quest for Meaning: Theories, Research, and Applications.* 2nd edn. New York: Routledge, 2012.

8   See, for example, Karen Gasper and Gerald L. Clore, 'Attending to the Big Picture: Mood and Global Versus Local Processing of Visual Information.' *Psychological Science* 13 (2002): 34–40; Joshua A. Hicks and Laura A. King, 'Meaning in Life and Seeing the Big Picture: Positive Affect and Global Focus.' *Cognition and Emotion* 21, no. 7 (2007): pp. 1,577–84.

9   Michael Sandel, *Democracy's Discontent: America in Search of a Public Philosophy.* Cambridge, MA: Belknap Press, 1998, p. ix (my emphasis).

10 Noam Chomsky, *Necessary Illusions: Thought Control in Democratic Societies.* London: Pluto Press, 1989, p. 33.

11 Henri Poincaré, *Science and Hypothesis.* London: Bloomsbury Academic, 2018, p. 103.

12 Christian Smith, *Moral, Believing Animals: Human Personhood and Culture.* Oxford: Oxford University Press, 2009, pp. 63–94.

13 Fernando Aguiar and Andrés de Francisco, 'Rationality and Identity'. *European Journal of Sociology* 43 (2002), pp. 119–31.

14 See McCloud's critique of the stereotypical view 'Religions are belief systems' in Brad Stoddard and Craig Martin, eds. *Stereotyping Religion: Critiquing Clichés.* London: Bloomsbury Academic, 2017, pp. 11–22.

15 Eric M. Orlin, *Foreign Cults in Rome: Creating a Roman Empire.* Oxford: Oxford University Press, 2010, pp. 191–214.

16 See the important study of Ying-Yi Hong, Michael W. Morris, Chi-Yue Chiu, and Verónica Benet-Martínez, 'Multicultural Minds: A Dynamic Constructivist Approach to Culture and Cognition.' *American Psychologist* 55, no. 7 (2000), pp. 709–20.

17 As noted by Caroline Gustavsson, 'Existential Configurations: A Way to Conceptualize People's Meaning-Making'. *British Journal of Religious Education* 42, no. 1 (2018), pp. 25–35.

18 C. P. Snow, *The Search.* Harmondsworth: Penguin, 1965, 33. Snow's 'Dutch Garden' refers to the formal organised garden introduced into England in the seventeenth century by William of Orange.

19 The significance of this point is brought out by Margaret Morrison, *Unifying Scientific Theories: Physical Concepts and Mathematical Structures*. Cambridge: Cambridge University Press, 2000, pp. 7–34.

20 Ludwig Wittgenstein, *Tractatus Logico-Philosophicus*. London: Routledge & Kegan Paul, 1992, 6.41. The original German reads: 'Der Sinn der Welt muss außerhalb ihrer liegen.'

21 Steven Weinberg, *Dreams of a Final Theory: The Search for the Fundamental Laws of Nature*. London: Hutchinson Radius, 1993, p. 196.

22 Sean M. Carroll, *The Big Picture: On the Origins of Life, Meaning, and the Universe Itself*. London: Oneworld, 2016.

23 John Polkinghorne, 'The Trinity and Scientific Reality', in *The Blackwell Companion to Science and Christianity*, edited by J. B. Stump and Alan G. Padgett, pp. 521–32; quote at p. 524.

24 Susan R. Wolf, *Meaning in Life and Why It Matters*. Princeton, NJ: Princeton University Press, 2010, pp. 7–10.

25 Pierre Hadot, *What Is Ancient Philosophy?* Cambridge, MA: Harvard University Press, 2002.

26 Pierre Hadot, *The Inner Citadel: The Meditations of Marcus Aurelius*. Cambridge, MA: Harvard University Press, 1998, pp. 312–13.

27 For the background, see Winrich Löhr, 'Christianity as Philosophy: Problems and Perspectives of an Ancient Intellectual Project.' *Vigiliae Christianae* 64, no. 2 (2010), pp. 160–88.

28 Susan R. Wolf, *Meaning in Life*. Princeton, NJ: Princeton University Press, 2010, pp. 10–11.

29 Keith Yandell, *Philosophy of Religion*. London: Routledge, 1999, p. 16.

30 Mary Midgley, *Evolution as a Religion*. 2nd edn. London: Routledge, 2002, pp. 17–18.

31 Hallam Tennyson, *Alfred Lord Tennyson: A Memoir*. 2 vols. London: Macmillan, 1897, vol. 2, p. 374.

32 Tennyson, 'The Ancient Sage', lines 66–7.

33 Richard Rorty, *Consequences of Pragmatism*. Minneapolis: University of Minneapolis Press, 1982, p. xlii.

34 Hannah Kent, 'Conversation with Philip Pullman', *Kill Your Darlings*, 1 July 2010. https://www.killyourdarlings.com.au/article/kill-your-darlings-in-conversation-with-philip-pullman.

35 Donald MacKinnon, 'The Function of Philosophy in Education.' *Blackfriars* 22 (1941), pp. 413–18.

36 Albert Einstein, *Out of My Later Years*. New York: Littlefield, Adams & Co., 1967, p. 29 (emphasis in original).

37 Mary Midgley, *What is Philosophy for?* London: Bloomsbury Academic, 2018, p. 193.

38 Mary Midgley, *Myths We Live By*. London: Routledge, 2004, p. 53.

39 Massimo Pigliucci, 'New Atheism and the Scientistic Turn in the Atheism Movement'. *Midwest Studies in Philosophy* 37, no. 1 (2013): 142–53; quote at p. 144.

40 Mary Midgley, 'Dover Beach: Understanding the Pains of Bereavement'. *Philosophy* 81, no. 316 (2006): 209–30; quote at p. 219.

41 Edward Feser, *Scholastic Metaphysics: A Contemporary Introduction*. Heusenstamm: Editiones Scholasticae, 2014, pp. 10–11 (my emphasis).

42 Steven Rose, 'The Biology of the Future and the Future of Biology.' In *Explanations: Styles of Explanation in Science*, edited by John Cornwell, pp. 125–42. Oxford: Oxford University Press, 2004, especially pp. 128–9.

43 Susan Sontag, *At the Same Time: Essays and Speeches*. New York: St. Martin's Press, 2007, p. 212.

44 For further exploration of these concerns, see Alex Worsnip, *Fitting Things Together: Coherence and the Demands of Structural Rationality*. Oxford: Oxford University Press, 2021.

45 Midgley, *Myths We Live By*, p. 40. Midgley here understands myths as 'imaginative patterns, networks of powerful symbols that suggest particular ways of interpreting the world'.

46 Mary Midgley, *Science and Poetry*. London: Routledge, 2001, pp. 170–213.

47 Iris Murdoch, *Metaphysics as a Guide to Morals*. London: Penguin, 1992, p. 7.

48 Ludwig Wittgenstein, *Notebooks, 1914–1916*. New York: Harper, 1961, p. 75.

49 The work of David E. Cooper is helpful here: see Cooper, 'Living with Mystery;' idem, *Convergence with Nature: A Daoist Perspective*. Totnes: Green Books, 2012, pp. 58–80.

Chapter 3 – The Case of Religious Belief

1   Yonatan Adler, *The Origins of Judaism: An Archaeological-Historical Reappraisal.* New Haven, CT: Yale University Press, 2023.

2   Alexander Bird, 'The Metaphysics of Natural Kinds'. *Synthese* 195 (2018): pp. 1,397–426.

3   Jonathan Jong, 'On (Not) Defining (Non)Religion'. *Science, Religion and Culture* 2, no. 3 (2015), pp. 15–24; quote at p. 18.

4   Talal Asad, *Genealogies of Religion.* Baltimore, MD: Johns Hopkins University Press 1993, p. 29.

5   Peter Harrison, *The Territories of Science and Religion.* Chicago: University of Chicago Press, 2015.

6   Donovan Schaefer, 'Blessed, Precious Mistakes: Deconstruction, Evolution, and New Atheism in America.' *International Journal for Philosophy of Religion* 76 (2014), pp. 75–94; quote at p. 83.

7   Asad, *Genealogies of Religion*, p. 29.

8   For example, Jonathan Kvanvig, 'Affective Theism and People of Faith'. *Midwest Studies in Philosophy* 37, no. 1 (2013), pp. 109–28.

9   Yuval Noah Harari, *Homo Deus: A Brief History of Tomorrow.* London: Collins, 2017, pp. 372–400.

10 Lars Kirkhusmo Pharo, 'The Concept of "Religion" in Mesoamerican Languages'. *Numen* 54, no. 1 (2007), pp. 28–70. For the context, see Alexus McLeod, *An Introduction to Mesoamerican Philosophy.* Cambridge: Cambridge University Press, 2023.

11 For the pervasiveness of this trend to see western particularism as a universal 'epistemic regime', see Tomoko Masuzawa, *The Invention of World Religions, or, How European Universalism was Preserved in the Language of Pluralism.* Chicago, IL: University of Chicago Press, 2005.

12 Brian K. Pennington, *Was Hinduism Invented? Britons, Indians, and the Colonial Construction of Religion.* Oxford: Oxford University Press, 2005.

13 Elaine M. Fisher, *Hindu Pluralism: Religion and the Public Sphere in Early Modern South India.* Berkeley, CA: University of California Press, 2017, p. 3.

14 See the analysis in Lionel M. Jensen, *Manufacturing Confucianism: Chinese Traditions & Universal Civilization.* Durham: Duke University Press, 1997; Anna Xiao Dong Sun, *Confucianism as a*

   World Religion: Contested Histories and Contemporary Realities.
   Princeton, NJ: Princeton University Press, 2015.

15   Robert Bartlett, The Natural and the Supernatural in the Middle
   Ages. Cambridge: Cambridge University Press, 2008, pp. 12–17.

16   Snezana Lawrence and Mark McCartney, Mathematicians and their
   Gods: Interactions between Mathematics and Religious Beliefs. Oxford:
   Oxford University Press, 2015.

17   Max Tegmark, Our Mathematical Universe: My Quest for the
   Ultimate Nature of Reality. New York: Alfred A. Knopf, 2013.

18   Mark Steiner, 'Penrose and Platonism'. In The Growth of
   Mathematical Knowledge, edited by Emily Grosholz and Herbert
   Breger, pp. 133–41. Dordrecht: Springer, 2000.

19   Roger Penrose, The Emperor's New Mind: Concerning Computers,
   Minds, and the Laws of Physics. Oxford: Oxford University Press,
   1989, xii. For fuller statements, see Roger Penrose, The Road to
   Reality: A Complete Guide to the Laws of the Universe. London:
   Vintage Books, 2005, pp. 17–21.

20   Peter van Nuffelen, Rethinking the Gods: Philosophical Readings
   of Religion in the Post-Hellenistic Period. Cambridge: Cambridge
   University Press, 2011.

21   Pierre Hadot, What Is Ancient Philosophy? Cambridge, MA: Harvard
   University Press, 2002, pp. 55–76.

22   Paul Elmer More, Pages from an Oxford Diary. Princeton, NJ:
   Princeton University Press, 1937, section XV (the work is
   unpaginated).

23   More, Pages from an Oxford Diary, section XVIII.

24   Salman Rushdie, Is Nothing Sacred? Cambridge: Granta, 1990,
   pp. 8–9.

25   Thomas Nagel, 'What Is It Like to Be a Bat?' Philosophical Review
   83 (1974), pp. 435–50.

26   Thomas Metzinger, Conscious Experiences. Exeter: Imprint Academic,
   1995, p. 215. Both Nagel and Metzinger are primarily interested in
   the question of 'consciousness'; I have here used their approaches to
   illustrate the importance of intellectual and experiential empathy in
   engaging beliefs.

27   Terry Eagleton, 'Lunging, Flailing, Mispunching.' London Review of
   Books, 19 October 2006.

28 Hannah Kent, 'Conversation with Philip Pullman', *Kill Your Darlings*, 1 July 2010. https://www.killyourdarlings.com.au/article/kill-your-darlings-in-conversation-with-philip-pullman.

29 Daniel Gustafsson, 'Atheist Aesthetics: A Critical Response'. In *Atheisms: The Philosophy of Non-Belief*, edited by Harriet A. Harris and Victoria S. Harrison, 142–56. London: Routledge, 2023. Quote at p. 142.

30 Victor Kumar, 'To Walk Alongside: Myth, Magic, and Mind in the Golden Bough'. *Hau: Journal of Ethnographic Theory* 6, no. 2 (2016), pp. 233–54. For C. S. Lewis's recasting of Frazer's approach, see Mattias Gassman, 'An Afterlife of a Scholarly Epic: Frazer's Golden Bough and Lewis's Argument from Myth'. *Journal of Inklings Studies* 11, no. 2 (2021), pp. 133–52.

31 'Hear O Israel, the Lord is our God, the Lord is One' (Deuteronomy 6:4). The Hebrew term 'Shema' derives from the opening word of this affirmation.

32 Ruth Abbey, 'The Articulated Life: An Interview with Charles Taylor'. *Philosophy of Management* 1, no. 3 (2001), pp. 3–9.

33 Wayne Proudfoot, 'William James on an Unseen Order'. *Harvard Theological Review* 93, no. 1 (2000), pp. 51–66, especially pp. 56–7.

34 Ryan S. Schellenberg, 'οἱ πιστεύοντες: An Early Christ-Group Self-Designation and Paul's Rhetoric of Faith'. *New Testament Studies* 65, no. 1 (2019), pp. 33–42; Teresa Morgan, *The New Testament and the Theology of Trust*. Oxford: Oxford University Press, 2022, pp. 1–38.

35 Keith Yandell, *Philosophy of Religion: A Contemporary Introduction*. London: Routledge, 1999, p. 16.

36 Ludwig Wittgenstein, *On Certainty*. Oxford: Blackwell, 1974, p. 336. For the general problem, see Alister E. McGrath, *The Territories of Human Reason*. Oxford: Oxford University Press, 2020, pp. 1–89. See also A. W. Moore, 'Varieties of Sense-Making'. *Midwest Studies in Philosophy* 37 (2013), pp. 1–10.

37 For reflections on the marginalisation of Hadot's approach in academic philosophy, see Matthew Sharpe, 'Towards a Phenomenology of Sagesse: Uncovering the Unique Philosophical Problematic of Pierre Hadot'. *Angelaki: Journal of Theoretical Humanities* 23, no. 2 (2018), pp. 125–38.

38   Crystal L. Park and Login S. George, 'Is Existential Meaning a Need or a Want?' *Evolutionary Studies in Imaginative Culture* 4, no. 1 (2020), pp. 43–6; quote at p. 45.

39   John Cottingham, 'What Difference Does It Make? The Nature and Significance of Theistic Belief.' *Ratio* 19, no. 4 (2006), pp. 401–20.

40   Cottingham, 'What Difference Does It Make?' p. 411.

41   For a good reflection on these issues, see Mark Wynn, *Emotional Experience and Religious Understanding: Integrating Perception, Conception, and Feeling.* Cambridge: Cambridge University Press, 2005, pp. 1–88.

42   Mark R. Wynn, *Renewing the Senses: A Study of the Philosophy and Theology of the Spiritual Life.* Oxford: Oxford University Press, 2013, p. 19.

43   David E. Cooper, *Convergence with Nature: A Daoist Perspective.* Dartington: Green Books, 2012, p. 9.

44   Charles Taylor, *Modern Social Imaginaries.* Durham, NC: Duke University Press, 2004, pp. 23–30.

45   Austin Farrer, in Jocelyn Gibb, ed. *Light on C.S. Lewis.* London: Geoffrey Bles, 1965, p. 37.

Chapter 4 – Making Judgements:
Belief, Explanation and Interpretation

1   Philip Rieff, *My Life among the Deathworks: Illustrations of the Aesthetics of Authority.* Charlottesville, VA: University of Virginia Press, 2006.

2   Anna-Kaisa Newheiser, Miguel Farias and Nicole Tausch, 'The Functional Nature of Conspiracy Beliefs: Examining the Underpinnings of Belief in the *Da Vinci Code* Conspiracy'. *Personality and Individual Differences* 51, no. 8 (2011), pp. 1,007–11.

3   Kyle Mantyla, 'The King Cobra Venom Pandemic: Stew Peters Unveils a New COVID-19 Conspiracy Theory', *Right Wing Watch,* 12 April 2022, https://www.rightwingwatch.org/post/the-king-cobra-venom-pandemic-stew-peters-unveils-a-new-covid-19-conspiracy-theory/.

4   Bruce Hoffman and David Dryer, 'Terrorism in the West: Al Qaeda's Role in "Homegrown" Terror'. *Brown Journal of World Affairs* 13, no. 2 (2007), pp. 91–9.

5 This hypothesis became particularly influential in the 1970s and 1980s. See Dick Anthony and Thomas Robbins, 'Conversion and "Brainwashing" in New Religious Movements', in James R. Lewis, ed., *The Oxford Handbook of New Religious Movements*. New York: Oxford University Press, 2004, pp. 243–97.

6 Anthony Lantian, Virginie Bagneux, Sylvain Delouvée and Nicolas Gauvrit, 'Maybe a Free Thinker but Not a Critical One: High Conspiracy Belief is Associated with Low Critical Thinking Ability'. *Applied Cognitive Psychology* 35, no. 3 (2021) pp. 674–84.

7 See Joseph P. Forgas and Roy F. Baumeister, eds, *The Social Psychology of Gullibility: Conspiracy Theories, Fake News and Irrational Beliefs*. London: Routledge, 2019.

8 https://www.newyorker.com/news/annals-of-communications/hasan-minhajs-emotional-truths

9 Aldous Huxley, *Ends and Means: An Inquiry into the Nature of Ideals*. New York: Harper, 1937, pp. 291–350, especially p. 312.

10 Jeremy Griffith, *A Species in Denial*. Sydney: World Transformation Movement, 2004.

11 Thomas Nagel, *The Last Word*. Oxford: Oxford University Press, 1997, p. 130.

12 This advice is found in Paul's first letter to the Christian community at Thessalonica, probably written about 51 CE: see 1 Thessalonians 5:21.

13 *Lumen Fidei*, no. 24. https://www.vatican.va/content/francesco/en/encyclicals/documents/papa-francesco_20130629_enciclica-lumen-fidei.html.

14 Philip K. Dick, *The Shifting Realities of Philip K. Dick: Selected Literary and Philosophical Writings*. New York: Pantheon Books, 1995, pp. 259–80.

15 Hermann Hesse, 'Die Sehnsucht unser Zeit nach einer Weltanschauung'. *UHU* 2 (1926), pp. 3–14.

16 Joseph Mileck, *Hermann Hesse and His Critics*: Chapel Hill, NC: University of North Carolina Press, 1972, p. 35.

17 See his analysis in Peter Gay, *Weimar Culture: The Outsider as Insider*. New York: Harper & Row, 1968.

18 See the important work of Andrea W. Nightingale, 'On Wondering and Wandering: Theoria in Greek Philosophy and Culture'. *Arion: A Journal of Humanities and the Classics* 9 (2001), pp. 23–58.

19 Andrea W. Nightingale, *Spectacles of Truth in Classical Greek Philosophy: Theoria in Its Cultural Context*. Cambridge: Cambridge University Press, 2004.

20 For the origins and development of this notion, see Peter Lipton, *Inference to the Best Explanation*. 2nd ed., London: Routledge, 2004.

21 Sherrie Lynn Lyons, *Species, Serpents, Spirits, and Skulls: Science at the Margins in the Victorian Age*. Albany, NY: SUNY Press, 2009, pp. 147–70.

22 Arthur Koestler, *The Ghost in the Machine*. London: Hutchinson, 1967, p. 178.

23 Richard Swinburne, *Was Jesus God?* Oxford: Oxford University Press, 2008, p. 16. See also Richard Swinburne, 'God as the Simplest Explanation of the Universe'. *European Journal for Philosophy of Religion* 2, no. 1 (2010), pp. 1–24.

24 G. K. Chesterton, 'The Return of the Angels'. *Daily News*, 14 March, 1903. For the full text, see Julia Stapleton, ed., *G. K. Chesterton at the Daily News*. 8 vols. London: Pickering & Chatto, 2012, vol. 2, pp. 22–6.

25 Dudley Barker, *G. K. Chesterton: A Biography*. London: Constable, 1973, p. 169.

26 Walther Dilthey, *Gesammelte Schriften*. 12 vols. Leipzig: Teubner Verlagsgesellschaft, 1961, vol. 5, p. 144.

27 Jonathan Sacks, *The Great Partnership*. London: Hodder & Stoughton, 2011, p. 32. Sacks served as Chief Rabbi in the United Kingdom from 1991 to 2013.

28 Neil Dewar, 'Interpretation and Equivalence; or, Equivalence and Interpretation'. *Synthese* 201, no. 4 (2023) p. 119.

29 For an influential critique, see Eliseo Vivas, 'Julian Huxley's Evolutionary Ethics.' *Ethics* 58, no. 4 (1948), pp. 275–84.

30 Thomas H. Huxley, *Evolution and Ethics and Other Essays*. London: Macmillan and Co., 1894, p. 80.

31 Thomas H. Huxley, 'Science and Religion.' *The Builder 17* (January 15, 1859), 35–36; quote at p. 35. Like Goethe before him, Huxley was generally critical of 'theology' and appreciative of 'religion'. For an excellent discussion of Huxley's complex views on science and religion, see Matthew Stanley, *Huxley's Church and Maxwell's Demon:*

From Theistic Science to Naturalistic Science. Chicago: University of Chicago Press, 2015.

32 Thomas H. Huxley, 'On the Reception of the Origin of Species', in Francis Darwin, ed., *The Life and Letters of Charles Darwin*. London: Appleton, 1904, vol. 1, p. 553.

33 Bertrand Russell, *History of Western Philosophy*. London: George Allen & Unwin, 1946, pp. 673–4.

34 Thomas H. Huxley, *Science and Christian Tradition*. London: Macmillan and Co., 1894, p. 310.

35 Thomas H. Huxley, in 'Agnosticism: A Symposium', in Charles Watts, ed., *The Agnostic Annual* (1884), pp. 5–6.

36 Anthony Kenny, *Faith and Reason*. New York: Columbia University Press, 1983, pp. 84–5.

37 Graham Oppy, *Atheism and Agnosticism*. Cambridge: Cambridge University Press, 2018, p. 63.

Chapter 5 – What Difference Does Believing Make?

1   Peter Hills, Leslie J. Francis, Michael Argyle and Chris J. Jackson, 'Primary Personality Trait Correlates of Religious Practice and Orientation'. *Personality and Individual Differences* 36, no. 1 (2004), pp. 61–73.

2   For the basics of this approach and its significance, see Martin Seligman and Mihaly Csikszentmihalyi, 'Positive Psychology: An Introduction'. *American Psychologist* 55 (2000), pp. 5–14.

3   Michael H. Connors and Peter W. Halligan, 'A Cognitive Account of Belief: A Tentative Road Map'. *Frontiers in Psychology* 5 (2015), article 1588.

4   For the physiological details, see Rüdiger J. Seitz, Raymond F. Paloutzian and Hans-Ferdinand Angel, 'Processes of Believing: Where Do They Come From? What Are They Good For?' *F1000 research* 5 (2017): 2573, pp. 4–10.

5   Rebecca M. Todd, Vladimir Miskovic, Junichi Chikazoe and Adam K. Anderson, 'Emotional Objectivity: Neural Representations of Emotions and their Interaction with Cognition'. *Annual Review of Psychology* 71, no. 1 (2020): 25–48; quote at p. 27.

6   John Cottingham, *Why Believe?* London: Continuum, 2009, pp. 113–24.

7   Gloria Gennaro and Elliott Ash, 'Emotion and Reason in Political Language'. *Economic Journal* 132, no. 643 (2022), pp. 1,037–59.

8   See, for example, William J. F. Keenan and Tatjana Schnell, 'Meaning–Making in an Atheist World'. *Archives for the Psychology of Religion* 33, no.1 (2011), pp. 55–78.

9   Agustín Fuentes, *Why We Believe: Evolution and the Human Way of Being.* New Haven, CT: Yale University Press, 2019, p. 116.

10 See Seitz, Paloutzian, and Angel, 'Processes of Believing.'

11 Colin McGinn, *Mindsight: Image, Dream, Meaning.* Cambridge, MA: Harvard University Press, 2004, pp. 42–55.

12 Stephen Asma, 'Imagination: A New Foundation for the Science of Mind'. *Biological Theory* 19 (2022), pp. 243–9; Cf. Emelie Jonsson, *The Early Evolutionary Imagination: Literature and Human Nature.* Cham, Switzerland: Palgrave Macmillan, 2021.

13 Hans Blumenberg, 'Licht als Metapher der Wahrheit'. *Studium Generale* 10, no. 7 (1957), pp. 432–47; Paola Potestà, *Gli occhi, il sole, la luce: metafore sulla visione tra scienza e arte dall' antichità greca al '400.* Florence: Fondazione Giorgi Ronchi, 2002.

14 Henry Miller, *Big Sur and The Oranges of Hieronymus Bosch.* New York: New Directions, 1957, p. 25.

15 Matthias Adam, *Theoriebeladenheit und Objektivität. Zur Rolle von Beobachtungen in den Naturwissenschafte.* Frankfurt am Main: Ontos Verlag, 2002, pp. 25–49.

16 E. F. Schumacher, *A Guide for the Perplexed.* London: Vintage, 2011, p. 11.

17 Bernard Williams, *Morality: An Introduction to Ethics.* Cambridge: Cambridge University Press, 1993, p. 80.

18 Mary Midgley, 'Pluralism: The Many Maps Model'. *Philosophy Now* 35 (2002), pp. 10–11; for a fuller discussion, see Mary Midgley, *Science and Poetry.* London: Routledge, 2001, pp. 170–213.

19 William Blitzstein, 'The Seven Identified Observations of Uranus made by John Flamsteed using his Mural Arc'. *The Observatory* 118 (1998), pp. 219–22.

20 Thomas Kuhn, *The Road since Structure: Philosophical Essays, 1970–1993.* Chicago: University of Chicago Press, 2000, p. 15.

21 Paul Kalanithi, *When Breath Becomes Air.* London: Vintage Books, 2017, p. 170.

22 Kalanithi, *When Breath Becomes Air*, p. 149. These words come from Beckett's 1953 work *The Unnamable*.

23 William James, *The Varieties of Religious Experience: A Study in Human Nature*. New York: Longmans Green, 1917, pp. 249–50. For a philosophical reflection of this new way of experiencing reality, see Mark Wynn, *Renewing the Senses: A Study of the Philosophy and Theology of the Spiritual Life*. Oxford: Oxford University Press, 2013, pp. 15–41.

24 Alex García-Rivera, *The Community of the Beautiful: A Theological Aesthetics*. Collegeville, MN: Liturgical Press, 1999, p. 179.

25 Augustine of Hippo, *Sermon* LXXXVIII.v.5. For comment, see Roland J. Teske, 'Augustine of Hippo on Seeing with the Eyes of the Mind', in Craig J. N. de Paulo, Patrick Messina and Marc Stier, eds, *Ambiguity in the Western Mind*. New York: Peter Lang, 2005, pp. 72–87.

26 Dirk-Martin Grube, 'Christian Theology Emerged by Way of a Kuhnian Paradigm Shift.' *International Journal of Philosophy and Theology* 79, no. 1–2 (2018), pp. 178–93.

27 Sophie Read, *Eucharist and the Poetic Imagination in Early Modern England*. Cambridge: Cambridge University Press, 2017, p. 101.

28 *The Works of George Herbert,* edited by F. E. Hutchinson. Oxford: Clarendon Press, 1945, p. 184.

29 Iris Murdoch, *The Sovereignty of Good*. London: Routledge, 1970, p.16.

30 Murdoch, *The Sovereignty of Good*, p. 17.

31 Nico H. Frijda, A. S. R. Manstead and Sacha Bem eds, *Emotions and Beliefs: How Feelings Influence Thoughts*. Cambridge: Cambridge University Press, 2000.

32 T. S. Eliot, *On Poetry and Poets*. London: Faber & Faber, 1957, pp. 19–20.

33 T. S. Eliot, *The Use of Poetry and the Use of Criticism*. Cambridge, MA: Harvard University Press, 1964, p. 149.

34 Patrick Baert, *The Existentialist Moment: The Rise of Sartre as a Public Intellectual*. Cambridge: Polity Press, 2015, pp. 1–13.

35 *The Selected Letters of Bertrand Russell: The Public Years 1914–1970*. London: Routledge, 2001, 85. The letter refers to Malleson by her stage name 'Colette O'Niel'.

36 The remark is recorded in David Brewster, *Life of Sir Isaac Newton*, new edn, revised by W. T. Lynn. London: Tegg, 1875, p. 303.

37 Richard Dawkins, 'Is Science a Religion?' *The Humanist* 57 (1997) pp. 26–39.

38 For example, see Dacher Keltner and Jonathan Haidt, 'Approaching Awe, a Moral, Spiritual and Aesthetic Emotion.' *Cognition and Emotion* 17 (2003): 297–314. Keltner and Haidt draw on Jean Piaget's account of the interaction of 'accommodation' and 'assimilation' in processing information.

39 William James, *The Varieties of Religious Experience*. London: Longmans, Green & Co., 1902, pp. 380–1.

40 James, *The Varieties of Religious Experience,* p. 58.

41 Matthew Arnold, *On the Study of Celtic Literature*. New York: Macmillan, 1907, 117–18. See further Peter Strasser, *Sehnsucht*. Munich: Wilhelm Fink Verlag, 2010, pp. 15–59.

42 Virginia Woolf, *Moments of Being: Unpublished Autobiographical Writings*. New York: Harcourt Brace Jovanovich, 1976, pp. 64–137; quote at p. 72. For comment on this notion, see Sierra M. Senzaki, 'Moments of Being, Moments of Nonbeing: Humanism and Posthumanism in Virginia Woolf's "A Sketch of the Past" and *To the Lighthouse*'. *Literature Interpretation Theory* 33, no. 3 (2022), pp. 153–73.

43 Sophie Grace Chappell, *Epiphanies: An Ethics of Experience*. Oxford: Oxford University Press, 2022, p. 8.

44 Aldous Huxley, *The Doors of Perception*. London: Penguin, 1954, p. 50.

45 James Pawelski, *The Dynamic Individualism of William James*. Albany, NY: SUNY Press, 2007, pp. 135–6.

46 Théodor Flournoy, 'Les principes de la psychologie religieuse'. *Archives de Psychologie* 5 (1902), pp. 33–57. Flournoy's controlling presupposition is that an empirical psychology must operate within the limits of the natural sciences, and exclude any reference to 'transcendence' as having any causal role in psychology.

47 J. B. S. Haldane, *Possible Worlds and Other Essays*. London: Chatto and Windus, 1927, p. 209.

48 For the origins and development of this framework, see Michael Casey, *A Thirst for God: Spiritual Desire in Bernard of Clairvaux's*

Sermons on the Song of Songs. Kalamazoo, MI: Cistercian Publications, 1988.

49   *The Prayers and Meditations of St Anselm*, translated by Benedicta Ward. Harmondsworth: Penguin, 1973, pp. 94–5.

50   Richard Dawkins, *The God Delusion*. Boston: Houghton Mifflin, 2006, p. 92.

51   Login S. George and Crystal L. Park, 'Meaning in Life as Comprehension, Purpose, and Mattering'. *Review of General Psychology* 20, no. 3 (2016): 205–20; quote at p. 206.

52   George and Park, 'Meaning in Life as Comprehension, Purpose, and Mattering'.

53   G. T. Reker and Paul T. P. Wong, 'Personal Meaning in Life and Psychosocial Adaptation in the Later Years', in *The Human Quest for Meaning*, edited by P. T. P. Wong, pp. 433–56. New York: Routledge, 2012.

54   Crystal L. Park and Login S. George, 'Is Existential Meaning a Need or a Want?' *Evolutionary Studies in Imaginative Culture* 4, no. 1 (2020), pp. 43–6.

55   *The Works of George Herbert,* edited by F. E. Hutchinson. Oxford: Clarendon Press, 1945, pp. 184–5.

56   Marilynne Robinson, *The Death of Adam: Essays on Modern Thought*. New York: Picador, 2005, p. 240.

57   Edith Wyschogrod, *Saints and Postmodernism: Revisioning Moral Philosophy*. Chicago: University of Chicago Press, 1990, p. 3.

58   See, for example, John M. Cooper, *Pursuits of Wisdom: Six Ways of Life in Ancient Philosophy from Socrates to Plotinus*. Princeton, NJ: Princeton University Press, 2012, pp. 17–22; Matthew Sharpe, 'Between Too Intellectualist and not Intellectualist Enough: Hadot's Spiritual Exercises and Annas' Virtues as Skills'. *Journal of Value Inquiry* 55 (2021), pp. 269–87.

59   Robert W. Yarbrough, *1–3 John*. Baker Exegetical Commentary on the New Testament. Grand Rapids, MI: Baker Academic, 2008, p. 89.

60   Richard A. Burridge, *Imitating Jesus: An Inclusive Approach to New Testament Ethics*. Grand Rapids, MI: Eerdmans, 2007, pp. 285–346.

61   Linda Zagzebski, *Exemplarist Moral Theory*. Oxford: Oxford University Press, 2017, pp. 30–59; 129–55.

62 On which see Ian James Kidd, 'Adversity, Wisdom, and Exemplarism'. *Journal of Value Inquiry* 52, no. 4 (2018), pp. 379–93.

Chapter 6 – When Beliefs Fail

1   Matthew McNaught, *Immanuel*. London: Fitzcarraldo, 2022.
2   For a good example, see A. J. Swoboda, *After Doubt: How to Question Your Faith Without Losing It*. Grand Rapids, MI: Brazos Press, 2021.
3   Kenneth I. Pargament, Bruce W. Smith, Harold G. Koenig and Lisa Perez, 'Patterns of Positive and Negative Religious Coping with Major Life Stressors'. *Journal for the Scientific Study of Religion* 37, no. 4 (1998): 710–24. For discussion, see Joanna Collicutt, *The Psychology of Christian Character Formation*. Norwich: SCM Press, 2015, pp. 232–3.
4   Romans 5:3–4. Paul's letter to Christians at Rome is thought to have been written about the year 57 or 58 CE.
5   Frank Newport, 'Slowdown in the Rise of Religious Nones,' GALLUP, 9 December 2022: https://news.gallup.com/opinion/polling-matters/406544/slowdown-rise-religious-nones.aspx.
6   For a good study, see Joel Thiessen and Sarah Wilkins-Laflamme, *None of the Above: Nonreligious Identity in the US and Canada*. New York: New York University Press, 2020.
7   Thiessen and Wilkins-Laflamme, *None of the Above*, pp. 59–60.
8   Aiyana K. Willard and Ara Norenzayan, '"Spiritual but not Religious": Cognition, Schizotypy, and Conversion in Alternative Beliefs'. *Cognition* 165 (2017), pp. 137–46.
9   Fredrik deBoer, *How Elites Ate the Social Justice Movement*. New York: Simon & Schuster, 2023, p. 153.
10 Thiessen and Wilkins-Laflamme, *None of the Above*, p. 91.
11 Anne Frank, diary entry for 15 July 1944; *Anne Frank: The Diary of a Young Girl*. New York: Bantam, 1993, p. 263.
12 Frank Brady and Frederick A. Pottle, eds, *Boswell on the Grand Tour: Italy, Corsica and France, 1765–1766*. London: Heinemann, 1955, p. 281.
13 John Gray, *Straw Dogs: Thoughts on Humans and Other Animals*. London: Granta, 2003, p. 92.

14 Aleksandr Solzhenitsyn, *The Gulag Archipelago 1918–56*. London: Harvill Press, 2003, p. 75.

15 Natalia Solzhenitsyna, 'Returning to "The Gulag"'. *New Criterion*, September 2012, pp. 4–12.

16 Eddie Harmon-Jones, *Cognitive Dissonance: Reexamining a Pivotal Theory in Psychology*. 2nd edn, Washington, DC: American Psychological Association, 2019.

17 Joel Cooper, *Cognitive Dissonance: Fifty Years of a Classic Theory*. Los Angeles, CA: Sage Publications, 2007, pp. 3–7.

18 For this event and its interpretation, see Leon Festinger, Henry W. Riecken, and Stanley Schachter, *When Prophecy Fails*. Minneapolis: University of Minnesota Press, 1956.

19 For the 'ordinariness' of those who committed genocide in Rwanda, see Mahmood Mamdani, *When Victims Become Killers: Colonialism, Nativism, and the Genocide in Rwanda*. Princeton, NJ: Princeton University Press, 2002.

20 Garrett A. Sullivan, *Memory and Forgetting in English Renaissance Drama: Shakespeare, Marlowe, Webster*. Cambridge: Cambridge University Press, 2005.

21 C. S. Lewis, *Surprised by Joy*. London: HarperCollins, 2002, p. 183.

22 Reinhold Niebuhr, *Moral Man and Immoral Society*. New York: Charles Scribner's Sons, 1932, p. 257.

23 Ludwig Wittgenstein, *Philosophical Investigations*. 4th edn. Oxford: Wiley-Blackwell, 2009, p. 115.

24 For this interpretation of Wittgenstein's use of *Bild*, see David Egan, 'Pictures in Wittgenstein's Later Philosophy'. *Philosophical Investigations* 34, no. 1 (2011), pp. 55–76.

25 Garry L. Hagberg, 'The Thinker and the Draughtsman,' in *Philosophy as Therapeia*, edited by Clare Carlisle and Jonardon Ganeri, 67–81. Cambridge: Cambridge University Press, 2010; quote at p. 67. More generally, see Martha Nussbaum, *The Therapy of Desire: Theory and Practice in Hellenistic Ethics*. Princeton, NJ: Princeton University Press, 1994.

26 Gordon Baker, 'Wittgenstein: Concepts or Conceptions?' *Harvard Review of Philosophy* 21, no. 1 (2012): 7–23; quote at p. 14.

27 For this notion, see Neil Levy, *Bad Beliefs: Why They Happen to Good People*. New York: Oxford University Press, 2022.

28 Robert W. Sussman, *The Myth of Race: The Troubling Persistence of an Unscientific Idea*. Cambridge, MA: Harvard University Press, 2014, p. 212.

29 Ernest Allen, 'Identity and Destiny: The Formative Views of the Moorish Science Temple and the Nation of Islam'. In *Muslims on the Americanization Path?*, edited by Yvonne Yazbeck Haddad and John L. Esposito, pp. 163–214. New York: Oxford University Press, 2000. Quote at p. 185.

30 Arthur Koestler, *Darkness at Noon*. New York: New American Library, 1948, p. 115.

31 Arthur Koestler, *The Invisible Writing*. London: Collins, 1954, p. 19.

32 Isaiah Berlin, *Karl Marx*. 5th edn. Princeton, NJ: Princeton University Press, 2013, p. 19.

33 Koestler, *The Invisible Writing*, p. 19.

34 Koestler, *Darkness at Noon*, p. 127

35 Koestler, *Darkness at Noon*, pp. 184–5.

36 Rafael Behr, '*Darkness at Noon* gave me a deep, life-long interest in politics', *Guardian*, 24 August 2014: https://www.theguardian.com/commentisfree/2014/aug/24/darkness-at-noon-arthur-koestler-interest-politics.

37 Emanuele Saccarelli, 'The Intellectual in Question: Antonio Gramsci and the Crisis of Academia'. *Cultural Studies* 25, no. 6 (2011), pp. 757–82.

38 George V. Coyne, 'The Jesuits and Galileo: Fidelity to Tradition and the Adventure of Discovery'. *Forum Italicum* 49, no. 1 (2015), pp. 154–65.

39 See Kenneth I. Pargament, *The Psychology of Religion and Coping: Theory, Practice and Research*. New York: Guilford Press, 1997.

40 John Sellars, *The Art of Living: The Stoics on the Nature and Function of Philosophy*. 2nd edn. London: Duckworth, 2009, pp. 6–10.

41 Martha Nussbaum, *The Fragility of Goodness: Luck and Ethics in Greek Tragedy and Philosophy*. Cambridge: Cambridge University Press, 2001, p. 45.

42 See, for example, Galatians 3:4; Philippians 1:28 and Romans 12:9–21. Cf. Sumney, 'Salvific Suffering in Paul,' pp. 199–202. For discussion, see Robert C. Tannehill, *Dying and Rising with Christ: A Study in Pauline Theology*. Berlin: De Gruyter, 1967; Michael

J. Gorman, *Participating in Christ: Explorations in Paul's Theology and Spirituality.* Grand Rapids, MI: Baker Academic, 2019.

43 Jerry L. Sumney, 'Salvific Suffering in Paul: Eschatological, Vicarious, and Mimetic'. In *Let the Reader Understand: Essays in Honor of Elizabeth Struthers Malbon*, edited by Edwin K. Broadhead, 195–212. London: Bloomsbury Publishing, 2018.

44 Johannes Brachtendorf, 'The Goodness of Creation and the Reality of Evil: Suffering as a Problem in Augustine's Theodicy'. *Augustinian Studies* 31, no. 1 (2000), pp. 79–92.

45 J. K. A. Smith, *How (Not) to Be Secular: Reading Charles Taylor.* Grand Rapids, MI: Eerdmans, 2014, p. 141.

46 Stephen Wykstra, 'The Humean Obstacle to Evidential Arguments from Suffering: On Avoiding the Evils of "Appearance"'. *International Journal for the Philosophy of Religion* 16 (1984), pp. 73–93.

47 C. S. Lewis, *The Problem of Pain.* London: HarperCollins, 2002, p. 153.

48 William Paul Young. *The Shack: Where Tragedy Confronts Eternity.* Newbury Park, CA: Windblown Media, 2007. For a critical analysis, see Christopher Douglas, 'This Is the Shack That Job Built: Theodicy and Polytheism in William Paul Young's Evangelical Bestseller'. *Journal of the American Academy of Religion* 88, no. 3 (2020), pp. 505–42.

49 Peter Sobczynski, 'The Shack', *RogerEbert.com.* https://www.rogerebert.com/reviews/the-shack-2017.

50 Nicholas Wolterstorff, *Lament for a Son.* Grand Rapids, MI: Eerdmans, 1987, p. 68.

51 Johann Baptist Metz, *Memoria Passionis; Ein provozierendes Gedächtnis in pluralistischer Gesellschaft.* Freiburg: Herder, 2006, 225.

52 For the details, see Alister E. McGrath, *C. S. Lewis: A Life. Eccentric Genius, Reluctant Prophet.* London: Hodder & Stoughton, 2013, pp. 63–4.

53 Jonathan Haidt, 'The Emotional Dog and Its Rational Tail: A Social Intuitionist Approach to Moral Judgment'. *Psychological Review* 108, no. 4 (2001), pp. 814–34.

54 David Hume, *A Treatise of Human Nature.* London: Penguin, 1969, p. 2.

55 Wykstra, 'The Humean Obstacle to Evidential Arguments from Suffering', p. 73.

56   C. S. Lewis, *Mere Christianity*. London: Harper Collins, 2001, pp. 38–9.

57   C. S. Lewis, *A Grief Observed*. New York: HarperCollins, 1994, pp. 5–6.

58   Lewis, *A Grief Observed*, p. 52.

59   Letter to Sister Madelva, 3 October 1963; in *The Collected Letters of C. S. Lewis*, edited by Walter Hooper. 3 vols. San Francisco: HarperOne, 2004–6, vol. 3, 1460.

60   Lewis, *A Grief Observed*, p. 44.

61   For example, see Ellen M. Ross, *The Grief of God: Images of the Suffering Jesus in Late Medieval England*. Oxford: Oxford University Press, 1997; Mitzi Kirkland-Ives, *In the Footsteps of Christ: Hans Memling's Passion Narratives and the Devotional Imagination in the Early Modern Netherlands*. Turnhout: Brepols, 2013.

62   Francis Spufford, *Unapologetic*. London: Faber and Faber, 2012, pp. 105; 107.

63   David M. Carr, *Holy Resilience: The Bible's Traumatic Origins*. New Haven, CT: Yale University Press, 2014, p. 3. See further Joanna Collicutt, 'Post-Traumatic Growth and the Origins of Early Christianity.' *Mental Health, Religion and Culture* no. 9 (2006), pp. 291–306.

64   Edith Weisskopf-Joelson, 'Logotherapy and Existential Analysis'. *Acta Psychotherapeutica et Psychosomatica* 6, no. 3 (1958): pp. 193–204; quote at p. 195.

65   Sarah Bachelard, *Experiencing God in a Time of Crisis*. Miami, FL: Convivium Press, 2012, p. 62.

66   See his classic study Viktor E. Frankl, *Man's Search for Meaning*. New York: Simon and Schuster, 1963.

67   Friedrich Nietzsche, *Götzen-Dämmerung; oder Wie man mit dem Hammer philosophiert*. Munich: Hanser, 1954, p. 7.

68   Jordan B. Peterson, *12 Rules for Life: An Antidote to Chaos*. Toronto: Random House Canada, 2018, p. 338.

Chapter 7 – The Dark Side of Believing:
Tensions, Intolerance and Violence

1   Alex Mahon, 'Beyond Z: The Real Truth About British Youth', Channel 4. https://www.channel4.com/press/news/

beyond-z-real-truth-about-british-youth-speech-alex-mahon-chief-executive-channel-4.

2   Guangwei Ouyang, 'Scientism, Technocracy, and Morality in China'. *Journal of Chinese Philosophy* 30, no. 2 (2003), pp. 177–93; Benjamin A. Elman, 'Toward a History of Modern Science in Republican China'. In *Science and Technology in Modern China, 1880s–1940s*, edited by Jing Tsu and Benjamin A. Elman. Leiden: Brill, 2014, pp. 15–38.

3   Ady van den Stock, *The Horizon of Modernity: Subjectivity and Social Structure in New Confucian Philosophy*. Leiden: Brill, 2016, especially pp. 197–266.

4   Xiaoguang Kang, 'A Study of the Renaissance of Traditional Confucian Culture in Contemporary China'. In *Confucianism and Spiritual Traditions in Modern China and Beyond*, edited by Fenggang Yang and Joseph B. Tamney. Leiden: Brill, 2012, pp. 33–74.

5   Marjorie Lipsham, 'Mātauranga-Ā-Whānau: Constructing a Methodological Approach Centred on Whānau Pūrākau'. *Aotearoa New Zealand Social Work* 32, no. 3 (2020), pp. 17–29.

6   Jerry Coyne, 'More from New Zealand, a nation whose science is circling the drain', whyevolutionistrue.com, January 23, 2022, https://whyevolutionistrue.com/2022/01/23/more-from-new-zea-land-a-nation-about-to-be-taken-over-by-insanity/.

7   The full title of Darwin's work is 'On the Origin of Species by Means of Natural Selection, or the Preservation of Favoured Races in the Struggle for Life'.

8   Alfred Russel Wallace, 'The Origin of Human Races and the Antiquity of Man Deduced from the Theory of "Natural Selection"'. *Journal of the Anthropological Society of London* 2 (1864): clxiv–clxvi; quote at pp. clxiv–clxv.

9   Wallace, 'The Origin of Human Races', p. clxix.

10   For reflections on and origins and development of Wallace's ideas, see Mark Clement, 'Evolution and Empire: Alfred Russel Wallace and Dutch Colonial Rule in Southeast Asia in the Mid-Nineteenth Century'. *Britain and the World* 9, no. 1 (2016): 55–75. See also Sarah Irving, *Natural Science and the Origins of the British Empire*. London: Routledge, 2016.

11 Charles Darwin, 'To Charles Kingsley, 6 February [1862]', Letter
    no. DCP-LETT-3439, *Darwin Correspondence Project,* https://
    www.darwinproject.ac.uk/letter/?docId=letters/DCP-LETT-3439.
    xml&query=DCP-LETT-3439.

12 Boaventura Sousa Santos, 'Epistemologies of the South and the
    Future'. *From the European South* 1 (2016): 17–29; quote at
    p. 18.

13 D. Wayne Orchiston, *Exploring the History of New Zealand
    Astronomy: Trials, Tribulations, Telescopes and Transits.* Cham,
    Switzerland: Springer Verlag, 2016, pp. 33–104.

14 Edward O. Wilson, *Consilience: The Unity of Knowledge.* New York:
    Alfred Knopf, 1998, p. 294.

15 Stephen Jay Gould, *The Hedgehog, the Fox, and the Magister's Pox:
    Mending the Gap between Science and the Humanities.* Cambridge,
    MA: Belknap Press of Harvard University Press, 2011, p. 190.

16 Dilip V. Jeste and Ellen E. Lee, 'The Emerging Empirical Science
    of Wisdom: Definition, Measurement, Neurobiology, Longevity,
    and Interventions', *Harvard Review of Psychiatry* 27, no. 3 (2019),
    pp. 127–40.

17 Thomas W. Meeks and Dilip V. Jeste, 'Neurobiology of Wisdom:
    A Literature Overview'. *Archives of General Psychiatry* 66, no. 4
    (2009), pp. 355–65.

18 Alkis Kotsonis and Gerard Dunne, 'Why Empathy Is an Intellectual
    Virtue.' *Philosophical Psychology* (2022). https://doi.org/10.1080/0
    9515089.2022.2100753.

19 Justin Steinberg, 'An Epistemic Case for Empathy'. *Pacific
    Philosophical Quarterly* 95, no. 1 (2014), pp. 47–71.

20 C. S. Lewis, *An Experiment in Criticism.* Cambridge: Cambridge
    University Press, 1992, pp. 140–1.

21 Lewis, *Experiment in Criticism*, p. 137.

22 See the classic study of Milton Rokeach, *The Open and Closed Mind:
    Investigations into the Nature of Belief Systems and Personality Systems.*
    New York: Basic Books, 1960.

23 Eugene V. Koonin, 'Why the Central Dogma: On the Nature of
    the Great Biological Exclusion Principle'. *Biology Direct* 10, no. 1
    (2015), 52; Takeuchi Nobuto and Kaneko Kunihiko 'The Origin

of the Central Dogma through Conflicting Multilevel Selection'. *Proceedings of the Royal Society B* (2019), 28620191359.

24 See the material gathered in Victor C. Ottati and Chadly Stern, eds. *Divided: Open-Mindedness and Dogmatism in a Polarized World.* New York: Oxford University Press, 2023.

25 Ruth Ben-Ghiat, *Strongmen: How They Rise, Why They Succeed, How They Fall.* London: Profile Books, 2020.

26 John Levi Martin, 'The Authoritarian Personality, 50 Years Later: What Questions are there for Political Psychology?' *Political Psychology* 22, no. 1 (2001), pp. 1–26.

27 Judy J. Johnson, *What's So Wrong with Being Absolutely Right? The Dangerous Nature of Dogmatic Belief.* Amherst, NY: Prometheus Books, 2009. See also Judy J. Johnson, 'Beyond a Shadow of Doubt: The Psychological Nature of Dogmatism'. *International Journal of Interdisciplinary Social Sciences: Annual Review* 5, no. 3, (2010), pp. 149–61.

28 Richard C. Roberts and W. Jay Wood, *Intellectual Virtues: An Essay in Regulative Epistemology.* Oxford: Oxford University Press, 2007, p. 195.

29 Sebastien Grenier, Anne-Marie Barrette and Robert Ladouceur, 'Intolerance of Uncertainty and Intolerance of Ambiguity: Similarities and Differences'. *Personality and Individual Differences* 39 (2005), pp. 593–600.

30 Greta B. Raglan, Maxim Babush, Victoria A. Farrow, Arie W. Kruglanski and Jay Schulkin, 'Need to Know: The Need for Cognitive Closure Impacts the Clinical Practice of Obstetrician/ Gynecologists'. *BMC Medical Informatics and Decision Making* 14 (2014), p. 122.

31 Ronald Weed, 'Putting Religion First: Diagnosing Division and Conflict in the Religious Violence Thesis'. *Political Theology* 15, no. 6 (2014), pp. 536–51.

32 Florence Burgat, 'La logique de la légitimation de la violence: animalité vs humanité', in François Héritier, ed., *De la violence.* 2 vols. Paris: Odile Jacob, 1999, vol. 2, pp. 45–62.

33 For a good example of this problem, see Kazi Nazrul Fattah and Suborna Camellia, 'Gender Norms and Beliefs, and Men's Violence Against Women in Rural Bangladesh'. *Journal of Interpersonal Violence* 35, no. 3–4 (2020), pp. 771–93.

34 Michael Shermer, *How we Believe: Science, Skepticism, and the Search for God*. New York: Freeman, 2000, p. 71.

35 For example, see Dawkins, *The God Delusion*, p. 273.

36 Bertrand Russell, *The Theory and Practice of Bolshevism*. London: George Allen & Unwin, 1921.

37 Emilio Gentile, *Politics as Religion*. Princeton, NJ: Princeton University Press, 2006, p. 1.

38 Martin Marty with Jonathan Moore, *Politics, Religion, and the Common Good: Advancing a Distinctly American Conversation About Religion's Role in Our Shared Life*. San Francisco: Jossey-Bass, 2000.

39 Julietta Singh, *Unthinking Mastery: Dehumanism and Decolonial Entanglements*. Durham, NC: Duke University Press, 2017, p. 6.

40 John Rawls, *Political Liberalism*. New York: Columbia University Press, expanded edition, 2005, p. xvii.

41 Shaun P. Young, ed. *Reflections on Rawls: An Assessment of His Legacy*. London: Routledge, 2016.

42 Rawls, *Political Liberalism*, pp. 58–9.

43 Rawls, *Political Liberalism*, p. xxxix.

44 Shanto Iyengar, Yphtach Lelkes, Matthew Levendusky, Neil Malhotra and Sean J. Westwood, 'The Origins and Consequences of Affective Polarization'. *Annual Review of Political Science* 22, no. 1 (2019), pp. 129–46.

Chapter 8 – Beliefs and Communities

1 David W. McMillan, 'Sense of Community'. *Journal of Community Psychology* 24, no. 4 (1996), pp. 315–25.

2 Robert Furbey, 'Beyond "Social Glue"? 'Faith' and Community Cohesion', in *Community Cohesion in Crisis? New Dimensions of Diversity and Difference*, John Flint and David Robinson, eds, Bristol: Bristol University Press, 2008, pp. 119–38.

3 Josje ten Kate, Willem de Koster and Jeroen van der Waal, 'The Effect of Religiosity on Life Satisfaction in a Secularized Context'. *Review of Religious Research* 59, no. 2 (2017), pp. 135–55, especially 140–1.

4 Peter L. Berger, *A Rumour of Angels*. New York: Basic Books, 1969, pp. 18–19.

5   A. Whiten, J. Goodall, W. C. McGrew, T. Nishida, V. Reynolds, Y. Sugiyama, C. E. G. Tutin, R. W. Wrangham and C. Boesch, 'Cultures in Chimpanzees'. *Nature* 399, no. 6737 (1999), pp. 682–5.

6   C. S. Lewis, *The Allegory of Love: A Study in Medieval Tradition.* Oxford: Clarendon Press, 1936, p. 1.

7   For example, Rainer Albertz and Rüdiger Schmitt, *Family and Household Religion in Ancient Israel and the Levant.* Winona Lake, IN: Eisenbrauns, 2012; David G. Orr, 'Roman Domestic Religion: The Evidence of the Household Shrines.' *Aufstieg und Niedergang der Römischen Welt* 16, no. 2 (1978), pp. 1,557–91.

8   Catherine Morgan, 'Politics without the Polis: Cities and the Achaean Ethnos, c.800–500 BC', in *Alternatives to Athens: Varieties of Political Organization and Community in Ancient Greece*, edited by Roger Brock and Stephen Hodkinson, Oxford: Oxford University Press, 2002, pp. 189–211.

9   Egbert Ribberink, Peter Achterberg and Dick Houtman, 'Deprivatization of Disbelief? Nonreligiosity and Anti-Religiosity in 14 Western European Countries'. *Politics and Religion* 6, no. 1 (2013), pp. 101–20.

10 Francis K. G. Lim and Bee Bee Sng, 'Social Media, Religion and Shifting Boundaries in Globalizing China'. *Global Media and China* 5, no. 3 (2020), pp. 261–74.

11 Berger, *A Rumour of Angels*, p. 50.

12 Peter L. Berger and Thomas Luckmann, *The Social Construction of Reality.* Harmondsworth: Penguin Books, 1971, p. 126.

13 Ronald Inglehart and Wayne E. Baker, 'Modernization, Cultural Change, and the Persistence of Traditional Values'. *American Sociological Review* 65, no. 1 (2000), pp. 19–51.

14 Catherine E. de Vries, 'How Foundational Narratives Shape European Union Politics'. *Journal of Common Market Studies* 61, no. 4 (2023), pp. 867–81.

15 Timothy Snyder, 'Europe's dangerous creation myth'. *Politico*, May 2019, https://www.politico.eu/article/europe-creation-project-myth-history-nation-state/.

16 Christian Smith, *Moral, Believing Animals: Human Personhood and Culture.* Oxford: Oxford University Press, 2009, pp. 63–94.

17 Ursula K. Le Guin, *Language of the Night: Essays on Fantasy and Science Fiction.* New York: Berkley, 1982, p. 22.

18 J. R. R. Tolkien, *Tree and Leaf.* London: HarperCollins, 2001, p. 56.

19 Stanley Hauerwas, 'The Demands of a Truthful Story: Ethics and the Pastoral Task', *Chicago Studies* 21, no. 1 (1982), pp. 59–71.

20 Dimitris Xygalatas, *Ritual: How Seemingly Senseless Acts Make Life Worth Living.* London: Profile Books, 2022.

21 Xygalatas, *Ritual*, pp. 61–2.

22 Rafael Nadal, *Rafa: My Story.* London: Sphere, 2011.

23 Peter M. Haas, *Epistemic Communities, Constructivism, and International Environmental Politics.* London: Routledge, 2016, p. 5.

24 See especially Linda Zagzebski, *Virtues of the Mind: An Inquiry into the Nature of Virtue and the Ethical Foundations of Knowledge.* Cambridge: Cambridge University Press, 1996.

25 See Reza Lahroodi, 'Collective Epistemic Virtues'. *Social Epistemology* 21 (2007), pp. 281–97; Reza Lahroodi, 'Virtue Epistemology and Collective Epistemology,' in *The Routledge Handbook of Virtue Epistemology*, edited by H. Battaly, pp. 407–20. New York: Routledge, 2019.

26 Richard C. Roberts and W. Jay Wood, *Intellectual Virtues: An Essay in Regulative Epistemology.* Oxford: Oxford University Press, 2007, p. 77.

27 See Miranda Fricker, 'Epistemic Oppression and Epistemic Privilege'. *Canadian Journal of Philosophy* 29 (1999), pp. 191–210; Fricker, *Epistemic Injustice: Power and the Ethics of Knowing.* Oxford: Oxford University Press, 2007.

28 Ian James Kidd, 'Epistemic Injustice and Religion'. In *Routledge Handbook of Epistemic Injustice*, Ian James Kidd, José Medina and Gaile Pohlhaus, eds, London: Routledge, 2017, pp. 386–96.

29 Shanto Iyengar, Yphtach Lelkes, Matthew Levendusky, Neil Malhotra and Sean J. Westwood, 'The Origins and Consequences of Affective Polarization'. *Annual Review of Political Science* 22, no. 1 (2019), pp. 129–46.

30 Russell Jacoby, *The Last Intellectuals: American Culture in the Age of Academe.* New York: Basic Books, 1987, p. 5.

31 Frances Ruane, 'Public Intellectuals in Times of Crisis: The Role of Academia'. In *Reflections on Crisis: The Role of the Public Intellectual*, edited by Mary P. Corcoran and Kevin Lalor, pp. 41–51. Dublin: Royal Irish Academy, 2012; quotes at pp. 43–4.

32 James D. G. Dunn, *The Partings of the Ways between Christianity and Judaism and their Significance for the Character of Christianity.* 2nd edn. London: SCM Press, 2006.

33 Lesley Hazleton, *After the Prophet: The Epic Story of the Shia–Sunni Split in Islam.* New York: Anchor, 2010.

34 Brad S. Gregory, *The Unintended Reformation: How a Religious Revolution Secularized Society.* Cambridge, MA: Belknap Press, 2012.

35 For this doctrine, see Alister E. McGrath, *Iustitia Dei: A History of the Christian Doctrine of Justification.* 4th ed. Cambridge: Cambridge University Press, 2015. For the role of doctrines in defining and distinguishing communities of belief, see Alister E. McGrath, *The Nature of Christian Doctrine: Its Origins, Development and Function.* Oxford: Oxford University Press, 2024, pp. 62–75.

Conclusion: Living in a
World of Uncertainty

1 David Rock, 'Hunger for Certainty'. *Psychology Today*, 25 October 2009. For the failure of the Enlightenment to provide such philosophical certainty, see the important study of Robert Pasnau, *After Certainty: A History of Our Epistemic Ideals and Illusions.* Oxford: Oxford University Press, 2017.

2 Carlo Rovelli, 'What We Believe About Certainty'. *New York Times*, 18 May 2021 (my italics). The full article merits close study, as it explains why Rovelli was uncertain about each of these beliefs, some of which rested on possibly unreliable personal testimony.

3 Voltaire, letter to Frederick II of Prussia, 28 November 1770; in *Oeuvres de Voltaire.* Paris: Alexandre Houssiaux, 1853, vol. 10, p. 522.

4 Alexander Pope, *Essay on Man*, I.ii.2.

5 Alexander Pope, *Essay on Man*, II.i.1–10.

6 Alexander Pope, *Essay on Man*, I.ii.24.

7 Frank P. Ramsey, 'Truth and Probability'. In *The Foundations of Mathematics, and other Logical Essays.* London: Routledge, 1931, pp. 156–98; quotes at pp. 184; 194.

8 I borrow this phrase from Timothy Chappell, 'Climbing Which Mountain? A Critical Study of Derek Parfit, *On What Matters.*' *Philosophical Investigations* 35, no. 2 (2012), pp. 167–81.

9   Bernard Lonergan, *Insight*. New York: Longman, 1957, p. 4.

10 Cory J. Clark, Brittany S. Liu, Bo M. Winegard and Peter H. Ditto, 'Tribalism Is Human Nature'. *Current Directions in Psychological Science* 28, no. 6 (2019), pp. 587–92.

11 There is a large literature. Useful entry points are Barbara Resnick, Lisa P. Gwyther and Karen A. Roberto, eds. *Resilience in Aging: Concepts, Research, and Outcomes.* 2nd edn. Cham, Switzerland: Springer Nature 2019; Hilary N. Weaver, ed. *The Routledge International Handbook of Indigenous Resilience.* London: Routledge, 2022; T. A. Balboni et al., 'Spirituality in Serious Illness and Health'. *Journal of the American Medical Association* 328, no. 2 (2022), pp. 184–97.

12 Andrew Briggs and Michael J. Reiss. *Human Flourishing: Scientific Insight and Spiritual Wisdom in Uncertain Times.* Oxford: Oxford University Press, 2021, pp. 115–202.

13 William A. Ulmer, 'Negative Capability: Identity and Truth in Keats'. *Romanticism* 25, no. 2 (2019), pp. 169–79.

14 Christian Smith, *Moral, Believing Animals: Human Personhood and Culture.* Oxford: Oxford University Press, 2009.

15 See, for example, Reuben Binns, 'Human Judgment in Algorithmic Loops: Individual Justice and Automated Decision-Making'. *Regulation & Governance* 16 (2022): 197–211; Gary H., Lyman and Nicole M. Kuderer, 'Perception, Cognition and Thought: Part III: Reasoning, Judgement and Decision-Making.' *Cancer Investigation* 41, no. 8 (2023), pp. 699–703.

16 Susan Sontag, *At the Same Time: Essays and Speeches.* New York: St. Martin's Press, 2007, p. 224.

17 Philip Pullman, *Northern Lights.* London: Scholastic, 1996, p. 145.